Managing Persistent and Serious Offenders in the Community

Managing Persistent and Serious Offenders in the Community

Intensive community programmes in theory and practice

Robin Moore, Emily Gray, Colin Roberts, Emily Taylor and **Simon Merrington**

WILLAN
PUBLISHING

Published by

Willan Publishing
Culmcott House
Mill Street, Uffculme
Cullompton, Devon
EX15 3AT, UK
Tel: +44(0)1884 840337
Fax: +44(0)1884 840251
e-mail: info@willanpublishing.co.uk
website: www.willanpublishing.co.uk

Published simultaneously in the USA and Canada by

Willan Publishing
c/o ISBS, 920 NE 58th Ave, Suite 300
Portland, Oregon 97213-3786, USA
Tel: +001(0)503 287 3093
Fax: +001(0)503 280 8832
e-mail: info@isbs.com
website: www.isbs.com

Paperback
ISBN-13: 978-1-84392-181-3
ISBN-10: 1-84392-181-2

British Library Cataloguing-in-Publication Data

A catalogue record for this book is available from the British Library

Typeset by GCS, Leighton Buzzard, Beds
Project management by Deer Park Productions, Tavistock, Devon
Printed and bound by T.J. International, Padstow, Cornwall

Contents

v

Figures and tables

Figures

Tables

Abbreviations

BJA	Bureau of Justice Assistance
CDRP	Crime and Disorder Reduction Partnership
CJA	Criminal Justice Act
CRO	Community Rehabilitation Order
CSO	Community Service Order
DJ	District Judge
DTO	Detention and Training Order
EM	Electronic Monitoring
HEIT	Heavy-End Intermediate Treatment
IAP	Intensive Aftercare Program
ICCP	Intensive Control and Change Programme
IDP	Intensive Drug Program
ILP	Intelligence-Led Policing
IMPACT	Intensive Matched Probation and After-Care Treatment
IP	Intensive Probation
IRIS	Intensive Recidivist Intervention Scheme
IRS	Intensive Rehabilitation Supervision
ISEM	Intensive Supervision with Electronic Monitoring
ISM	Intensive Supervision and Monitoring
ISP	Intensive Supervision Program
ISSO	Intensive Supervision and Surveillance Order
ISSP	Intensive Supervision and Surveillance Programme
IT	Intermediate Treatment
LRP	Learning Resources Program

MORI	Market & Opinion Research International
MST	Multi-Systemic Therapy
NOMS	National Offender Management Service
NACRO	National Association for the Care and Resettlement of Offenders
NPD	National Probation Directorate
OASys	Offender Assessment System
PNC	Police National Computer
PO	Persistent Offender
POP	Prolific Offender Project
PPO	Prolific and other Priority Offender
PSR	Pre-Sentence Report
PYO	Persistent Young Offender
RCT	Random Control Trial
RJ	Restorative Justice
ROM	Regional Offender Manager
SO	Supervision Order
SOP	Serious Offender Project
YAP	Youth Advocate Programme
YJB	Youth Justice Board
YOI	Young Offender Institution
YOIS	Young Offender Information System
YOP	Young Offender Project
YOT	Youth Offending Team

Acknowledgements

The ISSP case study at the heart of this book builds upon an evaluation for the Youth Justice Board running from 2001 until 2005. The evaluation was led by the Centre for Criminology, University of Oxford, but profited greatly from utilising the knowledge and research experience of a range of other departments, notably the Department of Educational Studies, the Department of Psychiatry, and SKOPE (ESRC Centre on Skills, Knowledge and Organisational Performance) in the Department of Economics. We would like to thank and acknowledge the important contributions of the rest of the research team, namely Ian Waters, Rosa Fernandez, Robert Rogers and Geoff Hayward. Particular thanks are due to the regional evaluators, without whose tireless efforts out in the field the evaluation would not have been possible: Helen Atkinson, Helen Barrs, Jacqueline Bell, Nicola Elson, Gilly Sharpe, Michael Staskevich and Alex Sutherland.

We would like to express our gratitude to the staff of the 41 ISSP schemes for their co-operation, understanding and assistance, and to the young people themselves and their parents for their co-operation in being interviewed and for their completion of the evaluation assessment tools. We are also grateful to the Youth Justice Board, particularly Ruth Allan and Mary Wyman, the Home Office and the electronic monitoring contractors for their support and the provision of essential data, and to the members of the ISSP steering and user groups for their valuable input. All opinions expressed by the authors however, are independent of the views of the Youth Justice Board and the Home Office.

On a more personal note, Robin would like to thank Louise for her support and encouragement.

Introduction

Karen is a 17-year-old white female, with an offending history of 18 recorded offences in the past 12 months. She is temporarily excluded from school and has significant problems with both alcohol and cannabis. Having been convicted of an offence of drunk and disorderly, she is placed on a six-month Intensive Supervision and Surveillance Programme (ISSP). While on the programme, she is placed on a catering course and is involved in sessions on education, reparation, offending behaviour, interpersonal skills, mental health, drugs/alcohol work, constructive leisure and counselling. She is also electronically tagged. Karen successfully completes the programme, but she admits ongoing problems with alcohol and continues offending, albeit at a significantly lower rate than prior to ISSP.

Paul is a 14-year-old black male. He has been a prolific offender since the age of 12, and has committed six recorded offences in the past 12 months. He has previously been subject to a custodial sentence and a variety of community sentences, with which he has a history of non-compliance. He has been assessed as having special needs and attends a pupil referral unit. He associates with pro-criminal peers, and has several fixed-term exclusions from school. He is also placed on a six-month ISSP for an offence of domestic burglary. He is electronically tagged and is involved in reparation (at a Farm Trust putting up fences), offending behaviour work, interpersonal skills sessions, family support and constructive leisure. The programme is terminated after five months following a conviction for a further domestic burglary, but he is given another ISSP that he completes. His caseworker is very optimistic that the programme has been successful for Paul.

As highlighted by these two case studies, persistent and serious young offenders in England and Wales can now be placed on an intensive community programme known as ISSP. The introduction of this programme in 2001 and its subsequent nationwide roll-out in late 2003 raise a number of important questions.

- How has such an intensive multi-modal community programme managed to establish itself? What are its origins?

- Does ISSP differ from earlier intensive community programmes?

- How does it fit into the broader political agenda? What are its theoretical foundations and how does it relate to broader penal theories?

- Which offenders are most suitable for ISSP?

- Can it be delivered in practice as intended in principle? Can the supervision and surveillance components be successfully combined?

- Can it tackle offenders' underlying problems and reduce re-offending? Can it help to bring about longer-term improvements?

- Can it help to reduce the levels of custodial sentencing? Can the confidence of sentencers and the public be maintained?

- Are the aims and objectives for the programme compatible?

- How should effectiveness be judged?

These questions are particularly important bearing in mind that intensive community programmes are now firmly established in the United States of America (US) and are becoming an increasingly integral part of penal policy in other jurisdictions. In England and Wales, an Intensive Control and Change Programme (ICCP) has also been piloted with young adult offenders, since subsumed within the provisions of the Criminal Justice Act 2003. Furthermore, the Carter Report (2003) has advocated 'Intensive Supervision and Monitoring' for persistent offenders of all ages, and a Prolific and other Priority Offender Scheme has been established in every Crime and Disorder Reduction Partnership (CDRP). While the expectations for these programmes are high, the research evidence regarding their effectiveness is mixed and a number of critical concerns remain. This book thus provides a timely review of the current literature, and presents findings from a recent national evaluation of ISSP. The emerging lessons for future penal policy are presented, and wider theoretical issues considered. In so doing, the book offers an 'empirically informed, theoretically grounded account' of intensive community programmes, filling a gap in the current literature which 'tends either to focus upon policy pronouncements, often from a critical perspective, with little regard to their operation in practice or to describe the evaluation of practical developments with little regard to theory' (Crawford and Newburn 2003: 1).

Chapter 1 considers the emergence and development of intensive community programmes for both young and adult offenders in the US and England and Wales, as well as in other jurisdictions. The political impetus behind the introduction of these programmes is clear, demonstrating a desire to tackle prison overcrowding while at the same time strengthening provision in the community and still appearing 'tough on crime'. The programmes have also benefited from their ability to combine elements from the welfare, justice and actuarial 'risk management' models of criminal justice, and from their multi-faceted theoretical foundations. It is noted, however, that there are some limitations to these foundations, particularly with regard to the rationales of incapacitation and deterrence. Furthermore, there are a number of tensions between the theoretical rationales themselves, and between the rationales and the more political aims. The programmes can also be viewed as a yet further illustration of a more general 'dispersal of discipline' (Cohen 1979).

Chapter 2 explores the evidence-base for intensive community programmes, building upon evaluation findings from the US, England and Wales and elsewhere. Notably, the impact upon re-offending has been variable, with the evidence suggesting most promise for those programmes that target high-risk offenders and have a strong rehabilitation component. As for the impact upon custody rates, the twin dangers of 'net-widening' and increased levels of breach have become increasingly apparent. A number of evaluations have also raised doubts regarding the compatibility of the differing aims and objectives.

The following three chapters present a case study from the national evaluation of the first 41 ISSP schemes (Moore *et al.* 2004; Gray *et al.* 2005). Chapter 3 illustrates that ISSP fits very well into the multi-faceted framework of the 'new youth justice', particularly through its combination of supervision and surveillance. It is the most robust multi-modal community programme currently available for young offenders in England and Wales, and is much more intensive than many of its predecessors. Its primary goal is to reduce re-offending, but the further desire to reduce custody rates has become more apparent over time, particularly with the widening of the target group to include offenders committing one-off serious offences. The evaluation itself provided a valuable opportunity to examine the potential of an intensive multi-modal programme to address the offending behaviour of a high-risk target group.

Chapter 4 demonstrates that all of the ISSP schemes were successful in attracting a reasonable number of referrals. Many of the young people on the programme were already damaged and deprived by their early life experiences and a high proportion were firmly engaged in a career of criminal behaviour. Many had developed strong pro-criminal attitudes, a distrust of adults in authority and a resistance to changing behaviour. Clearly, therefore, the ISSP teams were faced with a considerable challenge. But the group was not homogeneous. Offenders qualifying on grounds of seriousness and not persistence had fewer criminogenic needs and therefore a lower risk of re-offending, and also better social problem-solving skills and fewer pro-criminal attitudes. This suggests that they may not have required the same intensity or range of supervision as persistent offenders.

Chapter 5 considers how the programme was delivered in practice. This is particularly important, bearing in mind that, 'Practitioners, in particular, play a crucial role in mediating high-level policy such that it becomes reformulated "at the coalface"' (Young and Sanders 2003: 342). Requiring a multi-modal approach with appropriate surveillance, and a process for case management, heightened the challenge facing practitioners. A range of implementation difficulties were encountered but in a relatively short period of time most schemes were able to establish viable programmes. There was considerable variation in the style and quantity of intervention provided, and practitioners reported particular difficulties in accessing education, accommodation, mental health and drugs services in some locations. The electronic tag was the most commonly utilised form of ISSP surveillance, and combining human tracking with the tag was perceived to be a particularly stringent and effective form of surveillance. The young people viewed the tag as a dominant part of the programme, while practitioners emphasised the attempts at tackling underlying problems. Maintaining engagement with the young people, as well as resolving the tension with the desire for rigorous enforcement, was far from straightforward. The highest risk offenders were least likely to comply, and many of those cases that completed successfully had been breached at some stage. While the average cost per start, including both supervision and surveillance, was just over £12,000, the average cost per successful completion was almost £32,000, indicating how attrition can render a project like ISSP substantially more expensive.

Chapter 6 considers the impact of ISSP in terms of reducing re-offending rates, addressing underlying problems, satisfying sentencers and reducing custody rates. All forms of ISSP demonstrated a large reduction in offending frequency, but the comparison groups performed at least as well. It is acknowledged that reductions in re-offending can be partly explained by the statistical phenomenon known as 'regression to the mean', according to which extreme scores at the pre-test stage tend to move naturally towards the average at the post-test stage. However, ISSP made clear inroads into tackling the underlying problems of the young people on the programme, with greater progress being made with those who completed the programme successfully. The structure provided by the intensive supervision alongside re-engagement with local services and the work undertaken within the family provided young people with a strong basis from which to progress. The vast majority of sentencers believed ISSP had an appropriate balance of supervision and surveillance and provided a useful option for the youth courts. However, the introduction of ISSP had little direct impact, at a national level, upon the use of custody for young offenders. Sentencers were keen to emphasise that custody remained the only option in certain instances, and those sentenced to custody appeared to have been slightly higher risk. But even if ISSP was to consistently target only those at genuine risk of custody, it is recognised that any impact upon custody rates will be lessened by the use of custody for breach of the programme. Overall, the ISSP evaluation demonstrates that great care and prior thought needs to be given to the development of any type of intensive programme, and that the decisions made by policy-makers, practitioners, sentencers, and all those involved in programme delivery, need to take into account the potentially conflicting aims and objectives.

The final two chapters build upon the findings from the national evaluation of ISSP and earlier evaluations. The evidence-base for such programmes is clearly developing and the emerging lessons are presented in Chapter 7. The importance of setting realistic expectations and giving careful thought to both the theoretical model and the target group is emphasised. Implementation and delivery difficulties also need to be tackled, ensuring that the programme is 'conducted in practice as intended in theory and design' (Hollin 1995: 196). Notably, tensions can arise between the caring and the controlling aims. The need for intensive programmes to provide quality contact, rather than simply more contact, is highlighted, as is the associated requirement for a well-trained, supported and cohesive staff team. Bearing in mind the 'multi-modal' nature of many intensive programmes, establishing close liaisons with a range of departments and organisations appears critical, ideally resulting in 'inter-agency' working. Maintaining programme integrity would also appear essential, with strong leadership an important ingredient. Arguments in favour of graduated responses to non-compliances and a less stringent approach towards enforcement are presented, and it is submitted that incentives are needed to encourage and reward compliance, resulting in a more balanced carrot and stick approach. To ensure the longevity of the programmes, emphasis needs to be placed upon maintaining the confidence of the practitioners themselves, the local police, sentencers and the local communities. The importance of collecting precise evidence and information case on case and at aggregate level is also highlighted. Furthermore, there is a need to raise methodological standards and to employ integrated models of evaluation, combining quantitative and qualitative methods, and broader research designs, including economic analyses and longitudinal designs.

The concluding chapter considers the longer-term prospects of intensive community programmes, addressing some of the unresolved wider concerns. The first such concern focuses upon the targeting of intensive programmes, due to the difficulties of defining persistence and identifying 'high-risk' offenders. There are particular concerns that the attempted targeting of these offenders is resulting in the detrimental labelling of a sub-group of offenders as 'innately criminal' (Downes and Morgan 2002). More generally, it can be argued that the emphasis upon risk management needs to be constrained to ensure that risk is seen alongside other social principles and priorities, e.g. justice and rehabilitation. Applying Cohen's 'dispersal of discipline' thesis (1979), it is recognised that intensive community penalties can be seen as resulting in wider, denser and different nets. Furthermore, there are strong arguments in favour of a less punitive approach and lower levels of intervention, adhering to the sentencing principle of parsimony. Another concept employed by Cohen is that of 'blurring', highlighting the breakdown of the traditional institutional/non-institutional divide. One of the clearest examples of such blurring, and also adhering to a risk management approach, is the way in which politicians and policy-makers have promoted the surveillant aspects of intensive community programmes, particularly electronic monitoring (EM). Not only can it be argued that the benefits of EM have been overstated, there are some more fundamental fears that it can have detrimental effects. Finally, it is recognised that doubts remain as to the optimum approach for measuring effectiveness. Some commentators highlight the need to take into account a wide range of outcome measures, including improvements in the young person's attitudes or skills. Wider institutional and societal goals would also appear important. Notably, some commentators have argued that the contribution of intensive programmes to 'just deserts' should be viewed as the paramount concern. Such a stance has the clear attraction of adhering to the more general calls for the promotion of the concept of proportionality in sentencing.

Part I
The development of intensive community programmes

Chapter 1

Political and theoretical foundations

This chapter presents a historical overview of the development of intensive community programmes for young and adult offenders, both in the US and in England and Wales. A diverse range of programmes have been introduced in the US, while the numerous attempts at developing intensive programmes in England and Wales have coincided with a general intensification of community penalties. More recently, there has been a proliferation of intensive programmes in many jurisdictions, including England and Wales. While there has been a strong political impetus behind the introduction of these programmes, they have also benefited from their ability to combine elements from differing models of criminal justice and from their multi-faceted theoretical foundations. However, as will be shown, there are a number of tensions between these theoretical rationales and between the rationales and the more political aims.

A diverse range of programmes

The United States

Intensive community programmes are now well established in the US, with the Intensive Supervision Program (ISP) for adult offenders dating back to the 1960s. By 1990 an ISP had been initiated in every US state, and by 1994 it was estimated that over 120,000 offenders were the subject of such a programme. The result of this expansion is that the US has become the world leader in the development of intensive programmes. As Michael Tonry (1998: 691) concludes, 'although ad hoc intensive supervision in individual cases presumably occurs in every probation system, no other country has adopted widespread programs of intensive probation'. Notably, this expansion forms just one limb of an increasingly punitive approach by US authorities: 'In recent years, concern about the problem of crime and frustration over the seeming ineffectiveness of efforts to treat offenders has led to a tougher stance towards criminals. Longer prison sentences are being imposed, the death penalty has been resurrected, and more restrictive community-based sentencing has been implemented' (Hancock and Sharp 2004: 331).

The development of national standards for US intensive programmes has been hindered by the complexity of the US system. The correctional services and related statutory responsibilities vary from state to state and are distinct from federal provision. As Hancock and Sharp (2004: 6) state, 'There is no single criminal justice system in this country. We have many similar systems that are individually unique.' The majority of intensive community programmes have been developed and implemented at the local county or state level. Consequently, a diverse range of programmes has been introduced. More specifically, there have been differences in terms of both intake, i.e. the populations, which have been targeted, and process, i.e. the content and intensity of the programmes (see Chapter 2 for examples of individual programmes).

The variability in intake or targeting has had the following three dimensions: (i) age; (ii) stage in process; and (iii) risk of re-offending. With regard to the first of these dimensions, some of the programmes have targeted adult offenders, others have been confined to young adult offenders, and the remainder have targeted young offenders. Turning to the second dimension of 'stage in process', the intensive programmes have clearly positioned themselves at different points in the criminal justice process. Some of the programmes have targeted offenders pre-custody, sometimes even pre-sentence at the bail stage, but others have sought referrals at the post-custody stage. This is reflected in the following three-way classification devised by Joan Petersilia and Susan Turner, which also recognises that some pre-custody programmes are more concerned with diversion from custody than others.

- Prison-diversion, commonly referred to as 'front door' programs because their goal is to keep offenders from entering prison's front door.

- Early-release, commonly referred to as 'back door' programs because they hasten the prisoner's exit through the prison's back door.

- Probation-enhancement or case-management, programs created and controlled by probation managers, in which participants who are deemed high risk are selected from the pool of sentenced felony probationers. (Petersilia and Turner 1990: 12)

While the 'prison-diversion' programmes need to target those offenders at risk of custody, the final variation in targeting relates to a differing form of risk. This difference is indicative of the multi-faceted nature of risk, with a clear distinction now evident between those risks to which offenders are subject and those risks that can be seen as an attribute of offenders (Robinson 2003; McNeill and Batchelor 2004). The risks of custody and self-harm clearly fall into the former category, while the risks of re-offending and of serious harm to others fall into the latter. Increasing attention has been paid to this second category, and, notably, some intensive community programmes have specifically targeted those offenders deemed to be at low to moderate risk of re-offending, while others have targeted those offenders at high risk of re-offending.

The factors that have been taken into account in assessing the risk of re-offending have varied greatly, with some risk assessments having been more formalised than others. Specific eligibility criteria have included the seriousness of the current offence, the person's offending history, the person's sentencing and/or compliance history, the length of the current sentence, and the potential threat to others. A number of schemes have employed further suitability factors, extending to the offender's specific needs and/or motivation.

As indicated above, the intensive programmes in the US have varied greatly not only in their targeting but also in their programme content and intensity. Petersilia and Turner (1992: 611) have recognised that 'there is no generic ISP program. So many programs call themselves ISP that the acronym alone reveals little about any program's particular character. The only common characteristic of ISP programs is that they involve more supervision than routine probation programs.' For the purposes of this book, intensive community programmes are those that proclaim themselves as such and emphasise the increased levels of contact. Notably, however, there is no standard as to how much more supervision is required before a programme is deemed intensive. In some instances, a doubling of the

5

number of contacts from one to two a month seems to have sufficed, whereas in other instances, an expectancy of several contacts per day has been established. Somewhat clearer is the trend over time, which has been towards continually increasing levels of intensiveness.

> Before 1980, 'intensive supervision' generally meant no more than two or three contacts per month rather than the standard one; this situation existed in operations other than experimental programs or in other special circumstances. However, by 1983–1984 the number of contacts in intensive supervision programs had often become as many as two-to-four per week. As late as 1980, this quantity might have been criticized by various reformers and academicians as 'overly intrusive social control'. But, by the last half of the 1980s, this level of contact was common, was widely accepted, and was almost unquestioned. (Palmer 1991: 98)

Intensive programmes in the US have also varied in terms of their programme components. Such components, which have been combined in numerous ways, have been listed as follows:

1 Greatly increasing contact between supervisors and offenders.
2 Confining offenders to their homes.
3 Enforcing curfews.
4 Submitting offenders to random drug testing.
5 Requiring offenders to pay restitution to victims.
6 Electronically monitoring offenders.
7 Requiring offenders to pay for the privilege of being supervised.
   (Gendreau, Goggin and Fulton 2000: 197)

As can be seen, many of these components relate to the surveillance and monitoring of offenders, and, until relatively recently, these components were dominant among the US programmes. This trend was highlighted by Ted Palmer (1991: 98–9): 'As intensive supervision programs took shape in the early 1980s, the relative priority or emphasis placed on rehabilitation as a goal changed significantly. Specifically, its role was reduced in comparison to strategies focusing on short-term behaviour control … These intensive supervision programs might be called the *control/surveillance-centered programs of the 1980s*.' In other words, in many of the US programmes, supervision has actually meant monitoring, surveillance and control rather than treatment or rehabilitation. However, some of the more recent US models have incorporated, to a lesser or greater extent, a rehabilitative/treatment dimension. These models have been dubbed the second generation of intensive rehabilitation supervision programmes (Gendreau, Cullen and Bonta 1994). Nevertheless, diversity remains prevalent with the balance between control and treatment in these programmes ranging greatly.

England and Wales

Recent decades have also witnessed numerous attempts at developing intensive community interventions in England and Wales. Many of these attempts can be seen as examples of 'policy transfer' from the US to the UK (Newburn 2002a). Other such examples include 'zero tolerance', curfews, 'three strikes', private prisons and electronic monitoring. In contrast to the US, however, the intensive community initiatives in England and Wales have tended to be short-lived. There has, nevertheless, been a proliferation and a more general strengthening and intensification of community sentences for both young offenders and adult offenders. This can be traced back to the Children and Young Persons Act 1969, since described as 'the high point of "welfarism"' (Newburn 2002b), which introduced the Supervision Order for young offenders. This was followed three years later by the Criminal Justice Act 1972 which first placed the Community Service Order (CSO) on a statutory footing, and permitted the experimental use of day training centres by probation services. Following a short trial period, the CSO was made available nationally in 1975. Prior to this development, the Probation Order had been the main community sentence for adult offenders, having been introduced formally by the Probation of Offenders Act 1907.

In the following decade, the Criminal Justice Act 1982, which was seen as signifying a move away from welfare towards the concerns of justice, extended the availability of CSOs to 16-year-olds, while enabling courts to add further requirements to Supervision Orders, including night-time restrictions, and to Probation Orders, including attendance at a day centre (the latter probation requirements were commonly referred to as 4A and 4B orders). With regard to Supervision Orders, Rob Allen (1991: 45) noted that the new requirements were 'designed to bolster the credibility of supervision orders and arrest the decline in their use by magistrates'. Attempts to further promote the use of community sentences for 'top-end' cases were made through the Criminal Justice Act 1988 by imposing strict criteria upon the use of custodial sentences.

Moving into the 1990s, the Criminal Justice Act 1991 abandoned the terminology of 'alternatives to custody' and established community sentences as punishments in their own right, all within an explicit 'just deserts' model of sentencing. The focus was upon ensuring *appropriate* punishment, and the preceding White Paper (Home Office 1990: para 4.3) stated that, 'Punishment in the community should be an effective way of dealing with many offenders, particularly those convicted of property crimes and less serious offences of violence.' The Combination Order was introduced by the 1991 Act, combining probation and community service in a single sentence. The aim of this order was 'to provide a particularly demanding non-custodial measure for some of the petty persistent property offenders who had hitherto all too often been sentenced to custody' (Cavadino and Dignan 2002: 145). With hindsight, it can be seen as the beginning of a trend towards the 'creative mixing' of differing types of intervention (Bottoms, Rex and Robinson 2004).

The 1991 Act also placed the Curfew Order, supported by electronic monitoring, on a statutory footing, authorising its use either alone or in combination with other community penalties. It was introduced on an area-by-area basis by the Criminal Justice and Public Order Act 1994, before finally being extended to all courts in December 1999. In the meantime, the Drug Treatment and Testing Order had been introduced through the Crime and Disorder Act 1998, with national implementation following in 2000. Tony Bottoms, Sue Rex and Gwen Robinson (2004) recognise that both these orders can be seen as indicative of a dual emphasis upon 'punishment in the community' and 'public protection'. In the field of youth justice, the Crime and Disorder Act 1998 introduced both the Action Plan Order and the Reparation Order. The former was introduced as 'a short intensive programme of community intervention combining punishment, rehabilitation and reparation' (Home Office 1997a: 7). The Youth Justice and Criminal Evidence Act 1999 soon followed, establishing the Referral Order as the normal disposal for most young offenders convicted at court for the first time.

The pace of change, if anything, quickened in the early years of the twenty-first century. The Criminal Justice and Court Services Act 2000 enabled courts to allow the conditions of other community penalties to be monitored electronically, as well as introducing the Exclusion Order, requiring offenders to stay away from a certain place or places. The terminology of community penalties was toughened, with the Powers of Criminal Courts (Sentencing) Act 2000 renaming Probation Orders as Community Rehabilitation Orders (CROs),

CSOs as Community Punishment Orders and Combination Orders as Community Punishment and Rehabilitation Orders. More recently, the Anti-Social Behaviour Act 2003 increased the maximum number of 'specified activity' days from 90 to 180 for Supervision Orders, and lengthened the maximum duration of a Curfew Order from three to six months for offenders aged under 16.

More radical statutory provisions have now been introduced through the Criminal Justice Act 2003. All the previous developments for adult offenders have to be considered in the light of these provisions as they abolish all pre-existing community sentences and recreate them as 'requirements' that may be included in a new 'generic' community sentence. There are 12 such requirements and the courts have discretion to combine them as they see fit. Similar proposals have been considered for young offenders, with a new generic juvenile community sentence replacing the majority of the existing community sentences. For both young and adult offenders, this flexibility can be seen as the culmination of 'creative mixing', balancing the concerns of punishment, effectiveness and public safety (Bottoms, Rex and Robinson 2004). According to one view, the likely result is further intensification:

> The many divergent demands placed upon the probation service have led to the 'creative mixing' of different requirements imposed upon offenders. It seems probable that the possibility of combining the existing community penalties under the new single Community Order introduced by the Criminal Justice Act 2003 will exacerbate this tendency to intensify the requirements placed upon offenders. Indeed the tendency has already been identified as 'condition creep' or 'sentence stacking'. (Zedner 2004: 236)

All these statutory developments provide the context for the numerous attempts at developing intensive community programmes in England and Wales. As noted above, these initiatives have tended to be short-lived. Usefully, Anne Worrall and Rob Mawby (2004: 269) have identified the following three 'generations' of programmes for adult offenders: 'those which developed in the 1970s, those which were a feature of the 1980s and early 1990s but which continue in various forms to the present time, and those which emerged in the late 1990s and are proliferating in the early years of the twenty-first century'.

As in the US, there has been considerable diversity in both targeting and programme structure, with national standards maintaining a degree of discretion at the local level. Generally speaking, however, the programmes in England and Wales have tended to be more intensive than their US counterparts, and the need for some form of treatment/rehabilitation has been more consistently applied. Furthermore, the use of terminology has been more consistent with supervision referring to the treatment/rehabilitation components, rather than the accompanying surveillance/monitoring components. The programmes have also tended to target young, young adult or adult offenders at the pre-custody stage, with diversion from custody a more consistent objective.

The recent history of intensive programmes in England and Wales begins with the probation experiment known as IMPACT (Intensive Matched Probation and After-Care Treatment), which was initiated in the early 1970s. This initiative sought to treat high-risk adult offenders 'intensively' in the community with significantly lighter caseloads than normal. In the following decade, utilising the provisions of the Criminal Justice Act 1982, the Department of Health and Social Security funded a wide range of Intermediate Treatment (IT) projects that were intensive in nature, targeting those 'high-tariff' serious and/or persistent young offenders deemed to be at risk of custody. Further Intensive Probation (IP) experiments were also conducted in the 1980s and early 1990s in several probation areas, utilising the 4A and 4B orders of the 1982 Act. These experiments targeted those young adults aged between 17 and 25 years who had committed fairly serious offences such as burglary and who were considered likely to receive a custodial sentence.

In the late 1990s another model of intensive supervision, targeting persistent offenders, began its development. This approach, which had originally been pioneered in the city of Dordrecht (Van Zon 1994) in the Netherlands, was adopted in Burnley in the north-west of England as part of a Safer Cities partnership. The central element of the Burnley/Dordrecht initiative was the combination of targeted policing of prolific offenders and intensive probation supervision, with the local police and probation area working closely together. The independent evaluation, by a group from the University of Huddersfield, was largely positive about the approach adopted, reporting that it combined 'benefits to prolific offenders in helping with the problems that sustain them in crime, and benefits to the community in ensuring that those who persist in crime despite such help are promptly removed from the community' (Chenery and Pease 2000: 4). The approach then spread slowly to other locations in Lancashire and Staffordshire where they were typically described as

Intensive Supervision and Monitoring Projects (ISMs).

In May 2004 a Joint Inspection Report into Persistent and Prolific Offenders described positively the benefits of the early ISM projects, and concluded that 'all of the interventions inspected showed promising results with regard to rehabilitation and crime reduction which local stakeholders found convincing' (HM Chief Inspector of Constabulary *et al.* 2004: 31). It recommended the further development of ISMs, and suggested that 'funding streams for work with priority offenders should be easy to access via a national framework' (*ibid.*: 34). Then, in September 2004, the Home Office launched a national Prolific and other Priority Offender (PPO) Strategy, requiring a PPO scheme to be established in every CDRP in England and Wales. Worrall and Mawby (2004: 270) emphasise that these projects 'seek to provide a mix of frequent contact, access to treatment (particularly drugs treatment) and community facilities, and constant monitoring'. They further assert that the major departure they offer from other projects is 'their avoidance of the pitfall of relying on offenders to reduce their own rates of re-offending'. There are currently more than 40 such projects operating in different local police areas.

Alongside these developments, the Youth Justice Board (YJB) introduced the Intensive Supervision and Surveillance Programme (ISSP) in 2001, targeting persistent and serious young offenders. Shortly afterwards an Intensive Control and Change Programme (ICCP) was piloted in designated probation areas with young adult offenders. The ICCP has now been superseded by the requirements set out in the Criminal Justice Act 2003, which can be combined to provide an intensive community order, involving a 'significant restriction on liberty, which is delivered either via 4 or more different requirements, of which one must be supervision, or through a smaller number of very demanding, restrictive and/or punitive requirements'. The aim of this intensive order is 'to provide the courts with a robust and intensive community disposal that combines both punishment and, where appropriate, rehabilitation for offenders who represent the highest likelihood of re-offending, have multiples needs and who have committed a serious offence' (National Probation Service 2005a: 2).

In the field of youth justice, the seemingly ever-increasing intensification is further demonstrated by the development of schemes such as intensive fostering (Youth Justice Board 2004a), and the recommendations of the Office for Criminal Justice Reform that those young PPOs who are not eligible for ISSP should receive a programme of 'equivalent rigour and intensity' (Lee and Wildgoose

2005: 31). It has also been proposed that an Intensive Supervision and Surveillance Order (ISSO) should supersede the administrative ISSP.

Other jurisdictions

Interestingly, this recent proliferation of intensive programmes in England and Wales is mirrored in other jurisdictions. In Canada, the Youth Criminal Justice Act 2003 has established both the Intensive Support and Supervision Order and the Intensive Rehabilitative Custody and Supervision Order for juvenile offenders (Bala and Roberts 2004). In New Zealand, the priority interventions now include a number of intensive rehabilitation programmes, targeting differing age groups and risk levels, while in Western Australia, an Intensive Supervision Program was introduced in late 2004, targeting serious or persistent juveniles at the pre- and post-custody stages.

Moving back into Europe, a two-year intensive social, educational and employment training programme for young offenders was introduced in Denmark in 2001 (Vestergaard 2004). Also in Scandinavia, intensive supervision with electronic monitoring was introduced in Sweden on a permanent basis in 1999, operating as an alternative to short custodial sentences (National Council for Crime Prevention 1999). Finally, juvenile punishment has been piloted in Finland, consisting of youth service of 10 to 60 hours and intensive supervision for four to 12 months (Criminal Sanctions Agency 2003).

The political impetus

The proliferation of intensive community programmes in the US and the revived interest in such programmes in England and Wales has coincided with growing concerns regarding the levels of custodial sentencing. In the US, official custody figures for mid-2003 indicated that the state and federal prisons held nearly one and a half million offenders, while the local jails held over 750,000 persons, amounting to well in excess of two million people in total (Bureau of Justice 2004). This is the consequence of a steady rise in numbers, with the population growing an average 3.7 per cent per year between 1995 and 2003. As for England and Wales, there has been a similar surge in custodial sentencing, with over 77,000 people in custody at the end of November 2005, compared to a little over 45,000 in 1992. Looking at recently published prison population rates, the US emerges as the world leader with some 702 prisoners per 100,000 of the national population, with England and Wales the leader among the Western European countries with a rate of 137 per 100,000 (Councell 2003).

The drawbacks of custody

These increases have taken place despite the research evidence that suggests custody is relatively ineffective in reducing offending levels. In terms of the general incapacitative effect of custody, Home Office research in England and Wales (Tarling 1993) has estimated that a 25 per cent increase in custodial sentencing would be required to produce a 1 per cent fall in the level of crime. Custody is also relatively expensive. Towards the end of the twentieth century, Home Office (1999) figures indicated that the cost of a custodial sentence per person per month was £2,070, significantly higher than the corresponding costs of community rehabilitation and community punishment, which then stood at £183 and £141 respectively.

As for the effectiveness of custody in preventing individual offenders from re-offending, further Home Office (2003) statistics indicate that, of all prisoners discharged in 1999, 59 per cent were reconvicted within two years of their discharge, with a rate of 74 per cent for those young males under the age of 21. The criminological literature reveals particular concerns regarding the 'labelling effect' (Becker 1963). This phenomenon recognises that positive deterrent effects can be counteracted by the labelling of people as ex-prisoners and the consequent stigma that this carries, although how these positive and negative effects balance out in practice remains unclear. Such labelling has been viewed as a particular danger with young offenders: 'penal custody leads to broken links with family, friends, education, work and leisure and causes stigmatization and labelling. Rather than reintegrating young people into the communities where they must learn to live, custody results in increased alienation and greater risk of further offending' (Children's Society 1989). In addition, while the public may be protected in the short term, a multitude of crime is committed within prisons, and there is the potential for offenders to learn new 'tricks of the trade' while residing in these 'universities of crime'. Consequently, custody is often seen as an 'expensive way of making bad people worse' (Home Office 1990).

Furthermore, the warehousing of offenders in cramped conditions has obvious resource implications and limits the attempts that can be made at developing high-quality rehabilitation and treatment programmes. This was highlighted in the White Paper, *Justice for*

All (Home Office 2002: 106): 'High prison numbers mean staff have to spend more time supervising the additional offenders. This reduces the amount of time prisoners can spend outside their cells in education, training or work ... High prison numbers also lead to constant transfers to prisons all over the country. This means a prisoner may well have to move before he or she completes a rehabilitative programme.' Notably, at the end of October 2004, 82 of the 139 prisons in England and Wales were reported to be overcrowded (Prison Reform Trust 2004).

The overwhelming research evidence therefore contradicts the view that 'prison works', as was claimed by the then Home Secretary Michael Howard in the early 1990s (Downes 2001). A more reasoned consideration of the evidence has led the Coulsfield Inquiry (2004: 45) – an independent body of commissioners which considered submissions from a wide range of organisations and drew upon a body of research – to 'question whether a civilized, modern society should continue to use a model of custody developed in the nineteenth century – indeed not just to use it but expand it – particularly as it does not seem to be particularly effective in preventing re-offending'. The inquiry's report provides a useful overview of the counter-arguments to pro-custody claims:

- it exaggerates the effectiveness of prison as a means of controlling crime ... although prison incapacitates offenders while they are there, research evidence shows that increasing the severity of sentence does not have a deterrent effect – although increasing the likelihood of detection does;

- it underrates the damaging effects of imprisonment on both individuals and their families and contributes to the cycle of deprivation and crime in high-crime areas;

- its theoretical or philosophical basis does not fit with the reality that much of the prison population is young, underprivileged, illiterate and mentally ill;

- it involves abandoning some members of society and treating them as, in effect, outlaws with whose rehabilitation or reform society need not be concerned and who can simply be dealt with by straightforward punishment;

- overcrowded prisons can do little or nothing for reform or rehabilitation;

- whatever uncertainties there may be about the costs of some interventions, prison is vastly expensive compared with the alternatives;

- whatever the difficulties and limitations of the evidence about alternatives, it suggests that if properly targeted and resourced they can, at least sometimes, produce better results than imprisonment. (Coulsfield Inquiry 2004: 53)

These points should not be simply accepted at face value, however, and some qualifications can be made. Notably, punishment is never 'straightforward'. It has deeply rooted cultural significance, and this is particularly true of the prison. Furthermore, offenders are not 'abandoned' within prisons, as rehabilitative attempts continue to be made (although subject to the resource limitations set out above). Nevertheless, the UN Convention on the Rights of the Child has brought the acceptability of custody for young people in England and Wales into further question. Notably, Article 37 requires that the 'detention or imprisonment of a child shall ... be used only as a measure of last resort and for the shortest appropriate period of time'. Reporting on this convention in 2003, a House of Lords and House of Commons Joint Committee on Human Rights (2003) raised particular concerns over the levels of physical assault, self-harm and suicides in Young Offender Institutions (YOIs), the lack of adequate educational and rehabilitative opportunities available in these institutions, as well as the distances between some of the young people and their families. Highlighting the vulnerability, typical circumstances and life experiences of the young people, the Joint Committee held that when 'coupled with the conditions prevailing within custodial institutions, the high rates of re-offending may appear to be almost inevitable' (*ibid.*: 23). The Committee concluded that the Government should 're-examine, with renewed urgency, sentencing policy and practice (and in particular the use of detention and training order) and alternatives to custodial sentences, with the specific aim of reducing the number of young people entering custody' (*ibid.*: 21).

The attractions of intensive community programmes

This proposal highlights the need to consider the alternatives to custody. The political support for intensive community programmes at a time of prison overcrowding is no coincidence, as those programmes that fall within the 'prison-diversion' category are seen as having the greatest potential to limit and possibly even reduce the levels of custodial sentencing. In an attempt to ensure that these programmes target offenders at genuine risk of a custodial sentence, policy-makers have repeatedly stressed that the initiatives are both tough and stringent, promoting the view that they are credible alternatives to custody, rather than less punitive and less demanding community penalties. In contrast, the 'probation enhancement' or 'case management' programmes operate as alternatives to non-intensive probation, rather than custody. Consequently, they can only have an indirect impact upon custody rates by preventing further offending from which a custodial sentence might have resulted (Petersilia and Turner 1990).

Politicians and policy-makers have seemingly paid particular attention to public opinion, becoming increasingly eager to avoid the perception that they are 'soft on crime'. Populist punitivism has come to the fore, emerging initially in the US in the early 1960s, and then developing in the UK in the late 1970s/early 1980s with a real expansion in the 1990s (Newburn 2002a). Such punitivism poses significant problems in terms of limiting the use of custody. Not only is this viewed as the most punitive sanction, for some it is seen as the only genuine punishment. The media typically promotes such a view: 'In the pages of the popular press, imposition of a community sentence is commonly portrayed as a failure to punish; community rehabilitation (formerly probation) is condemned as a "let-off"; and community punishment (formerly community service) is deemed a benefit rather than a detriment at times when work is scarce' (Zedner 2004: 199).

Yet, in contrast to these conventional community sentences, intensive community programmes, which are both 'tough' and 'stringent', can be promoted as an altogether different proposition. For policy-makers, therefore, intensive programmes offer a potential solution to their dilemma of wanting to reduce custody levels while not appearing soft on crime (Gendreau, Cullen and Bonta 1994). But while the rhetoric may be tough, the programmes have the further attractions of avoiding the damaging effects of imprisonment and enabling offenders to maintain their links with their family and the wider community. Furthermore, additional rehabilitative components can be provided alongside the more controlling and punitive aspects of the programmes, with the ultimate goal of reducing re-offending.

The political attractiveness of intensive community programmes is thus further guaranteed through their potential ability to reduce both re-offending and custody rates. Which of these two goals is promoted can also be varied according to the political priorities of the time.

There are numerous important assumptions here, however, that will need to be revisited. For example, will the public and sentencers perceive intensive programmes as 'tough' and 'stringent'? Will the damaging effects of labelling be avoided? Will practitioners be able to successfully marry the rehabilitative and controlling aspects of the programmes? Will the programmes successfully target those who would otherwise have received a custodial sentence or will the use of custody increase through more active and punitive breaching policies and practices?

The literature indicates that other subsidiary factors have encouraged the expansion of intensive community programmes. In the US, their proliferation has signified an attempt to restore confidence in probation and community sentences more generally, overcoming a poor public relations image (Lurigio and Petersilia 1992: 9). The need to maintain credibility has also been evident in England and Wales, as recognised by David Garland:

> Over the last thirty years, probation has had to struggle to maintain its credibility, as the ideals upon which it was based have been discredited and displaced. Under pressure from government it has tightened its procedures, highlighted its supervisory capacities, downplayed its social work affiliations, intensified its controls, and represented itself as a community punishment. 'Intensive probation orders' have been deployed, involving heavier restrictions and reporting requirements, and probation supervision has increasingly been 'blended' with more explicitly penal measures, such as curfews, partial custody, and fines. (Garland 2001: 177)

In the US, commentators have further suggested that doubts about the effectiveness and value of community sentences have 'seeped into the daily work attitudes of probation officers themselves' (Clear 1997: 121). In consequence, achievement of the above 'institutional aim' is intended to increase the levels of esteem of the probation officers themselves, fulfilling a further 'professional aim' (Tonry 1990).

Theoretical context

While the political impetus behind the introduction of intensive community programmes has been strong and figured prominently, the programmes have benefited further from their ability to combine elements from differing models of criminal justice, displaying 'echoes of both the old "welfare" and "justice" models as well as signs of the influence of "new" penological thinking' (Newburn 2002c: 456). Beginning with the two older models, although certain eras have been portrayed as welfare-orientated or justice-orientated, 'neither model has been fully realized in practice' (Muncie 2004: 266), and intensive community programmes provide a clear example of how the two models can be combined. More specifically, adhering to the welfare model, the programmes offer the scope to address offenders' needs and tailor treatment appropriately, while following the justice model, they can contribute to the provision of proportionality in sentencing.

Taken together, the welfare and justice models are seen by Malcolm Feely and Jonathan Simon (1994: 173) as representing the 'old penology', and they argue that a 'new penology' has come to the fore, which they describe as 'actuarial', being 'concerned with techniques for identifying, classifying, and managing groups assorted by levels of dangerousness'. Kempf-Leonard and Peterson (2002: 432) provide the following elaboration: 'In short, actuarial justice presents a theoretical model of criminal justice processing in which the pursuit of efficiency and techniques that streamline case processing and offender supervision replace traditional goals of rehabilitation, punishment, deterrence, and incapacitation, and the focus on due process or crime control procedures.' Once again there is a fit between this model and intensive community programmes, as the programmes provide a potential method for managing high risk offenders. Kempf-Leonard and Peterson (2002: 433) further note that 'if a policy or procedure draws more heavily from the logic of actuarialism, eventually, it is more likely to be evaluated solely in terms of its cost-effectiveness and efficiency in management'. It is thus as significant, that many intensive programmes have been promoted on the basis of their potential cost-effectiveness compared to custody.

Intensive community programmes can be seen, therefore, as exemplifying a 'hybrid formation' of criminal justice models, supporting the view of Garland (2001: 167) that 'new practices and mentalities co-exist with the residues and continuations of older arrangements'. There is a further potential fit between the proliferation of intensive community programmes and Stanley Cohen's 'dispersal of discipline' thesis (1979). The thrust of his analysis is that community corrections widen the net 'by expanding networks of social control and diffusing surveillance. It pulls more people into the system and it 'thins the mesh' by subjecting them to more intense supervision. The combined effect is greater 'penetration': the system of social control extends ever more deeply into society, augmenting existing control mechanisms (most notably the prison) rather than acting as alternatives to them' (Zedner 2004: 201).

The relevance and strength of this theory in relation to intensive community programmes depends upon the degree to which they target those offenders who would previously have received less demanding community sentences rather than custodial sentences. Nevertheless, it is very apparent that the proliferation of intensive programmes offers more support to the 'dispersal of discipline' theory than to the rival 'juridical revival' theory outlined by Tony Bottoms. In the juridical system, Bottoms (1983: 176) states, 'there is no specific penal administrative apparatus designed to mould offenders into obedient subjects' and 'just enough punishment is applied to act as a deterrent to the offender and to others'. In contrast, intensive programmes often seek to combine surveillance and supervision, commonly presented as control and care, and their theoretical foundations are multi-faceted, attempting to fuse consequentialist forward-looking theories of deterrence, incapacitation and rehabilitation with backward-looking retribution and a promotion of 'just deserts'.

In considering these differing rationales, the following four-way classification of interventions, designed by John Muncie in his consideration of youth justice, provides a useful starting point:

1 *welfare-based interventions* designed to help young people in trouble and to secure their rehabilitation and reintegration into mainstream society;

2 *justice-based interventions* designed to give young people the same legal rights as those afforded to adults and divert them from the damaging effects of court and custodial processing;

3 *risk management interventions* designed to identify those 'at risk of offending' and secure their 'restoration' through pragmatic, cost-effective and proven methods;

4 *authoritarian interventions* designed to punish offenders and prevent further offending through punitive deterrence. (Muncie 2004: 250)

Notably, intensive community programmes can be classified as welfare-based, risk management or authoritarian interventions, depending upon their particular make-up. The remaining classification, 'justice-based', is also relevant as there is a clear link to the political desire for intensive programmes to reduce custody rates. More important from a theoretical perspective, however, is the ability of the programmes to contribute to 'just deserts', and this provides a preferable fourth classification of proportionate interventions. As shown below, there would appear to be some tensions between these classifications, and with the more political agenda.

A welfare-based intervention

While differing definitions and models of rehabilitation have been developed (Lewis 2005), criminal justice interventions are often seen as rehabilitative when the following criteria are fulfilled:

> (1) the intervention is planned or explicitly undertaken, not a chance or unwitting occurrence; (2) the intervention targets for change some aspect about the offender that is thought to cause the offender's criminality, such as his or her attitudes, cognitive processes, personality or mental health, social relationships to others, educational and vocational skills, and employment; and (3) the intervention is intended to make the offender less likely to break the law in the future. (Cullen and Gendreau 2000: 112)

The attraction of rehabilitation, therefore, is that it represents a more determined attempt to achieve 'longer-term offender change', rather than simply having 'a narrow, short-term, in-program crime-control focus' (Petersilia and Turner 1990: 11). While many of the US intensive programmes of the 1980s tended to prioritise deterrence (Gendreau, Cullen and Bonta 1994), a number of the more recent models have incorporated rehabilitative/treatment components, attempting to address welfare needs. Such components have also been a feature of many of the programmes in England and Wales, although there has been considerable variance in the balance between deterrence and rehabilitation. This balance has often been portrayed as leading to an uncomfortable allegiance between control and care, particularly in the area of youth justice due to heightened welfarist concerns.

More generally, rehabilitation was a primary doctrine in both the US and England and Wales during the 1950s and 1960s, with a prominent belief that it was possible to 'cure' criminality. However, this belief fell from favour in the late 1970s, largely due to mixed research findings in both jurisdictions (e.g. Lipton, Martinson and Wilks 1975;

Brody 1976), and particularly an essay by Robert Martinson (1974), which was interpreted as concluding that 'nothing works'. However, Martinson's analysis included a number of qualifications and he later retracted his most negative statements, adopting the more cautious position that 'treatments will be found to be "impotent" under certain conditions, beneficial under others, and detrimental under still others' (Martinson 1979).

A body of research has since developed that demonstrates that some things work to some extent with some offenders. This research includes a number of meta-analytic studies (e.g. Lipsey 1992; 1995), which measure statistically the average effect on recidivism across a range of evaluations, accounting for such factors as the risk levels of the offenders and the type of treatment, as well as the methodology employed. Such an approach is not without its weaknesses, however, as the results are influenced by which studies are included and how they are coded. Nevertheless, meta-analysis has greater statistical power than traditional narrative reviews, and has usefully revealed that recidivism is, on average, ten percentage points lower for treatment groups than control groups (Cullen and Gendreau 2000).

The meta-analytic studies have also revealed considerable variations in effectiveness, and this has, in turn, led to the development of the 'What Works' principles, attempting to distinguish the most effective programmes from the least effective ones (McGuire 1995). Significantly, these principles do not represent a return to the welfarist era of the 1950s and 1960s, with Garland (2001) arguing that the objectives are now more constrained, reflecting the increasing importance afforded to dimensions of risk. To this extent, there is a degree of overlap between viewing intensive community programmes as welfare-based or risk management interventions.

> The practice of rehabilitation is increasingly inscribed in a framework of risk rather than a framework of welfare. Offenders can only be 'treated' (in drug-abuse programmes, anger-management groups, offence-reduction programmes, etc.) to the extent that such treatment is deemed to be capable of protecting the public, reducing risk, and becoming more cost-effective than simple, unadorned punishment. Rehabilitation is thus presented as a targeted intervention inculcating self-controls, reducing danger, enhancing the security of the public. In the new framework rehabilitation is viewed as a means of managing risk, not a welfarist end in itself. (Garland 2001: 176)

21

The following 'What Works' principles (McGuire 1995) can be seen as particularly relevant to the development of intensive community programmes:

- **Risk classification**: the level and intensity of intervention should be matched to the risk of re-offending.

- **Criminogenic needs**: offending-related needs should be addressed as a priority.

- **Community base**: community-based interventions yield, on balance, more effective outcomes than those in custodial settings.

- **Treatment modality**: programmes should be multi-modal, addressing the multiple needs of offenders with multiple services – also known as the 'breadth principle' (Palmer 1992). They should be skills orientated and use behavioural, cognitive or cognitive-behavioural methods.

- **Programme integrity**: the stated aims should be linked to the methods used. There should be adequate resources and well-trained staff, and an agreed plan for monitoring and evaluation.

Further research has revealed that persistent offenders, often the target group for intensive community programmes, tend to fall into the high-risk category with multiple criminogenic needs, encompassing family factors, education/employment factors, community factors and personal/individual factors (Audit Commission 2004). Positively, intensive programmes offer the scope for a multi-modal approach, addressing the multiple needs of offenders with multiple services. Such approaches have become increasingly popular, as exemplified by the development and expansion of Multi-Systemic Therapy (MST) in the US. Cullen and Gendreau (2000: 153) summarise its philosophy, noting that 'its approach is social-ecological in the sense that it views individuals as enmeshed in multiple systems, including the family, peer group, school, and community. Interventions thus must be "multisystemic", targeting for change criminogenic aspects of the individual and the contexts in which he or she is situated.'

The 'What Works' principles are continually evolving, and James McGuire (2002: 3) notes that 'the focus is now upon more complex questions of what works when, where, and with whom; and why the various combinations of such elements form the patterns that they do'. It is particularly important to recognise that the 'What Works' principles, as well as the more general agenda in England and Wales, are not set in stone, and that some question marks remain. George Mair (2004: 29–30), for example, concludes that 'the reality is that the What Works initiative – a massive undertaking in criminal justice experimentation and one which carries huge risks for the National Probation Service – is not based on solid ground, is being implemented in not particularly conducive circumstances and shows what at best might be described as not very encouraging results'. Reviewing the recent research findings, a Home Office report (Debidin and Lovbakke 2004: 48) has highlighted the following three problems: the rapid expansion of programmes, the ineffective targeting of programmes, and higher than expected attrition rates.

The 'What Works' agenda has so far seen a particular and deliberate promotion of cognitive-behavioural interventions in preference to other types of provision. Such cognitive-behavioural work, which can be delivered within the framework of an intensive community programme, is indicative of a further change in emphasis for rehabilitation. As Garland (2001: 176) states, 'Where once the individual's personality or social relations formed the object of transformative efforts, that object is now offence behaviour and the habits most closely associated with it'. Put simply, the emphasis is now upon 'teaching' rather than 'treating', as demonstrated by the following summary of cognitive-behavioural work:

> Cognitive skills and behavioural programmes are a broad description given to approaches that seek to reduce re-offending by modifying anti-social ways of thinking and associated behaviour. 'Cognitive-behaviourism' is not a unified, distinct psychological theory or method but, rather, a term derived from three distinct theories:
>
> - **Behaviourism**: which stresses the role of external, environmental factors in shaping an individual's actions, typically through positive reinforcement or punishment;
>
> - **Cognitive theory**: in which the role of an individual's thought processes, such as reasoning, memory and problem solving are stressed; and
>
> - **Social learning theory**: which emphasises the role of social factors and the importance of learning through interaction with others. (Utting and Vennard 2000: 39-40)

There remains, however, a wide range of theoretical models of treatment, all of which can be employed within the framework of an intensive community programme, and attention has recently 'been moving from sole focus on offenders' cognitive deficits to community integration. There have been some significant achievements, for example in raising the profile of basic skills and developing a more consistent framework to tackle basic skills needs' (Debidin and Lovbakke 2004: 66). Intensive community programmes can clearly tap into such achievements. More specifically, local probation areas have entered into partnerships with Learning and Skills Councils and Job Centre Plus agencies, as well as local Drug Action Teams (Knott 2004). For young offenders, there are now a number of programmes in England and Wales that seek to reintegrate young offenders into mainstream schooling or involve them in further education. There are also family-based interventions and mentoring schemes, the latter involving frequent contact with an appropriate role model, providing both friendship and non-judgemental support.

There has also been increasing support in England and Wales for various forms of Restorative Justice (RJ). Perhaps the best-known definition of RJ is that it is a 'process whereby the parties with a stake in a particular offence come together to resolve collectively how to deal with the aftermath of the offence and its implications for the future' (Marshall 1996: 37). Adam Crawford and Tim Newburn (2003: 22) build upon this definition, identifying three 'central elements' of RJ: 'the notion of stakeholder inclusion, the importance of participatory and deliberative processes and the emphasis upon restorative outcomes'. These elements of the RJ process can, once again, be incorporated within an intensive community framework.

To summarise, therefore, the intensity and flexibility of intensive community programmes suggest promise for rehabilitation as a coherent theoretical rationale. Notably, there is the potential to deliver multi-modal interventions with a range of treatment components, suitably tailored to the individual offender. However, it is important to recognise that the rationale sits somewhat uneasily alongside the political emphasis upon punitiveness. Put simply, there is a potential tension, not unique to intensive community programmes, between control and care.

A proportionate intervention

While rehabilitation, along with deterrence and incapacitation, are forward-looking rationales for intensive community programmes, in the sense that they are concerned with preventing further offending, either in the short term or over a more sustained period, a further attraction of intensive programmes is that they can fulfil more backward-looking retributivist tendencies. The importance of this aspect is highlighted by Todd Clear (1991: 39): 'A simple conceptual test shows that these interventions, while *potentially* rehabilitative, are used *because they are punitive.*' More specifically, the programmes can help ensure that the offender receives his or her 'just deserts' by enabling courts to tailor the punishment to the current offence. Desert theory is summarised by Andrew Ashworth (2002: 1078) as follows: 'The political premise is that all individuals are entitled to equal respect and dignity; an offender deserves punishment, but does not forfeit all rights on conviction, and has a right not to be punished disproportionately to the crime committed.'

There has been a long-standing perception, among much of the public and many sentencers, that the divide between standard community sentences and custody is too wide, and that the courts have lacked an appropriate middle option. Intensive community programmes can potentially fill this gap: 'If community-based programs can be made sufficiently punitive, but in a manner that is neither abusive nor lingering in its effect, then we will have successfully expanded the range of existing penalties to better fit the diversity of criminal behavior. The choice between prison and probation has never been a very satisfactory one' (McCarthy 1987: 3).

Ensuring 'just deserts' would appear, therefore, to provide an alternative rationale for intensive community programmes. However, this argument potentially supports the view that while intensive programmes are more punitive than conventional community penalties, they are less punitive than custody. This raises the spectre of Cohen's 'dispersal of discipline' thesis, suggesting that some of those offenders referred on to the programmes would have previously received less intensive community supervision. In this sense, there would appear to be a clear tension with the political agenda as this prescribes that the programmes should be viewed as genuine alternatives to custody and equally punitive, targeting those who would previously have received a custodial sentence. A further tension would appear to exist between 'just deserts' and the welfare-based rationale, as the latter's emphasis upon tackling underlying needs could, in some instances, require more prolonged and intensive intervention than is justified by the seriousness of the current offence. Finally, there would appear to be a more specific tension between 'just deserts' and the 'What

Works' principle of risk classification, as the latter prescribes more intensive provision for persistent offenders, who tend to be at high risk of re-offending, thus prioritising the offenders' criminal history rather than offence seriousness.

A risk management intervention

The 'new penology' of actuarial justice promotes a 'risk management' approach to dealing with offenders. This term is summarised by Gwen Robinson (2002: 6) as follows: '[It] essentially implies a shift of focus away from individuals in favour of categories or aggregates of potential or actual deviants; and from a position of rehabilitative or "transformative" optimism, in favour of more limited, "managerial" goals.' Similarly, Lucia Zedner (2004: 9) states that risk management 'is a device for identifying and classifying groups sorted by level of dangerousness and managing them through surveillance, prevention, and incapacitation'. Notably, intensive community programmes can be seen as incapacitative in two differing senses. First, stringent enforcement policies can be established, ensuring that any breaches of the programme and/or further offending result in swift revocation to custody. Second, the surveillance component of the programme can itself be seen as incapacitative: 'intensive supervision from the perspective of crime control and reduction entails transferring the technology of control from the institution to the community, thereby continuing a reliance on the philosophy of incapacitation as offenders are diverted from secure correctional placement' (Armstrong 1991: 17–18). Other commentators have been keen to emphasise, however, that incapacitation in the community does not equal incarceration: 'Most of the current intermediate sanction models are built on the general premise of creating jail cells in the community. The fact that communities are open systems where people have considerable freedom of movement, and not closed-system total institutions (as are prisons), is conveniently ignored by policymakers' (Cochran 1992: 309–10).

A feature of incapacitative measures in recent years, in line with the principles of risk management, has been the targeting of both persistent offenders and those thought to represent a risk of serious harm. For the latter group, Pratt (1989: 244) acknowledges that there 'is an official and recognised separation between serious/violent/ dangerous "*hard core*'" offenders, for whom custody is thought essential, and "*the rest*" non-violent/minor offenders, and so on, for whom non-custody is thought to be appropriate'. The further targeting of persistent offenders follows research findings that suggest that a small proportion of offenders are responsible for a large proportion of all offending. For example, in England and Wales, the Carter Report (2003) has reported that persistent offenders, defined as those who accumulate at least three convictions during their criminal careers, form about 10 per cent of the active offender population at any one time and over their careers accumulate at least 50 per cent of all serious offences. More recently, analysis of the 2003 Crime and Justice Survey, a self-report offending survey of households, found that 2 per cent of the whole sample or 26 per cent of active offenders were responsible for 82 per cent of all offences measured. The researchers concluded, therefore, that 'focusing crime reduction measures on high rate offenders could bring disproportionate returns' (Budd, Sharp and Mayhew 2005: 36).

Those intensive community programmes that target persistent offenders and/or those that represent a risk of serious harm are thus in line with other recent initiatives that seek to reserve incapacitative measures for the so-called most 'deserving' offenders. It is important to emphasise, however, that the ability to manage offenders through incapacitation is often overplayed, ignoring other research findings that suggest it has limited potential as a form of public protection. Using Home Office figures for 1999, Ashworth notes that only 2.2 per cent of all offences resulted in a conviction in court, leading him to question how such a small tail (sentence) can wag such a large dog (offending). He concludes that 'increasing the incarceration of the small proportion of offenders who are convicted and sentenced is not a fruitful way of ensuring greater public protection' (Ashworth 2004: 523).

Thus, while risk management through incapacitation and surveillance provides one of the rationales for intensive community programmes, its limitations need to be recognised. There is also an uneasy tension between risk management and a more welfarist agenda, as the former categorises offenders and has limited managerial goals, while the latter emphasises individualisation and has greater rehabilitative aspirations. As shown above, this has led to a degree of compromise, with rehabilitation being reinscribed within a framework of risk.

An authoritarian intervention

For those offenders referred on to an intensive community programme, the surveillance components aim to raise their expectancy, while on the programme, of any further offending being both detected and punished, potentially with custody. In this way, it is hoped that such offending will be deterred, at least in the short term. This rationale dominated the US programmes of the 1980s: 'Although exceptions exist, the distinctive feature of ISPs is an abiding faith in the power of the threat of punishment to effect prosocial conformity' (Gendreau, Cullen and Bonta 1994: 72). As for any longer-term marginal deterrent effect, this will clearly depend upon the individuals' perceptions of the programme and its potentially punitive characteristics relative to custody.

The ability of intensive community programmes to deter further offending, even in the short term, needs to be considered in the light of the more general evidence regarding the effectiveness of deterrence. The theory clearly assumes it is possible to change offenders' subjective choices, but, as Andrew von Hirsch and colleagues (1999: 7) highlight, this requires a number of preconditions to be met:

- The offender must realise that the probability of detection and punishment has changed.
- The offender must take these altered risks into account when deciding whether to offend.
- The offender must believe that there is a non-negligible likelihood of being caught.
- The offender must believe that the punishment will be applied to him if he is caught.
- The offender must be willing to alter his or her choices regarding offending in the light of the perceived change in certainty of punishment.

The literature on deterrence indicates that, in reality, these preconditions are not easily satisfied. For example, offences that are committed to feed a drug habit do not tend to be associated with rational thought, while many violent offences occur in the heat of the moment, when feelings of anger and hostility override any more reasoned contemplation of potential consequences. More generally, James McGuire (2002: 9) notes that, 'Findings from a number of studies based on interviews, or *in vivo* observational work, suggest that prior to committing an offence most individuals are preoccupied with the execution of the act rather than deliberation upon or fear of consequences should they be caught.'

McGuire further acknowledges that deterrence is at its weakest 'where individuals perceive themselves as having little or nothing to lose'. Those high-risk offenders with established criminal histories, often the target group for intensive community programmes, would appear to fall within this category. Thus, similarly to incapacitation, there are significant limitations to deterrence as a rationale for intensive programmes. A hard-line approach with an emphasis upon deterrence also sits somewhat uneasily alongside a more welfarist agenda, which prioritises the need to tackle offenders' underlying problems.

Summary

This chapter has demonstrated that a diverse range of intensive community programmes have been introduced in both England and Wales and the US. They have differed greatly in terms of their targeting and programme structure, with very few standards in place, even as to what is meant by 'intensive'. The political impetus behind the introduction of the programmes has figured prominently, based upon the perceived need to tackle prison overcrowding while, at the same time, strengthening provision in the community and still appearing 'tough on crime'. The programmes have also benefited from their ability to combine elements from the justice, welfare and actuarial models of criminal justice, although they can be further viewed as adhering most closely to the 'dispersal of discipline' thesis. Their theoretical foundations are multi-faceted, attempting to fuse consequentialist forward-looking rationales of deterrence, incapacitation and rehabilitation with backward-looking retribution and a promotion of 'just deserts'. Consequently, the programmes can be promoted as welfare-based interventions, proportionate interventions, risk management interventions and/or authoritarian interventions.

However, these theoretical foundations have their limitations, particularly with regard to the rationales of incapacitation and deterrence. Furthermore, there are a number of tensions between the theoretical rationales and with the more political aims. Notably, a welfarist agenda and a more punitive, authoritarian approach are uncomfortable bedfellows, with the former also differing from risk management due to its prioritisation of the individual and its greater rehabilitative aspirations. Equally significantly, an emphasis upon 'just deserts' potentially conflicts with (i) the political desire for the programmes to be viewed as genuine alternatives to custody, (ii) the welfare-based model's support for prolonged intervention when required, and (iii) the 'What Works' principle of risk classification that focuses upon the risk of re-offending rather than the seriousness of the current offence.

Given these theoretical uncertainties, the need for empirical analysis is clear. Particularly important questions are whether intensive programmes can be implemented in practice as intended in theory, whether they can successfully target high-risk offenders, whether they can marry the elements of control and care, whether they can tackle the offenders' underlying problems and deliver reductions in re-offending and custodial sentencing, both in the short term and longer term, and whether they can maintain the confidence of practitioners, police officers, sentencers and local communities.

Chapter 2

Empirical findings

The following consideration of the evidence-base relating to intensive community programmes builds upon evaluation findings from the US, England and Wales and other jurisdictions. The analysis is complicated by the fact that the programmes have varied greatly in terms of both their targeting and programme structure. The aims and objectives of the programmes have also differed. Most notably, while the majority of programmes have emphasised the need to reduce re-offending rates, others have paid equal regard to reducing levels of custodial sentencing. The difficulties in reviewing the evidence are further compounded by the variable reliability and validity of the research itself. Differing methodologies have been adopted and sample sizes have varied greatly. Bearing in mind all of these considerations, it is perhaps not surprising that the impact of individual programmes upon re-offending and/or custody rates has been found to be variable.

Evidence from the United States

As was shown in the previous chapter, intensive community programmes are now well established in the US. Numerous evaluations of individual programmes have been conducted, but these studies have varied greatly in both their size and methodological rigour. Reviewing a wide range of studies of criminal justice interventions, James McGuire (2002: 11) concludes that their quality has been 'much lamented', and he highlights the following weaknesses in their reliability and internal validity: (i) small sample sizes, (ii) non-equivalence of comparison groups, (iii) limited follow-up periods and (iv) high levels of follow-up attrition. Some or all of these weaknesses apply to a number of the studies of intensive programmes.

The two dominant aims of intensive community programmes have been to reduce re-offending rates and/or custody rates, with the emphasis placed upon each depending upon the current political priorities and policy interests. Usefully, in assessing the quality of the evaluations Lawrence Sherman and colleagues (1997) have developed a five-level scientific methodological rigour scale, which has been adapted by the Home Office (Friendship *et al.* 2004: 7) for reconviction studies as follows:

Level 1   A relationship between intervention and reconviction outcome (*intervention group with no comparison group*).

Level 2   Expected reconviction rates (or predicted rates) compared to actual reconviction rates for intervention group (*risk predictor with no comparison group*).

Level 3   Comparison group present without demonstrated comparability to intervention group (*unmatched comparison group*).

Level 4   Comparison group matched to intervention group on theoretically relevant factors, e.g. risk of reconviction (*well-matched comparison group*).

Level 5   Random assignment of offenders to the intervention and control conditions (*Randomised Control Trial*).

The results below (summarised in Table 2.1) are provided by some of the more sizeable and methodologically rigorous evaluations, all but two of which benefited from the random assignment of cases to either the treatment or control groups, corresponding to level 5 above. Such Random Control Trials (RCTs) have been described as the 'gold standard', although it has been recognised that insufficient attention can be paid to issues of programme integrity and context, resulting in 'contradictory or inconclusive results' (Wilcox 2005). Sample sizes in the studies are also variable, seemingly overlooking the fact that to measure an expected reduction in reconviction of five percentage points, for example, requires a minimum sample size for the treatment and comparison groups of at least 1,300. When the required sample sizes are not achieved, the statistical reliability of any reductions in reconviction is reduced and should thus be treated with caution (Friendship *et al.* 2004).

As will be shown, the results of the evaluations and the interpretations placed upon them are somewhat mixed. The programmes themselves also vary greatly, with differing levels of intensity and differing combinations of programme components, the latter impacting upon the balance between care and control. The target groups also vary. Notably, three of the programmes target young offenders, while five target adult offenders; four of the programmes target the offenders pre-custody, three target the offenders post-custody and one targets the offenders both pre- and post-custody. When reviewing the results, it is also important to consider their external validity, recognising that the findings may not be automatically transferable to the prevalent conditions of other jurisdictions, including England and Wales: 'the characteristics of offenders, the nature of prison regimes and interventions, labour markets and benefit systems in North America differ in many respects from those in England and Wales, meaning that what works abroad may not necessarily work for England and Wales' (Friendship *et al.* 2004: 4).

California (Contra Costa)

In July 1978, Contra Costa County's Probation Department initiated the 'Serious 602 Offender Project' (SOP), a three-year demonstration project of intensive supervision for young offenders charged with serious offences and who were deemed a 'physical threat to others' (Fagan and Reinarman 1991: 344). The demonstration included an experimental design, in which eligible cases were randomly assigned to the experimental group (intensive supervision) or the control group (regular probation). The final sample sizes were 267 SOP cases and 102 control cases. The SOP clients were overwhelmingly male with an average age of 15.0 years. The mean number of prior arrests was 10.5, about 11 per cent of which related to offences categorised as 'serious'.

The SOP caseloads were limited to 20 'active' cases, enabling the officers to maintain weekly contacts during an expected supervision period of six months. The project provided individual counselling, family counselling, school follow-up, group activities and specialised drugs misuse services. However, the main distinction between SOP and regular probation was in the degree of the supervision rather than the content. The primary goal of the SOP was to 'reduce the rate of recidivism of project cases by a statistically significant amount when compared to the control group' (*ibid.*: 359). Analysis revealed, however, that there was 'a general reduction in the prevalence of crime regardless of level of supervision' (*ibid.*: 382). The evaluators thus concluded that most serious offenders could be supervised through regular supervision, but, for those offenders who required more control and intervention, a new form of supervision was needed that offered 'stronger sanctions and more meaningful interventions' (*ibid.*: 359, 360).

Michigan

The Wayne County Juvenile Court in Detroit, Michigan, developed three intensive supervision programs (ISPs) as alternatives to custody for relatively serious but primarily non-violent young offenders facing their first custodial sentence. During the period from February 1983 to March 1985, 511 juveniles met the eligibility criteria and were randomly assigned to the evaluation. The three ISPs received 326 offenders, leaving 185 control group cases that were committed to the state for placement as they would have been prior to the evaluation. The young offenders had an average age of 15.4 years, and an average of 3.2 prior charges. In about half the cases, the current charge was found to be 'quite serious' (Barton and Butts 1990: 241).

The three ISPs provided an average of at least ten contacts per month. Behavioural supervision and individual counselling were provided in nearly every case, while school placement assistance and social skills training were provided frequently. It was 'expected, but not formally required' that each young person would remain on the program for about one year (*ibid.*: 242). Just under half the cases (46 per cent) 'successfully graduated', which occurred when the staff were satisfied with the young person's 'continued cooperation and behavioral improvements' (*ibid.*: 243). During a two-year follow-up period, 78 per cent of the experimental cases reappeared in a juvenile or adult court at least once. Comparisons with the control group revealed that, 'At about one-third the cost, the programs were no less effective than commitment in controlling subsequent offending or producing other measurable outcomes' (*ibid.*: 251).

New Jersey

The New Jersey's ISP aimed to deliver appropriate, intermediate punishment in the community, prevent criminal behaviour, improve the use of scarce prison resources, and be monetarily cost-beneficial and cost-effective when compared to ordinary incarceration. Data were collected from 1983 to 1987, with a primary dataset of 554 individuals who were referred onto ISP by 31 December 1985 (Pearson 1988). A random sample of 500 offenders who were sentenced to prison for ISP-eligible crime before ISP was instituted formed a full comparison sample. Of these 500 cases, 130 formed a close comparison sample, having been found to be closely matched to the ISP sample in terms of prior criminal behaviour and socio-demographic background factors.

Applicants had to serve at least two months in prison before entering ISP. Although the caseload was not intended to include the most dangerous offenders, the current offences tended to be serious and most participants had at least one prior felony conviction. Over half had a drug problem. The delivery of the programme was found to adhere closely to the original plan, with an eventual caseload in the range of 375 to 500 offenders and a median number of contacts in the first six months of 31 per month. Payments of fines, restitution and fees were implemented, the vast majority of the offenders satisfied the requirements of employment and 16 hours' community service per month, and those with identified problems attended specialised counselling/treatment services.

ISP officers actively looked for violations, and of the first 554 offenders referred on to the programme, excluding the 64 cases that were still live, 41 per cent had been returned to prison before completion. Nevertheless, the evaluators concluded that ISP saved about 200 prison days per offender, equating to a saving of roughly $7,000 to $8,000 per offender. Notably, ISP participants had significantly lower recidivism rates than those in the close comparison sample. For example, at the end of two years, 12 per cent of the ISP group had an arrest that led to a conviction, compared to 23 per cent of the close comparison group. The evaluators note, however, that 'because random assignment to a true control group was not permitted by ISP policymakers, it is possible that some or all of the observed significant decrease was due to the selective screening component of the Intensive Supervision Program, instead of (or in addition to) its supervision and counseling components' (Pearson 1988: 443).

California (Contra Costa, Ventura and Los Angeles)

Three counties in California – Contra Costa, Ventura and Los Angeles – took part in an ISP demonstration, funded by the Bureau of Justice Assistance (BJA) and evaluated by the RAND corporation (Petersilia and Turner 1990). Each site developed its own eligibility criteria, with eligible offenders being randomly assigned to either the experimental ISP group or the control group (routine probation). The evaluation ran from January 1987 to July 1988, resulting in sample sizes of 170 offenders in Contra Costa, 166 offenders in Ventura, and 152 offenders in Los Angeles. More than half the offenders had been previously incarcerated, nearly half had serious drug abuse problems, and three-quarters were at 'high' or 'intensive' risk of recidivism.

The evaluation found that the programmes were 'intensive' in the sense that the offenders received more probation contacts than those on routine probation. However, the programmes were primarily surveillance rather than service-orientated, with participation in rehabilitative programs varying across the three sites from 16 per cent to 78 per cent. During a one-year follow-up period, about a quarter of the offenders had no technical violations or new arrests, about 40 per cent had technical violations, and about a third had new arrests. Comparisons with the control group revealed that 'ISP was not associated with a reduction in new arrests' (*ibid.*: 95). Similarly, there were no significant differences in the severity of the arrest offences.

Texas

The Texas Board of Prisons and Paroles developed an ISP programme to intensify the supervision of persons currently on parole who were evidencing poor parole performance and who possessed a serious prior criminal record, increasing their chances of a recall to custody. A randomised field experiment was established with eligible offenders being randomly assigned to either the experimental ISP group or the control group (routine parole supervision). The study began in August 1987 and continued until July 1988, during which time 221 offenders in Dallas and 458 in Houston were assigned to the study conditions (Turner and Petersilia 1992). More than 90 per cent of the offenders were male, and their average age was 31 years. They averaged eight to nine prior arrests and six to eight prior convictions, 85 per cent had served at least their second prison term, and nearly all were classified as 'high' or 'intensive' risk.

The ISP programme was designed to last nine to 12 months, with an emphasis upon deterrence rather than rehabilitation. The evaluators found that, while it was more intensive than routine parole, the average number of total face-to-face and phone contacts fell short of the target of ten per month, with an average of 6.5 in Houston and 4.8 in Dallas. Despite particular attention being paid to employment issues, offenders were no more likely to be employed during the one-year follow-up period. Having conducted comparisons with the control group, the evaluators reached the conclusion that 'ISP was not associated with a reduction in proportion of persons being arrested, the seriousness of the crimes for which they were arrested, the total number of arrests during the one-year follow-up period, or the annualized arrest rate. However, ISP offenders had more technical violations ... and their technical violations were more serious' (*ibid*.: 46). As a result of these violations, prison overcrowding was not alleviated, with ISP offenders spending more time in prison during the one-year follow-up than those assigned to routine parole.

Washington, Iowa, New Mexico, Georgia and Virginia

As part of its intensive supervision demonstration, the BJA funded another seven ISPs in five different states. These programmes targeted serious adult drug offenders, on probation or parole, and they incorporated risk assessment, counselling and team supervision, with particular emphasis upon surveillance, urinalysis, and appropriate treatment. These drug ISPs were again evaluated by the RAND Corporation, with the assessment period beginning in December 1987 and continuing until May 1989, with a one-year follow-up period until May 1990 (Petersilia, Turner and Piper Deschenes 1992). Once again, offenders were randomly assigned to ISP or the control program, with final sample sizes for these two groups of 281 and 268 respectively.

The offenders were predominantly male, and their mean ages ranged across the seven sites from 26 to 30 years. More than two-thirds were of either 'high' or 'moderate' risk, and in all but two sites the majority evidenced dependency upon drugs. All seven ISP sites successfully delivered more face-to-face contacts, telephone and collateral contacts, and drug tests than the control programmes, although the average number of monthly face-to-face contacts ranged from about three to just under 23. Participation in counselling also differed from a high of 100 per cent to a low of 12 per cent. Turning to the one-year outcome analysis, the proportion of ISP offenders arrested for new crimes ranged from about 11 per cent to just over 48 per cent. Crucially, when comparing the outcomes for the ISP and control groups, no significant differences were found. This was 'despite the fact that ISP offenders not only received more surveillance-orientated contacts but in many instances were more involved in treatment-orientated programs as well' (ibid: 35). The Georgia sites tested the benefits of adding electronic monitoring, but there was no evidence of additional benefits over and above human monitoring.

Oregon

The Clackamas County Intensive Out-Patient Drug Program (IDP) in Oregon provided intensive substance abuse treatment and intensive supervision of offenders in the community, with the goal of reducing both their substance abuse and their recidivism. The programme consisted of 14 weeks of surveillance plus treatment, followed by 14 weeks of aftercare. Individual components included an eight-to-one offender/counsellor ratio, continuous electronic monitoring, weekly drug treatment, life structuring and community self-help group sessions, drug and alcohol testing, and a daily programme fee. To evaluate the effectiveness of this approach, a quasi-experimental comparison group design was employed, with comparison groups taken from two different programmes administered in the same county (Jolin and Stipak 1992). Stratified random sampling was employed to match the groups on clients' risk assessment scores, resulting in 100 offenders in each of the comparison groups and 70 offenders in the treatment group.

Analysis revealed that the percentage of IDP clients using drugs fell from 95 per cent at entry to 32 per cent at termination. Using logistic regression to further control for differences between the groups revealed that for all clients the IDP group had higher recidivism but for successful completers the IDP group had lower recidivism. The evaluators concluded as follows: 'Because the comparison programs did not include a treatment component, these findings suggest that recidivism may diminish if (a) offenders receive treatment specific to their substance abuse problem as part of their sentence, and if (b) those offenders remain in the program to completion' (*ibid.*: 167).

Colorado, Nevada and Virginia

The Intensive Aftercare Program (IAP) targeted high-risk, incarcerated juvenile offenders who had demonstrated high recidivism rates. Its premise was that effective intervention required not only intensive supervision and services but also a focus on reintegration with a highly structured and gradual transition into the community. It also involved individualised case planning, the use of small caseloads, continuity in case management and service delivery, and the use of a system of graduated rewards and sanctions. The programme was evaluated over a five-year period (1995 to 2000) across three

Table 2.1 Empirical studies in the United States

Programme	Sample sizes	Offender profiles	Programme structure	Outcomes
Probation for young offenders (California: Contra Costa)	Random assignment of 267 SOP cases and 102 control cases.	• Average age of 15.0 years. • Average of 10.5 prior arrests. • 11% of prior arrests for serious offences.	• Six-month supervision period with weekly contacts. • Counselling, school follow-up, group activities, drug misuse services.	• 'A general reduction in the prevalence of crime regardless of supervision.'
Probation for young offenders (Michigan)	Random assignment of 326 ISP cases and 185 control cases.	• Average age of 15.4 years. • Average of 3.2 prior charges. • Current charge 'quite serious' in approx. 50% of cases.	• Usually a one-year programme with an average of at least ten contacts per month. • Behavioural supervision, individual counselling, school placement assistance, social skills training.	• 46% ISP cases 'successfully graduated', and 78% reappeared in court during two-year follow-up. • ISP was 'no less effective' than commitment.
Post-custody parole (New Jersey)	554 ISP cases and 130 matched comparison cases.	• Current offences generally serious. • Most had one prior felony conviction. • Over half had a drug problem.	• Average of 31 contacts in first six months. • 16 hours' community service per month, employment requirement, counselling/treatment services, financial payments.	• 41% ISP cases recalled to prison before completion. • After two years, 12% of ISP group had an arrest compared to 23% of comparison cases.

Table 2.1 continues overleaf

Table 2.1 continued

Programme	Sample sizes	Offender profiles	Programme structure	Outcomes
Probation (California: Contra Costa, Ventura and Los Angeles)	Random assignment of 488 cases (ISP and control).	• More than half previously incarcerated. • Nearly half had serious drug abuse problems. • Three-quarters were at high risk of recidivism.	• Surveillance-orientated. • Participation in rehabilitative programmes varied from 16% to 78% across the sites.	• In a one-year follow-up period, 40% had technical violations and a third had new arrests. • There were no significant differences between the ISP and control groups.
Post-custody parole (Texas)	Random assignment of 679 cases (ISP and control).	• Average age of 31 years. • Average of 8–9 prior arrests and 6–8 prior convictions. • 85% had served at least two prison terms. • Nearly all classified as high risk.	• Nine to 12 month programme with an average of 6.5 and 4.8 contacts per month across the two sites. • Emphasis upon deterrence.	• ISP was not associated with a reduction in arrests, and there was an increase in technical violations.
Probation or parole for drug offenders (Washington, Iowa, New Mexico, Georgia, Virginia)	Random assignment of 281 ISP cases and 268 control cases.	• Mean ages ranged from 26 to 30 years across the sites. • More than two-thirds were of 'high' or 'moderate' risk. • The majority were drug-dependent.	• The average number of face-to-face contacts ranged from three to 23. • Emphasis upon surveillance, urinalysis and appropriate drug treatment. Counselling participation ranged from 11% to 48%.	• In a one-year follow-up period, 11% to 48% of the ISP offenders were arrested for new crimes. • No significant differences were found between the ISP and control groups.

Probation for drug offenders (Oregon)	70 treatment (IDP) cases and 2 x 100 matched comparison cases.	• 95% IDP offenders were using drugs.	• 14 weeks' surveillance plus treatment, with 14 weeks' aftercare. • Counselling, electronic monitoring, weekly drug treatment, life sessions, drug/alcohol testing, daily programme fee.	• Percentage using drugs fell to 32%. • The IDP group had higher recidivism than the comparison groups, but for completers only, the IDP group had lower recidivism.
Parole for young offenders (Colorado, Virginia and Nevada)	Random assignment of 230 IAP cases and 205 control cases.	• The young offenders were at high risk of re-offending. • In Nevada, two-thirds had 11 or more prior referrals, 80% had a prior commitment to secure care, and 55% were gang members.	• Small, IAP-specific caseloads, and individualised case planning. Institutional length of stay averaged between 6.7 and 10.3 months, and the aftercare length of stay averaged between 5.8 and 8.4 months. • Transitional activities, with continuity in case management and service delivery. A system of graduated rewards and sanctions.	• No significant differences in (1) the nature of the most serious subsequent offence, (2) the mean number of felony arrests, criminal arrests, or total arrests, or (3) the number of days to first felony or criminal arrest. • No evidence that program maturation resulted in lower recidivism rates, or that IAP was more or less successful with particular types of offenders.

sites (Colorado, Clark County in Nevada and the City of Norfolk in Virginia) by the National Council on Crime and Delinquency (NCCD: Wiebush *et al.* 2005). An experimental design was employed with random assignment to either the experimental (IAP) or control (traditional services) group. The final sample sizes were smaller than originally anticipated, with 230 IAP cases and 205 control cases.

The evaluators found that, although all three sites had 'implementation weaknesses, they operated programs that successfully incorporated most of the core features on the national IAP model' (*ibid.*: iii). In each site, the young offenders on IAP were significantly more likely than the control cases to be involved in vocational training for at least two months, and, in two of the sites a substantially larger percentage of IAP cases were in school for at least two months. Nevertheless, few statistically significant differences were found in 12-month reconviction rates, confirmed by multivariate analysis: 'In all three sites, there were no differences between the groups in (1) the nature of the most serious subsequent offence, (2) the mean number of felony arrests, criminal arrests, or total arrests, or (3) the number of days to first felony or criminal arrest' (*ibid.*: v). There was no evidence that program maturation resulted in lower recidivism rates, or that IAP was more or less successful with particular types of offenders. The evaluators emphasised, however, that in two of the sites, 'evaluation issues regarding confounds to the experiment and small sample size do not allow definitive statements about the efficacy – or lack thereof – of IAP' (*ibid.*: viii). They thus concluded that, 'With the experience and knowledge gained from the ... initiative, and with more favorable conditions (e.g., larger samples), the model may still demonstrate its ability to affect recidivism' (*ibid.*: viii–ix).

Evidence from England and Wales

Recent decades have also witnessed numerous attempts at developing intensive community programmes in England and Wales. A number of these programmes have been evaluated, and, as in the US, the studies indicate considerable diversity in programme structure and intensity. Generally speaking, however, the programmes in England and Wales have tended to be of greater intensity, and the need for some form of treatment/rehabilitation has been more consistently applied. With regard to targeting, IMPACT and the Prolific Offender Projects (POPs) targeted adult offenders, Intensive Probation (IP) targeted young adult offenders, while Intermediate Treatment (IT) and ISSP both targeted young offenders. In all instances, the offenders were generally targeted pre-custody.

Similarly to the US, the size and methodological rigour of the evaluations, the results themselves, and the interpretations placed upon them vary greatly. The evidence-base for England and Wales is clearly less well developed, and only two of the following studies (IMPACT and Kent ISSP) benefited from the random assignment of cases. In one of these instances (Kent ISSP), the sample sizes were very small; a common weakness of UK criminal justice studies (Friendship *et al.* 2004). The larger studies are summarised in Table 2.2.

IMPACT

The general aim of IMPACT was to treat high-risk offenders 'intensively' in the community with significantly lighter caseloads than normal. To be eligible for the programme, the offender had to be aged 17 years or over, be placed on probation for two or three years, and have two or more previous convictions since the age of 14. Treatment was intensified by reducing the caseload of the experimental officers from about 40–45 cases to approximately 20 cases. This was achieved by reducing the officers' other duties, such as preparing social inquiry reports, and by a more extensive use of other resources. Treatment was also diversified by encouraging and supporting the development of alternative methods and the use of other resources such as ancillary workers, voluntary workers, and other agencies. There was a particular emphasis upon situational treatment in the form of more direct practical intervention in the areas of family, work and leisure.

The impact of the treatment was evaluated by a Home Office research team through random allocation of cases to experimental and control groups in four areas: Dorset, London, Sheffield and Staffordshire (Folkard *et al.* 1974; Folkard, Smith and Smith 1976). Data were collected for 244 experimental cases and 161 control cases. For the sample as a whole (experimental and control cases), two-thirds to three-quarters of the offenders were found to be aged 17 to 29. Many had previously been placed on probation and the most frequent current offence was theft. The experimental officers believed that their work was more effective than it had been prior to the experiment and that their relationships with clients had been enhanced. From the analyses of the treatment, the evaluators concluded that the experimental cases had received more contacts than the control cases, and that the officers had successfully employed a more 'situational' style of supervision, with more contacts outside the office and greater involvement with family and associates.

However, analysis of reconviction rates over a one- and two-year follow-up period revealed no significant differences between the experimental and control group cases, leading the researchers to conclude that there was 'no solid evidence' to support the claim that IMPACT produced more beneficial results (Folkard, Smith and Smith 1976: 16–17). Further statistical analysis revealed that subsequent offending was associated with the number of previous convictions, probation officers' assessment of criminal tendencies, unemployment at the beginning of the order, and associating with delinquent companions. Furthermore, 'a differential treatment effect for different types of offender was apparently demonstrated'. Those offenders with moderate or high criminal tendencies and average or few personal problems 'did significantly worse (in terms of one-year reconviction rates) under intensive situational treatment than under normal probation supervision'. There was also a 'suggestion' that those offenders with low criminal tendencies and many personal problems had a more successful outcome under the experimental treatment, but this was not statistically significant (*ibid.*: 23).

The experimental officers were also asked for their views regarding the suitability of offenders for the programme. While their responses 'varied greatly', those deemed unsuitable included those who were unmotivated to change, those who were extremely hostile to probation, those who were severe alcoholics and those with gross personality deficiencies (Folkard *et al.* 1974: 44).

Intermediate treatment

The term 'Intermediate Treatment' (IT) was first used in the 1968 White Paper *Children in Trouble*. In its original manifestation, IT was to be available both as a requirement of a Supervision Order, and as a form of community-based treatment or activity to other consenting offenders and non-offenders. In reality, many programmes in the 1970s targeted relatively minor offenders (Bottoms *et al.* 1990). But in the 1980s, following the implementation of the Criminal Justice Act 1982 which enabled courts to add further requirements to Supervision Orders, the Department of Health and Social Security funded a wide range of IT projects that were intensive in nature. These projects targeted those 'high-tariff' serious and/or persistent young offenders deemed to be at risk of custody. Between 1983 and 1987, 110 such projects offering nearly 4,000 places were set up by voluntary bodies in 62 local authority areas (Allen 1991).

The impact of IT upon both custody rates and re-offending rates was assessed by a research team from the University of Cambridge (Bottoms 1995). The study collected data for the following cases: 103 heavy-end IT (HEIT) cases, 40 other IT cases, 141 custody cases, and 142 straight Supervision Orders cases. For the sample as a whole (all groups), the mean age was 15.7 years, while for the HEIT group, the average number of charges/convictions in the prior 14 months was 7.0. The cases were collected from a large northern city, a southern shire county, and two metropolitan boroughs during the period September 1987 to April 1990. In the two metropolitan boroughs, the projects tended to consist of group and individual work, an 'offending curriculum', the teaching of social skills and various constructive activities; in the large city there was an emphasis upon tracking, accompanied by weekly meetings at the centre's premises; while in the shire county, the programmes were more individualised, potentially comprising of community service, a motor project, an offending curriculum, individual counselling and a befriending scheme.

The evaluators found that the HEIT projects were, on the whole, successful in targeting serious and persistent offenders at genuine risk of a custodial sentence, rather than those who would previously have received a less intensive non-custodial penalty. This confirmed monitoring by NACRO (National Association for the Care and Resettlement of Offenders) which revealed that those sentenced to heavy-end IT schemes were similar in terms of the type and number of previous disposals and the type of offence committed to those receiving custodial sentences (Allen 1991: 48). However, while there was a substantial reduction in the number of young people sent to custody during the 1980s (a fall from 7,900 in 1981 to 2,200 in 1989), the Cambridge evaluators found that there was 'no automatic or necessary relationship between the development of a strong HEIT programme and the reduction of custodial sentencing levels' (Bottoms 1995: 34).

Offenders and parents rated HEIT very positively, although offenders disliked the extent of the restrictions upon their activities. When re-offending was measured over a 14-month follow-up period, there was 'no evidence ... that any one main treatment type was statistically significantly better or worse at preventing reoffending than any other treatment' (Bottoms 1995: 18). Similarly, all treatment samples showed a reduction in self-perceived problems.

Medway

Further evaluations were conducted at specific IT projects. One such evaluation was conducted at the Medway Close Support Unit, which targeted those young offenders who would otherwise have been sentenced to custody or care. It reduced their opportunities to offend by placing them in supervised activities for six days and five evenings each week over a 90-day period. The structured daily routine incorporated elements of work, leisure, education and punishment, requiring full school attendance or full-time employment, and imposing an evening curfew.

The Home Office funded evaluation found that the Unit was seen in a 'reasonably positive light' by the majority of offenders, parents and sentencers (Ely, Swift and Sutherland 1987: 155). The courts made 75 orders to the Unit for 67 young males over a three-year period from 1979 to 1981, resulting in a relatively small sample size for the study. Sixteen of the offenders (24 per cent) were prosecuted for offences committed during the 90-day period, usually towards its end, five of whom (8 per cent) were given a custodial sentence. In a two-year follow-up period, 22 re-offended (33 per cent) and were sentenced to custody or care. The focus of the evaluation related to the effectiveness of the Unit as an alternative to custody, looking at changes in the numbers receiving various sentences from 1974 to 1981 and comparing the characteristics of the young people. The evaluators found that there was a marked reduction in the proportion of young people sent to custody, and that the characteristics of the young people sentenced to the Unit closely resembled the profiles of those sentenced to custody or care. They thus concluded that the Unit had attracted a 'proportion of those who would otherwise have received custodial sentences' (*ibid.*: 181). They noted, however, that magistrates had difficulty in restricting its use solely to those at risk of custody, preferring to use it 'as a sentence in its own right' (*ibid.*: 159).

Intensive Probation

Further experiments in Intensive Probation (IP) were conducted in several probation areas in the 1980s and early 1990s, utilising the so-called 4A and 4B orders which had been introduced by the Criminal Justice Act 1982. These IP schemes targeted those young adults aged between 17 and 25 years who had committed fairly serious offences such as burglary and who were considered likely to receive a custodial sentence. Individualised programmes were provided, ensuring frequent contact with a project worker, with a focus upon confronting offending behaviour. Comparing IP to previous intensive programmes, the evaluators of eight of the IP areas concluded: 'In the past intensive meant more social work, more counselling, more guidance; while today, intensive tends to mean a more rigorous and demanding approach to working with offenders' (Mair *et al.* 1994: 3).

During the evaluation of the eight areas, 1,677 people were referred to IP, 45 per cent of whom were then sentenced on to the programme. Risk assessment scores suggested that, 'on the whole', the offenders were at risk of a custodial sentence (*ibid.*: 118). Notably, 51 per cent of referrals had more than five previous convictions and 54 per cent had previous experience of custody. The evaluators found that offenders appreciated the attention they received, were generally positive about IP and felt that it had prevented them from re-offending. The quality of organisation and management appeared important, and there were some concerns regarding the transitional period from IP to normal supervision. The evaluators' general conclusion was that 'IP worked well in some areas and not so well in others; it worked well in some manifestations and not so well in others' (*ibid.*: 124).

Port Talbot

Further evaluations were conducted at specific IP sites. The 'Afan Alternative' project, based in Port Talbot, began in late 1980. During a five-year period until June 1985, 79 clients both started and finished their involvement with the project. In 66 of these cases – a relatively small sample size – two-year reconviction data were obtained. The project objectives encompassed 'not only the provision of an alternative to custodial sentences for young male offenders but also the intention to provide a more constructive and useful experience than the custodial sentences they would otherwise have served' (Raynor 1988: 26).

The evaluators measured the impact of the project upon both sentencing trends and re-offending rates. With regard to the former, the evaluators found 'a significant shift in sentencing in Port Talbot soon after the introduction of the project which did not occur at that time in the rest of the County where the decline in custodial sentencing was less marked and more gradual' (*ibid.*: 89–90). Although there was some reversion in 1984–85, the evaluators noted that the sentencing shift remained significant over a seven-year period. Furthermore, comparing the profiles of the offenders referred on to the schemes to those receiving custodial sentences and standard community penalties, the evaluators concluded that recruitment was 'at a level where the risk of custodial sentences was substantial ... [with] no significant evidence of net-widening or of recruitment below the intended level' (*ibid.*: 104).

Thirteen per cent of the offenders referred on to the scheme breached their orders through failure to comply, two of whom received a custodial sentence. Of those followed-up, two-thirds reported lower overall levels of difficulty in their lives at the end of the project than at the beginning (n=57). Exactly half were reconvicted in the following two-year period (n=66), but, crucially, comparative analysis revealed that 'project members were reconvicted significantly less than young men with similar ages, similar criminal histories and similar current offences who received custodial sentences' (*ibid.*: 113). The greatest period of risk appeared to be the time following completion of the project, when the offenders were still receiving standard probation.

Hereford and Worcester
The Hereford and Worcester Young Offender Project (YOP) started in 1984, targeting young adult male offenders who might otherwise have received a youth custody sentence. It was an intensive programme of supervision and activity for 17- to 20-year-old unemployed young men, which commenced with a three-day per week requirement of attendance at a specified centre for the first seven weeks of the programme. One full week was spent at an adventure-training centre and all participants were expected to be involved in purposeful leisure activities in their own community throughout. The programme included a mixture of social skills training, group work elements and drug and alcohol education, as well as practical assistance in problem areas such as employment, accommodation and financial management. Following the intensive period, the participants were required to maintain regular contact with their designated probation supervisor for the remainder of their probation order. Strict compliance rules were applied to all parts of the order.

The evaluation encompassed those offenders attending during the first two years of the project, with two comparison groups being constructed: (i) those young offenders recommended for YOP in the Social Inquiry Reports prepared for the courts but who were given youth custody sentences (Custody A); and (ii) those young offenders who were not recommended for the programme but who also received youth custody sentences (Custody B). Analysis of the three samples revealed that the YOP sample (n=53) were similar to or marginally higher in their tariff position than the Custody A sample (n=56) on all dimensions, but that the Custody B sample (n=51) had been convicted of more serious principal offences. It was concluded that the YOP offenders would almost certainly have received custodial sentences if the YOP requirement had not been recommended in their Social Inquiry Reports and the courts had not been willing to consider a probation order with specified requirements as an alternative (Roberts 1989).

A two-year reconviction study was undertaken. The differences in reconviction rates revealed a short-term benefit for the two custodial samples resulting from the incapacitation effects of custody, which was largely negated by the frequency and seriousness of re-offending when the young offenders were released back into the community. After two years, 30 per cent of the YOP sample had not been reconvicted, compared with 6 per cent of the Custody A sample and 19 per cent of the Custody B sample. Although small sample sizes, statistical analysis confirmed a greater reduction in the likelihood of reconviction by the YOP offenders compared to both custodial samples, and indicated that the effect was most marked in relation to those offenders with more previous convictions.

Leeds

An IP scheme, known locally as 'the Edge', was established in Leeds in February 1989. As with all IP schemes, it targeted young adult offenders deemed to be at risk of custody. In addition, offenders needed to be deemed suitable, taking into account their motivation, attitudes to offending and specific needs. Once referred on to the scheme, each offender received an eight-week individualised programme, with the most frequent attendance requirements at the beginning of this period. Programme components included one-to-one counselling, offending behaviour work and social skills sessions. Attempts were also made to tackle other problems such as homelessness, unemployment and financial need.

A research team from the University of Leeds assessed the impact of the project upon both sentencing practice and reconviction rates (Brownlee and Joanes 1993; Brownlee 1995). From May 1989 to December 1993, the scheme received 585 referrals, with attendance on the programme becoming a condition of the court sentence in 227 of these cases. The evaluators found that those referred on to the programme differed little on relevant criteria from those sentenced to immediate custody despite a project recommendation. They thus concluded that the scheme was successfully attracting those at serious risk of custody and that a 'genuine diversion effect' was taking place (Brownlee and Joanes 1993: 228).

The reconviction study included those who attended the Edge during its first 12 months of operation. Using a research design similar to that used by Roberts (1989) for the Hereford and Worcester YOP, this sample was compared to those who received custodial sentences during this period, either following a recommendation for attendance at the Edge or with no referral for assessment having been made. In a two-year follow-up period, 73 per cent of those attending the Edge had been reconvicted. Notably, this was for a small sample size of just 45. The comparison groups revealed, however, that custodial sentencing was 'not demonstrably more effective in preventing or deterring reconviction once the initial incapacitating effects of custody were removed' (Brownlee 1995: 609). The evaluators argued that given 'the fact that custodial sentencing is significantly more expensive (and arguably more personally damaging to those who undergo it), the case for community-based punishments remains persuasive' (*ibid.*: 610).

Prolific Offender Projects

The Prolific Offender Projects (POPs) combined intensive attention from both the police and probation services in an attempt to reduce property crime, particularly theft and burglary. More precisely, the projects' characteristics were as follows:

- The projects were staffed by designated police and probation personnel, and were located on either police or probation premises.

- Offenders were required to meet local criteria that categorised them as 'prolific'.

- Offenders were required to be the subject of court-ordered community rehabilitation or a post-custodial licence.

- The projects provided high levels of police monitoring and programmes of intensive probation supervision, with approximately four appointments per week. Attention was paid to addressing offending behaviour and other needs such as housing, substance misuse, leisure, education and employment.

- There was an agreed mechanism of information exchange between all participating agencies.

- There was an agreed procedure for swift enforcement in the event of non-compliance or further offending. (Worrall and Walton 2000: 35)

Burnley
The first of these projects to be evaluated was the original scheme in Burnley, Lancashire, after it had been in operation for three years. By then 47 offenders had been involved in the programme, with an average of 45 previous offences per offender. Participation was initially voluntary, but project attendance could be incorporated into their court sentences or prison licences at a later stage. While there was a substantial fall in burglary offences reported in the target area and the number of crimes attributable to the targeted offenders almost halved, the researchers reported that there was no significant difference in the monthly rate of offending of the participants compared with a matched sample of offenders of a similar age and with similar offending histories (Chenery and Pease 2000). The evaluators argued, however, that both reconviction and non-reconviction could, under different circumstances, 'be counted as successes' (*ibid.*: 4), and that one possible reason for the high rate of offending in the POP sample was 'a function of increased probability of offences coming to light' (*ibid.*: 39). They concluded that 'in the real world, reconviction of those who persist in criminality despite help offered constitutes a success, certainly as far as public protection is involved' (*ibid.*: 38). The same research group also undertook an evaluation of a second project in Blackpool, with largely similar findings (Chenery and Deakin 2003).

Newcastle-under-Lyme
An evaluation of the Newcastle POP by the University of Keele found that intensive supervision and individualised treatment packages had been successfully delivered (Worrall and Walton 2000). 'Fast-track' drugs assessment and treatment procedures were established, and assistance was available for accommodation tenancies, constructive leisure activities, college courses and job searches. Positive feedback was received from both offenders and workers, although some offenders needed longer to respond than others and some responded better the second time round. The evaluators compared the progress of the first 29 offenders on the project with a 'similar' group of offenders, who had not been exposed to the project, and concluded that the project had a beneficial impact upon re-offending rates of over 50 per cent (*ibid.*: 35). Clearly, though, these sample sizes are very small.

Stoke-on-Trent
The University of Keele also evaluated the Stoke-on-Trent Targeted Policing Initiative POP, which operated between June 2000 and

September 2002. The project identified offenders who were committing high volumes of acquisitive crime, assessing them for suitability through interviews and by using a scoring matrix. This matrix took into account factors including 'criminal type', the category of crime and its locality, criminal intelligence, current crime trends, victims targeted, and the impact of the offender on the locality, on fear of crime and on the volume of crime (Worrall *et al.* 2003). The offenders were referred on to the project by consenting to participate as a condition of a Community Rehabilitation Order or they participated on licence following release from custody. In the evaluation period, 22 offenders were recruited to the project, eight of whom participated as part of their licence conditions. Their ages ranged from 19 to 43, two were female, their previous convictions ranged from eight to 129, and they had histories of drug and substance misuse.

The intensive supervision included a minimum of four appointments per week, accompanied by close police monitoring. The appointments included a weekly office visit, a weekly home visit, consultations with a substance misuse nurse/doctor, a monthly Multi-Agency Planning and Assessment meeting, employment/work assessment interviews, healthy lifestyle sessions, and attendance at a day-centre. Five of the 22 offenders completed their designated period on the programme without being breached and recalled to prison or resentenced. The offenders saw the daily contact with a probation officer as providing helpful support, sometimes contrasting to their previous experiences of the probation service. Matching the 22 offenders to their own individual comparators, the evaluators concluded that 'following recruitment to the project, a participant may be 45 per cent less likely to be reconvicted than he/she would have been had he/she not gone on the project' (Worrall *et al.* 2003: 12). Once again, however, the sample sizes are very small.

Oxford

The Intensive Recidivist Intervention Scheme (IRIS) was initiated in the Oxford area of the Thames Valley Police in September 2003. The scheme was based at the city police station, but was a partnership project between the police, probation and other local agencies, and had a dedicated full-time team consisting of experienced police officers, a seconded probation officer and a civilian who worked closely with local service providers and voluntary agencies. Suitable local persistent and prolific offenders were identified by a scoring matrix and then informed in person of their IRIS status. Offenders could engage with the team on a voluntary basis, but many became subject to requirements to participate as part of a community sentence or custodial licence.

The evaluation compared the first 20 offenders on the project during its first year of operation against a matched comparison group of local offenders who were not subject to IRIS oversight (Roberts 2006). In the 24 months prior to the start of IRIS, the 20 offenders had between them accumulated 269 court convictions for separate offences, with 384 offences having been taken into consideration, the majority of them for offences of burglary, theft of vehicles, theft from vehicles, theft from shops, robbery, serious motoring offences, assault and criminal damage. They had collectively experienced 75 separate custodial sentences in their careers, and all had recently been in breach of community sentences and prison licences.

Despite the small sample sizes, there were statistically significant reductions in the number, frequency and seriousness of offences known to have been committed by the IRIS offenders, the largest reductions being for burglaries (72 per cent) and thefts of vehicles (83 per cent). There were also reductions of known re-offending in the comparison group but not on the scale observed in the IRIS group. Looking at monthly offending, the rate for the IRIS offenders fell from 2.1 to 0.8 per month (a reduction of 60 per cent), while the rate for the comparison group fell from 1.1 to 1.0 per month (a reduction of 5 per cent). The reductions in known offending by the IRIS group made a small but significant contribution to the level of serious acquisitive crime recorded in the Oxford local police area, and an even greater contribution to improvements in the rates of detection. It appeared that those IRIS offenders who did re-offend were more likely to be detected, arrested and convicted, and were more likely to be recalled to prison and remanded in custody.

Another key objective of the project was to improve the compliance of the IRIS offenders with court orders, community sentence requirements, prison licence conditions and curfews. In the IRIS group, breaches of court-ordered bail reduced from 1.8 to 0.15 per month in the first year of operation. The breaches of community sentence requirements reduced from 1.8 to 0.5 per month, prison licence breaches dropped from 0.45 to 0.25, and curfew breaches from 0.25 to 0.05 per month. These improvements in compliance occurred even though the IRIS offenders were subject to vastly greater levels of supervision and monitoring than the comparison group. In the comparison group, the combined rate per month for all such orders and requirements actually increased from 0.26 to 0.37 per month, an increase of 42 per cent.

Home Office Prolific and other Priority Offender evaluation

The Home Office has commenced an evaluation of a large sample (n=7,801) of Prolific and other Priority Offenders (PPOs), describing the similarities and differences in local PPO projects across England and Wales. The majority are based on close police and probation partnerships, but some involve Youth Offending Teams (YOTs) and deal with ISSP cases. So far only early findings have been published, indicating both the increasing scale of such projects and considerable diversity in type (Dawson 2005).

In general, PPO schemes were adopting a two-stage procedure to the selection of appropriate offenders: identification of potential offenders, followed by the application of a scoring matrix to prioritise cases. However, the criteria used in the matrices varied considerably between schemes, usually according to local priorities and crime reduction targets. The PPO cohort was compared with a sample of all offenders who were sentenced during 2003. This revealed that the PPO cohort had received an average of 24 convictions, compared to ten convictions for the general sample over the previous five years, and more of these prior convictions were for acquisitive offences. The PPO cohort had been more criminally versatile during their criminal careers, with a wider range of convictions for different types of offence, and had, on average, started their offending careers at a significantly younger age. The PPO cohort were almost three times more likely to have serious drug misuse problems and were, on average, rated as 'high risk' offenders, whereas the general sample were, on average, rated as 'medium risk'.

All the schemes studied had interventions that contained 'Catch and Convict' tactics alongside 'Rehabilitate and Resettle' elements, typically including dedicated tracking, prior notification to police custody staff, increased surveillance, fast-tracked prosecutions, increased use of police intelligence, more home and prison visits, fast-tracking into programmes and drug treatment, increased contact by case managers and active breaching and prison recall procedures. The PPO schemes were reported to have considerably improved inter-agency communication and data sharing on the targeted offenders, and this was viewed as crucial to the effective delivery of key parts of most programmes.

Limited reconviction analysis has so far been conducted. In the six months leading up to their PPO designation, the cohort had been collectively responsible for 22,484 recorded convictions, compared with 20,188 recorded convictions in the first six months on the schemes, representing a fall of 10 per cent. There are numerous possible explanations for this short-term reduction other than the influence of the PPO schemes, and at present there is no comparison group. Considerable further research is thus needed to disentangle the effects of the PPO programmes from other factors, as well as measuring any impact over a longer period. Nevertheless, Worrall and Mawby (2004: 281) have boldly written that these projects, 'if implemented carefully, represent the development of a model of partnership working that balances the care and control of prolific offenders. They have the potential to support offenders, reduce their offending and bring wider benefits.'

Kent ISSP

A variant forerunner of the national Intensive Supervision and Surveillance Programme (ISSP) was established in Kent in 1997, based on a similar scheme that had been implemented in Groningen in the Netherlands. The eligibility criteria required the offenders (i) to be 15 to 17 years old; (ii) to have been charged or cautioned on three or more occasions within a 12-month period with an imprisonable offence; and (iii) to have previously been detained in custody or to have failed to complete a sentence requiring community work. The programme itself was multi-systemic, and had four compulsory components and three ancillary components that were to be provided where necessary. These components were as follows:

- *Compulsory*
  - Joint and frequent supervision by police and social services.
  - Improved diagnosis, assessments and individual treatment plans.
  - Improved sharing of information between police, social services and education professionals.
  - Regular multi-agency review of cases.

- *Ancillary*
  - Family group conferencing.
  - Victim reparation and mediation.
  - Mentoring.

An evaluation team tested the hypothesis that the programme 'would have no measurable impact on the reconviction rates of programme participants, but that it might reduce the number of offences for which they were arrested by 30 per cent in the first twelve months after joining the programme' (Little *et al.* 2004: 228). To test this hypothesis, a north–south regional divide was created, with ISSP being offered in the south but not in the north. In the south, all eligible and consenting young people were randomly allocated to either ISSP or to standard services. In the north, all eligible young people were provided with standard services and then matched with the ISSP cases. While a methodologically strong approach, unfortunately the study suffered from small groupings, with final sample sizes of 24 ISSP cases, 24 randomly allocated control groups cases, and 31 matched control group cases.

In a two-year follow-up period, 87 per cent of the ISSP sample was reconvicted and, as hypothesised, there were no significant differences between the groups. However, multivariate analysis confirmed a 'statistically significant impact of ISSP by reducing the risk of criminal behaviour (as expressed in terms of volume of offending) by between 4.7 and 6.2 times depending on the comparison' (*ibid.*: 237). The evaluators thus concluded that 'concerted action can have a modest impact on levels of criminal behaviour of the most persistent offenders' (*ibid.*: 239).

ICCP

The most recently published research on intensive community programmes in England and Wales is a Home Office study on the Intensive Control and Change Programme (ICCP), which was introduced into 11 pilot probation areas from April 2003 to March 2004. The programme was reserved for young adult offenders aged from 18 to 20 years. Of the 433 offenders included in the evaluation, 90 per cent were white and 93 per cent were male. They had an average of 27 previous convictions, a medium to high risk of re-offending, and higher levels of accommodation and education, training and employment needs than 18- to 20-year-olds serving other community sentences (Partridge *et al.* 2005).

The Home Office set out the following requirements for the programme: a minimum of 25 hours of contact per week for the first three months; mandatory curfews with electronic tagging; and five core supervision components, encompassing accredited offending behaviour programmes, mentoring, one-to-one supervision, education, training and employment, and community punishment. However, the evaluation found differences in the intensity, content and rigour with which the different components of ICCP were delivered. Generally, great emphasis was placed upon the control elements in the initial stages of the programme, although there was evidence of significantly different levels of compliance, breach and completion rates. Overall, 26 per cent of the offenders had their orders revoked or terminated and a further 27 per cent had breached the programme but were awaiting their court hearings. The lower-risk offenders, who had the fewest criminogenic needs, were more likely to complete the programme. Unfortunately it was not possible, due to the small sample sizes, to distinguish between the influences of different local policies upon breach and revocation or the benefits of particular models of delivery.

The study was only preliminary and did not attempt to measure any outcomes in relation to re-offending or other measurable benefits for the offenders. The study did, however, explore the views of sentencers, including magistrates, justices' clerks and Crown Court judges. The majority thought 'ICCP was a good alternative to custody for young offenders especially those with chaotic lifestyles' (Partridge *et al.* 2005: ix), but many of the judges also considered that 'it would only work for less serious offenders with less established criminal histories' (*ibid.*: ix), and several judges 'did not actually perceive ICCP orders to be of much relevance to the sorts of young offenders coming before the Crown Court given the limit of twelve months on anticipated custody sentences' (*ibid.*: 45). The study reviewed court sentencing data in the 11 pilot areas and compared it with non-ICCP areas, finding that there had been an overall 15 per cent reduction in the use of custody across all the ICCP areas, but that there had been an average 9 per cent fall in the non-ICCP areas. The researchers concluded that 'it was not possible to be sure that the difference between the reduction in the pilot areas compared with the others was not due to chance' (*ibid.*: 49).

Evidence from other jurisdictions

Intensive community programmes are not confined to the US and England and Wales, with a recent proliferation of such programmes in many other jurisdictions. Once again the programmes vary greatly in terms of both their targeting and programme structure, with the results of the evaluations themselves also differing. Of the three evaluations set out below, the first programme targets young offenders pre-custody, the second targets adult offenders pre-custody, and the third targets adult offenders post-custody. An electronic monitoring component is a feature of both the adult programmes.

Table 2.2 Major empirical studies in England and Wales

Programme	Sample sizes	Offender profiles	Programme structure	Outcomes
Probation (IMPACT)	Random assignment of 244 experimental cases and 161 control cases.	• For the sample as a whole (experimental and control cases), two-thirds to three-quarters were aged 17–29. • Many had previously been placed on probation and the most frequent current offence was theft.	• Officer caseloads reduced from 40–45 cases to approximately 20 cases. • Emphasis upon 'situational' treatment, with more direct involvement in the areas of family, work and leisure.	• No significant differences in one and two-year reconviction rates. • A 'suggestion' that those offenders with low criminal tendencies and many personal problems had a more successful outcome under the experimental treatment.
Probation for young offenders (IT)	103 heavy-end IT (HEIT) cases, 40 other IT cases, 141 custody cases and 142 straight SO cases.	• For the sample as a whole (all groups), the mean age was 15.7 years. • For the HEIT group, the average number of charges/convictions in the prior 14 months was seven.	• In the two metropolitan boroughs, the projects consisted of group and individual work, an 'offending curriculum', the teaching of social skills and various constructive activities; in the large city there was an emphasis upon tracking with weekly meetings; while in the shire county, the programmes were more individualised.	• HEIT 'on the whole' successfully targeted serious and persistent offenders at genuine risk of custody. • There was 'no automatic or necessary relationship' between HEIT and custody levels.

Probation for young adults (IP)	1,677 offenders referred to IP, 45% of whom were sentenced onto the programme. No comparison group.	• 51% had more than five previous convictions and 54% had previous experience of custody.	• Individualised programmes involving frequent contact with a project worker and an emphasis upon confronting offending behaviour.	• 'On the whole' the offenders were at risk of a custodial sentence. • 'IP worked well in some areas and not so well in others.'
Probation for young adults (Leeds IP)	227 IP cases. Compared to a custodial group of unknown size.	• Unknown	• An eight-week individualised programme, with most frequent attendance requirements at the beginning. • One-to-one counselling sessions, offending behaviour sessions and social skills sessions.	• The scheme 'successfully' attracted those at serious risk of custody, with a 'genuine diversion effect' taking place. • 73% of a small sub-sample (n=45) were reconvicted over a two-year follow-up period, but custody was 'not demonstrably more effective in preventing or deterring reconviction'.

Table 2.2. continues overleaf

59

Table 2.2 continued

Programme	Sample sizes	Offender profiles	Programme structure	Outcomes
Probation for young adult offenders (ICCP)	433 ICCP cases. No comparison group.	• 90% were white and 93% were male. • They had an average of 27 previous convictions, and a medium to high risk of re-offending.	• A minimum of 25 hours of contact per week for the first three months. • Mandatory curfews with electronic tagging. • Five core supervision components, encompassing accredited offending behaviour programmes, mentoring, one-to-one supervision, education, training and employment, and community punishment.	• 26% of the offenders had their orders revoked or terminated and a further 27% had breached the programme but were awaiting their court hearings. • There was an overall 15% reduction in the use of custody across all the ICCP areas, but and an average 9% fall in the non-ICCP areas. This difference was possibly 'due to chance'.

Scotland

The Freagarrach programme targeted the most persistent juvenile offenders in Clackmannanshire, Falkirk and Stirling. To qualify, the young person needed to be aged from 12 to 16 years (raised to 18 in 1999), to have at least five offending episodes within the previous 12 months and to have at least one offending episode within the last two months. The evaluation began in August 1995 and ran until the end of March 2000 (Lobley, Smith and Stern 2001). By the end of this period, there had been 121 starts by 106 young people, 94 of whom were male and 12 were female. The average age of the young people at the start of the programme changed over time, from 14.5 in the first year to 16 in the fourth and 15.5 in the fifth. Of the 95 young people for whom follow-up data were available, two-thirds had been charged with an offence by the age of 12, with an average number of charges in the prior year of 18. Over half of those of school attending age were currently excluded from school, and about 25 per cent were in some form of local authority care. Two-thirds had problems with both drugs and alcohol.

The guideline period of attendance was initially six months, but the actual average length of attendance was found to be 11.5 months in 1995–96 and 7.5 months in 1998–99. The length of contact was determined according to the young person's needs, and it was not unusual for young people to attend for over a year, and three stayed for over two years. There were three face-to-face contacts every week, with each contact lasting between 1.5 and 2.5 hours. Attendance was voluntary, but the evaluators reported that the young people willingly kept in contact apart from an estimated nine offenders who never formed a relationship with the staff. The core offending behaviour work was approached either in groups or individually depending on the young person's capabilities and learning style. Education and employment issues were also addressed, and families were supported through formal parents' groups and other informal contacts. Staff succeeded in many cases in achieving at least a partial return to school, but they were less successful in helping young people into employment or vocational training. The expectation that victim–offender mediation would develop on a substantial scale was not fulfilled, while leisure pursuits were limited by the scarcity of available resources. Nevertheless, the young people expressed 'overwhelmingly positive views of the project and its staff' (Lobley, Smith and Stern 2001: 4), and there were indications that attendance helped to improve their family relationships.

With regard to the impact upon re-offending, the evaluators found that: 'The 81 young people on whom at least twelve months' figures are available had a total of 801 charges or convictions against them in the twelve months before starting at Freagarrach, and 681 in the twelve months after starting, a reduction of 15 per cent in the total volume of recorded offending' (*ibid*.: 65). Two comparison groups were collected (sample sizes of 52 and 39) but the offenders in these groups were found to be generally less persistent, limiting their comparability. Nevertheless, the evaluators concluded that 'there were indications that over a two-year period young people who attended Freagarrach offended less seriously than those in the comparison group'. Further analysis led them to suggest that 'a constellation of factors, including employment, training and a supportive family' were associated with a reduced risk of offending (*ibid*.: 63).

Sweden

An Intensive Supervision Experiment with Electronic Monitoring (ISEM) was carried out in Sweden between 1994 and 1998. The pilot was initially limited to certain regions before being expanded nationwide during 1997 and 1998. At the same time, the target group was expanded from those persons sentenced to a maximum of two months in prison to those sentenced to a maximum of three months. Any offender sentenced to such a period in custody could apply for ISEM, with the number of days matching the period that would have been spent in custody. Home monitoring was carried out through the use of an electronic tag, which was supplemented by unannounced visits several times a week. These visits usually included a breath test, while drug use was checked through urine/blood tests where necessary. The offender was allowed to leave home for employment, training, health care and the weekly corrective-influence sessions. Non-compliances with the programme usually resulted in a transfer to custody.

The nationwide part of the experiment was evaluated by the National Council for Crime Prevention (1999). They found that 75 per cent of the target group applied for ISEM, of which 85 per cent were allowed to participate. Consequently, in 1997, some 3,800 offenders participated. The most common reason for refusing ISEM was a lack of co-operation with the initial investigation. For those on the programme, the evaluators found that, 'generally speaking', both they and their families were 'positively disposed' towards the programme (*ibid*.: 71). The probation service made an average of three visits a week to the offenders' homes, and the offenders spent an average of 30 hours per week at their workplace. About six per cent failed to complete, usually for violating the drug/alcohol ban or for other non-compliances. Of those on ISEM during the regional trial (1994–95), 26 per cent re-offended within three years, compared to 28 per cent of a corresponding group who served their sentences in prison. The evaluators thus state that 'a cautious interpretation might be that ISEM as an implementation procedure does not generally affect the convicted person's tendency to reoffend' (*ibid.*: 71). They, nevertheless, conclude that 'ISEM is a form of sentence implementation that is not encumbered by the negative consequences associated with imprisonment, that demands fewer resources, and that is in many ways, if not entirely, as intrusive as a prison term' (*ibid.*: 72).

Canada

Fifty-four offenders were released from custody onto Intensive Rehabilitation Supervision (IRS), in the form of the Learning Resources Program (LRP), with electronic monitoring attached (the IRS group). The selection criteria for this treatment group included a non-violent and non-sexual offence, a sentence of less than six months, and an assessment of moderate risk. They were joined on the LRP by 17 probationers but these offenders were not the subject of EM (the probationers group). As the random assignment of offenders was not possible, the evaluators adopted a quasi-experimental methodology, with a comparison non-treatment sample of 100 offenders drawn from two prisons in areas where IRS was not available. Comparability was ensured through matching on eligibility and risk/needs factors (the inmates group), with further analysis revealing very few differences between the groups (Bonta, Wallace-Capretta and Rooney 2000).

The LRP adopted a highly structured, cognitive-behavioural approach, operating four mornings per week for a total of nine hours. Anger management, criminal thinking and substance abuse groups were all provided, alongside individual counselling to deal with more specific personal needs. Analysis revealed that the IRS offenders received an average of 65 hours of treatment, with 87 per cent completing the programme, while the probationers received an average of 74 hours, with 53 per cent completing. The differing completion rates reflected the fact that, for the IRS group, failure to attend could result in return to custody, while for the probationers group attendance was voluntary. The recidivism rates were 32 per cent for the IRS offenders, 35 per cent for the probationers, and 31 per cent for the inmates, but further analysis revealed a statistically significant interaction between treatment and risk level: 'The high-risk offenders who received relatively intensive levels of treatment showed lower recidivism rates than untreated high-risk offenders (31.6% vs. 51.1%)', while 'the low-risk offenders who received intensive levels of treatment demonstrated higher recidivism rates (32.3%) than nontreated low-risk offenders (14.5%)' (*ibid.*: 325).

Reviewing the impact upon re-offending

As indicated by the studies set out above, particularly from the US, the early reconviction findings from some of the more rigorous evaluations were not particularly promising. Reviewing the research literature, Gendreau, Goggin and Fulton (2000: 198) thus determined that 'when it comes to the matter of reducing offender recidivism, the conclusion is inescapable, ISPs have had little effect on offenders' future criminal activity'. Similar results were found in relation to the IMPACT experiment and the 'high-tariff' IT projects in England and Wales (Folkard, Smith and Smith 1976; Bottoms 1995). It is particularly informative that it has tended to be in the developmental and smaller-scale projects that significant positive outcomes have been recorded. One possible interpretation is that their small sample sizes and inadequate comparison groups render their findings at best tentative and sometimes overstated. In contrast, large-scale projects tend to be multi-sited and subject to highly variable delivery practices and performance. Perhaps, therefore, we should not be surprised that these large-scale projects produce disappointing and inconclusive results.

It also needs to be considered whether limited positive effects should be expected when programmes are targeting the most persistent and high-risk offenders. There would appear to be the need for some realism, as the evaluators of the Kent ISSP concluded: 'Almost by definition, persistent offending behaviour is extremely resistant to change ... it was unrealistic to expect that young people convicted several times prior to beginning ISSP would never be convicted during involvement with the programme and in the 24 months that followed' (Little *et al.* 2004: 228–9). These evaluators hypothesised, however, that there would be a reduction in the volume of offending, and a 30 to 50 per cent reduction was detected (*ibid.*: 225). As this hypothesis indicates, there is a clear need to distinguish between 'prevalence', referring to whether the offender is reconvicted or not, and 'incidence', referring to the volume or frequency of re-offending.

Consideration of the impact upon re-offending is complicated by the fact that individual evaluations have used differing measures of recidivism, as well as deviating greatly in their methodological standards. This problem is not confined to evaluations of intensive community programmes, with Michael Maltz (1984) having identified the following nine categories of measurement from a survey of various research findings:

- Arrest: number of arrests; recorded police contact, court appearance; time elapsed before the first re-arrest; did conviction result?
- Reconviction: jail or prison sentence; seriousness of offence; sentence.
- Incarceration: type of facility; seriousness of offence.
- Parole violation: nature of the violation; seriousness of the infraction; was it police-initiated?
- Parole suspension: new offence; number of suspensions.
- Parole revocation: new offence; seriousness of the offence; average number of good days on parole.
- Offence: seriousness; number; new offence.
- Absconding: was an absconder warrant issued?
- Probation: proportion re-detained; length of time detained; number of violations; violation warrant.

Despite the difficulties in drawing conclusions from studies that have employed differing methodological standards and alternative forms of measurement, there would appear to have been some more positive results, and it is here that the variability in targeting criteria and programme content are of particular significance. With regard to the latter, Gendreau, Goggin and Fulton (2000: 199–200) have drawn a distinction between those programmes with a treatment component (e.g. counselling; supervised activities) and those with no treatment component. Analysing the research findings in more detail and employing a meta-analysis on studies with control group comparisons, they report that the experimental effects are remarkably consistent: 'Under the "no treatment" condition ISPs produced a 7% increase in recidivism … ISPs that appeared to have had some treatment component tended to produce a slight decline in recidivism of 3%. ISPs that employed more treatment reported a 10% decrease in recidivism.' Such a distinction was earlier suggested by Gendreau,

Cullen, and Bonta (1994: 77): 'The empirical evidence regarding ISPs is decisive: without a rehabilitation component, reductions in recidivism are as elusive as a desert mirage.' They thus concluded (*ibid.*: 74) that 'A persuasive case can be made for abandoning intensive supervision programs that seek only to control and punish offenders in favor of programs that give equal primacy to changing offenders.'

These findings can be considered in the context of the wider knowledge regarding the theoretical foundations set out in Chapter 1. The more recent 'What Works' literature suggests that some forms of treatment work to some extent with some offenders. But those intensive programmes without a treatment component place much faith in the power of deterrence, which assumes that offenders make rational choices and that these choices are influenced by the threatened punishments. In contrast, there is much evidence, confirmed by a number of meta-analyses (e.g. Lipsey 1992; 1995) that the reality is often very different:

> The failure of ISP's to produce striking results in reducing recidivism would not surprise those familiar with the relevant criminological and psychological research. Underlying ISP's is the theory of deterrence – that is, the notion that offenders can be compelled to behave prosocially by the threat of enhanced punishment. This idea has achieved little empirical support in the criminological literature. (Gendreau, Cullen and Bonta 1994: 73)

Turning to the differences in targeting, the Canadian study set out in the previous section highlights the importance of distinguishing between high-risk and low-risk offenders. As shown, the authors found a reduction in recidivism for the higher-risk offenders only, leading them to conclude that 'the importance of matching treatment intensity to offender risk level and ensuring that there is a treatment component in intensive supervision programs is reaffirmed' (Bonta, Wallace-Capretta and Rooney 2000: 312). This clearly supports the 'What Works' principle of 'risk classification', which stipulates that the level and intensity of the intervention should be matched to the risk of re-offending.

Reviewing the impact upon custodial sentencing

To have a direct impact upon custody rates, the 'prison-diversion' intensive community programmes need to successfully target those offenders who are at genuine risk of custody rather than those who might have been dealt with more leniently. This avoids what has become commonly known as the 'net-widening' effect, using this concept in its qualitative sense in which offenders within the system are subjected to 'levels of intervention which they might not have previously received' (Cohen 1985: 44). In his 'dispersal of discipline' thesis, Cohen actually employed the alternative concepts of 'denser nets' and 'mesh-thinning' to describe such an effect, with 'net-widening' being used to describe an overall expansion of penal control, bringing new offenders into the system. Nevertheless, 'net-widening' is now commonly used in both senses, and, usefully, McMahon (1990: 124) distinguishes between the traditional quantitative and 'mesh-thinning' qualitative aspects of the concept.

Assessing whether the right offenders are being targeted is clearly difficult: 'Any claim to certainty that a person who is on ISP would have otherwise been in prison can only be based upon shaky evidence' (Clear 1997: 128). Nevertheless, the high-tariff IT projects that were introduced in England and Wales in the 1980s have been viewed as the 'most important factor' in reducing custody rates for young people during this period (Pitts 2002: 418). However, closer analysis by Tony Bottoms (1995) revealed no direct relationship. So-called net-widening has also accompanied the introduction of intensive programmes in the US, leading Michael Tonry (1998: 683) to comment that 'the availability of new sanctions presents almost irresistible temptations to judges and corrections officials to use them for offenders other than those for whom the program was created'. Tonry further notes that those programmes particularly in danger of net-widening are those in which the judges control the referrals. Support for this conclusion is provided by the evaluations in England and Wales of IT (Ely, Swift and Sutherland 1987) and IP (Mair *et al.* 1994), with both studies finding that sentencers tend to favour a wider use for intensive programmes.

In assessing the relationship between intensive programmes and custody rates, one also needs to take into account the impact of breach, since a potential consequence of breach is imprisonment. Recent research findings, particularly in the US, indicate that high levels of breach have been common: 'As higher risk offenders are placed in such programs, higher violation rates must be expected especially if the programs vigorously enforce their technical conditions' (Petersilia and Turner 1992: 650). John Muncie (1999: 278), in his critique of decarceration in the 1960s, has referred to this risk as 'jeopardy': 'the risk of accelerating routes into custody through breaches of the conditions of community sentences'. The research evidence would suggest that such an acceleration has in many instances occurred: 'It appears that, at best, the various intermediate punishment programmes serve only as temporary alternative to incarceration, and may, in fact, generate a need for expanded incarceration capacities' (Blomberg and Lucken 1994: 68–9).

Most worryingly, if the dangers of net-widening and increased breaching are combined then a number of those offenders sent to custody for breach would have previously been the subject of regular community supervision. Consequently, the potential for intensive programmes to deliver cost savings is seriously curtailed:

> Let us say that an ISP 'costs' $5,000 per year, while prison 'costs' $20,000. A hundred cases getting two years on ISP then will cost one million dollars; these same cases getting a year in prison will cost $2 million. But if the ISP has a 50 per cent failure rate, and failures average 6 months on ISP and then serve their year in prison, then the ISP under these terms costs a total of $1.65 million. If only 80 per cent of the ISP cases are diverted from prison, the program costs of prison and ISP are essentially equal. (Clear 1997: 129)

There seems, therefore, to be a clear disparity between the aims of reducing both custody rates and costs and the research evidence regarding actual impact. One can also take a wider perspective, recognising that intensive programmes represent one strand of a more general decarceration movement. It cannot be disputed that this movement has so far failed, with record numbers being held in custody in both the US and England and Wales. This follows increases in both custody rates and the lengths of custodial sentences (Friendship et al. 2004). Rod Morgan (2002) reaches the following persuasive conclusion: 'toughening the language of community penalties, introducing additional sentencing options, and loading those penalties up with additional conditions which, if breached, lead offenders brought back to court, has not displaced custody but, rather, fuelled an ever-more punitive, interventionist and costly trend'. In other words, there is much evidence to support Cohen's 'dispersal of discipline' thesis.

In addition to the problems of 'net-widening' and 'jeopardy', Muncie lists further 'contradictions' as having contributed to the failure of the decarceration movement:

- lack of purpose – the contradiction between the punitive, reparative and welfare aims of community-based programmes ...

- dubious rationales – the development of community programmes motivated purely by financial and economic, rather than progressive concerns ...

- political vulnerability – whatever progressive elements are present in an anti-custody ethos, they are forever prey to knee-jerk and reactionary overhaul. (Muncie 1999: 278)

All three contradictions are apparent in the recent history of intensive programmes in England and Wales. Their purpose has been multi-faceted and, in some senses, contradictory (see pp. 17–29); the limited cost-effectiveness of custody has been repeatedly emphasised; and the programmes have arrived and then disappeared in differing political climates. A number of political initiatives have in fact encouraged the use of custody and the imposition of longer sentences, e.g. the 'three-strikes' laws in the Crime (Sentences) Act 1997. Certain political pronouncements have also proved unhelpful, notably the declaration by Michael Howard in the early 1990s that 'prison works'. In consequence of all these factors, the commanding position of the prison remains intact: 'The prison dominates our criminal justice system as the cardinal penalty, against which all other penalties must be assessed. Despite repeated efforts by penal policymakers, politicians, and lobbyists to displace the prison from its central position, it continues to have a powerful hold over our collective imagination' (Zedner 2004: 7).

Reviewing other findings

While many empirical studies have concentrated upon the impact of intensive community programmes upon re-offending rates and/or custody rates, a number of studies have reported other outcome findings. Notably, some programmes appear to have made inroads into tackling the underlying problems and criminogenic risk factors of the offenders (e.g. Raynor 1988; Latessa and Vito 1988; Jolin and Stipak 1992). In some instances, positive feedback has been gained from all relevant parties, with the intensive contact encouraging productive relationships between offenders and practitioners. For example, in their evaluation of IP in England and Wales, George Mair and colleagues (1994: xi) found that, 'Sentencers tended to be very positive about IP, although they had differing views about its objectives. Probation officers, especially those who worked on IP schemes, were also enthusiastic. Offenders appreciated the attention given to them by IP workers.' Some of those programmes targeting young offenders have also been reported to be popular with parents (e.g. Bottoms 1995).

Less positively, a number of evaluations have raised doubts regarding the compatibility of the differing aims and objectives that intensive community programmes are expected to meet. More specifically, bearing in mind that imprisonment is a potential consequence of breach, there would appear to be a clear tension between using intensive programmes as an alternative to custodial sentences and increasing the likelihood of custody through a promotion of rigorous enforcement. For practitioners, the difficult dilemma is between their desire to maintain engagement with the offender and ensure programme completions with their recognition of the need to maintain the credibility of the programme itself. It is perhaps not surprising, therefore, that individual studies have found evidence of officers differentiating between breaches and/or ignoring them, and, in contrast, pursuing a policy of breaching as early as possible (Goodstein and Sontheimer 1997; Hill 1992; Latessa and Vito 1988).

The optimum target group for reducing custody rates is also likely to be different from that for reducing re-offending rates. To satisfy the former objective, the emphasis should be upon those genuinely at risk of a custodial sentence, requiring consideration of the seriousness of the current offence, but to achieve a significant reduction in offending frequency, greater inroads could be made with persistent petty offenders who have committed high volumes of crime in the pre-intervention period.

Attempting to achieve a multitude of objectives would thus appear to carry the risk of diluting the inroads that are made into achieving each objective individually. In their evaluation of IP, Mair and colleagues (1994: 5) noted that 'IP may not be able to satisfy equally well all of the demands which may be made of it. Will it be able to reduce offending, reduce the prison population, provide effective punishment, keep sentencers satisfied, and reduce costs all at the same time?' Evidence from the US would appear to support such caution, with evaluation results struggling to match the expectations that have been set: 'During the mid 1980s, intermediate sanctions such as intensive supervision ... were oversold as being able simultaneously to divert offenders from incarceration, reduce recidivism rates, and save money, while providing credible punishments that could be scaled in intensity to be proportionate to the severity of the offender's crime. Like most propositions that seem too good to be true, that one wasn't' (Tonry 1998: 80). Perhaps one should not be overly surprised: as Troy Armstrong (1991: 4) comments, 'if this multitude of goals are achievable under one program approach, intensive supervision would have to be considered the wonder child of the criminal justice system'.

Summary

A large number of evaluations, in the US, England and Wales and elsewhere, have attempted to assess the effectiveness and impact of various intensive community programmes. The two dominant goals have been to reduce re-offending rates and the levels of custodial sentencing, but analysis of the more methodologically rigorous studies indicates mixed results, with a number of evaluations raising doubts as to whether these aims are fully compatible. Reductions in re-offending have apparently been limited by the weaknesses in the deterrence rationale, with the evidence suggesting most promise for those programmes that target high-risk offenders and have a strong rehabilitation component. As for the impact upon custody rates, the twin dangers of 'net-widening' and increased levels of breach have become increasingly apparent. One can also take a wider perspective, recognising that a more general decarceration movement has so far failed. More positively, some evaluations indicate that intensive community programmes can make inroads into tackling the underlying problems of offenders, while proving popular with offenders, their families, practitioners and sentencers.

Notwithstanding this climate of uncertainty, intensive community programmes are becoming an increasingly integral part of penal policy in many jurisdictions, following the lead of the US. In England and Wales, the Intensive Supervision and Surveillance Programme (ISSP) has now been introduced nationwide, targeting persistent and serious young offences both pre- and post-custody. Notably, the programme is far more intensive than many of its predecessors and seeks to deliver an appropriate balance between control and care. This programme, and its accompanying national evaluation, provides the focus for the next part of the book. Given the theoretical tensions and empirical uncertainties so far set out, there is an obvious need for careful consideration of the results of this evaluation and its wider implications.

Part II
Case Study: The Intensive Supervision and Surveillance Programme

Chapter 3

The introduction of ISSP

As was shown in Chapter 1, there were numerous attempts at developing intensive community programmes in England and Wales during the latter decades of the twentieth century, most notably the Intensive Matched Probation and After-Care Treatment (IMPACT), Intermediate Treatment (IT) and Intensive Probation (IP) initiatives. While these programmes were fairly short-lived, a more sustained initiative has materialised in the twenty-first century in the form of the Intensive Supervision and Surveillance Programme (ISSP). This programme, established by the Youth Justice Board (YJB) for England and Wales, is significantly more intensive than many previous initiatives and is multi-modal, combining supervision with surveillance in an attempt to ensure an appropriate balance between control and care. To assess whether ISSP was delivered in practice as intended in principle, and whether the objectives for ISSP were being met, the YJB commissioned a multi-dimensional evaluation of the first 41 schemes, conducted by the University of Oxford. Through a broad model of evaluation, involving a range of quantitative and qualitative techniques, it was hoped that the immediate and wider impact of ISSP would be captured.

Youth Justice in England and Wales

During the latter half of the twentieth century, the tensions between the welfare and justice models of criminal justice were particularly pronounced in the field of youth justice. As Adam Crawford and Tim

Newburn recognise, 'Since the Second World War there have been a significant number of shifts in government policy towards young offenders, often with policy swinging between an emphasis upon "care/welfare" and "control/punishment", as the political mood has changed.' However, despite welfarism dominating during the 1960s, they continue that in comparison to the rest of Europe, England and Wales 'has traditionally adopted a more punitive and less welfare-orientated approach to youth justice' (Crawford and Newburn 2002: 477).

Following the election of the Labour Government in 1997 with its slogan of 'Tough on crime, tough on the causes of crime', the welfare vs. justice debate has to some extent been surpassed by the establishment of a 'new youth justice'. The key components of this new approach can be found in the Crime and Disorder Act 1998. Significantly, the Act established both the YJB and 155 multi-disciplinary Youth Offending Teams (YOTs). The YJB is a non-departmental public body with overall responsibility for monitoring performance and setting standards for the youth justice system, while the YOTs have the role of co-ordinating services in their local authority areas. These YOTs are further guided by the new overarching aim for the youth justice system, as set out in the 1998 Act, which is 'to prevent offending by children and young people'.

Various commentators have attempted to identify the key themes and characteristics of this 'new youth justice'. Newburn (2002c: 460), for example, has stated that: 'New Labour youth justice, which combines the rhetoric and practice of criminality prevention and crime reduction with that of "what works" and "evidence-based policy", attempts to concern itself with the causes of crime and the delivery of justice whilst simultaneously focusing on probabilistic calculations of risk and harm minimization.' In other words, there is a combination of the old welfare and justice models with the new penological thinking of actuarial justice (see pp. 17–18). Similar analysis has led Allison Morris and Loraine Gelsthorpe (2000) to highlight the following five strands to the new youth justice: (i) proportionality; (ii) managerialism; (iii) risk assessment and actuarial justice; (iv) community; and (v) restorative justice. Consequently, the theoretical foundations of youth offending interventions have become multi-faceted:

> Youth justice in the twenty-first century has evolved into a particularly complex state of affairs. It is designed to punish the offender while keeping their welfare paramount. It is at one and

the same time about crime prevention and retribution. It makes claims for restoration and reintegration whilst seeking some of the most punitive measures of surveillance and containment in custodial and community settings. (Muncie 2004: 248)

As will be shown, ISSP fits very well into this multi-faceted framework, particularly through its combination of supervision and surveillance. Furthermore, ISSP adheres closely to the 'What Works' principles, which have proved highly influential in guiding the youth justice reforms. The Audit Commission report *Misspent Youth* (1996), and particularly its evidence regarding the poor quality and content of Supervision Orders, has also had a major impact upon the thinking behind ISSP. The report concluded that 'persistent offenders should receive more intensive supervision in the community'. The seeds for ISSP were sown, and following the Spending Review of 2000, the YJB invited YOTs across England and Wales to apply for funds to 'pilot' the programme. The first 41 schemes were launched in July 2001 and within six months all 41 schemes were operational. Nationwide roll-out quickly followed in October 2003.

Multi-dimensional objectives

Previous evaluations have questioned the compatibility of the aims and objectives with which intensive community programmes have been set, indicating that attempting to achieve a multitude of objectives can dilute the inroads that are made into achieving each objective individually (see p. 71 above). Despite this evidence, the YJB set out multi-dimensional objectives for ISSP. Initially, three key objectives were specified:

1 To reduce the rate of re-offending in the target group of offenders by 5 per cent and reduce the seriousness of any re-offending.

2 To tackle underlying problems of the young people concerned in an effective manner and with a particular emphasis on educational needs.

3 To demonstrate that supervision and surveillance is being undertaken consistently and rigorously, and in ways which will reassure the community and sentencers of their credibility and likely success. (Youth Justice Board 2000: 1–2)

These objectives filtered into the more general aims of the YJB, which were to reduce re-offending by young offenders by 5 per cent, compared to the predicted rate, by March 2004, and to promote interventions that reduced the risk factors associated with offending (Youth Justice Board 2002a). The first objective for ISSP seemingly recognised that when dealing with a high-risk group of offenders, for whom some further offending is likely, it is more realistic to seek to make inroads into the frequency and seriousness of their offending rather than its 'prevalence', referring to whether the offender is reconvicted or not. The second objective emphasised the need for some form of rehabilitation or treatment, adhering to a welfare model of intervention, while the third objective supported a rigorous approach, adhering more closely to the risk management and authoritarian models of intervention. It was clear from these objectives that practitioners were expected to deliver both care and control, ensuring an appropriate balance between the two.

A common objective of previous intensive community programmes in England and Wales has been to divert offenders from custody and reduce the levels of custodial sentencing. While not initially explicit, this became an increasingly important and transparent objective for ISSP. Notably, the introduction of eligibility shortcuts in April 2002 was intended to counter any increase in the use of custody resulting from other policy initiatives (see next section). Furthermore, the YJB explicitly stated its preference for ISSP over short DTOs (Youth Justice Board 2002b), assumingly taking into account the high costs of custody and more specific concerns regarding the detrimental effects of imprisoning young people, including bullying, limited educational provision, self-harm and occasional suicides. Finally, one of the YJB's targets for 2003/04 to 2005/06 was to ensure that, by March 2005, at least 4,000 young offenders a year were intensively supervised in the community and to reduce the number of under-18s remanded and sentenced to secure facilities by 10 per cent (Youth Justice Board 2003a). In setting out this target, the YJB were clearly hopeful that ISSP would not become another illustration of the 'dispersal of discipline' thesis and would avoid up-tariffing offenders who would previously have received less intrusive community sentences. Seemingly, however, there was little recognition that the optimum target group for reducing custody rates was likely to be different from that for reducing re-offending rates.

The target group

Previous intensive community programmes have varied greatly in their targeting. This variability has had the following three dimensions: (i) age; (ii) stage in process; and (iii) risk of re-offending. With regard to the first of these dimensions, ISSP targets young offenders aged ten to 17. Turning to the second dimension of 'stage in process', unlike many of its predecessors, ISSP targets offenders both pre- and post-sentence and pre- and post-custody. More precisely, the three routes on to the programme are: (i) as a condition of bail supervision and support; (ii) as part of a community penalty, either a Supervision Order or a Community Rehabilitation Order (CRO); and (iii) as a condition of community supervision in the second half of a DTO. ISSP is thus not currently an order in its own right, and there have been no new legislative powers relating specifically to the programme, although an Intensive Supervision and Surveillance Order (ISSO) is under consideration.

For those serving a community sentence the programme lasts for six or four months, depending upon whether the order is part of a Supervision Order or CRO respectively. For those bailed or in the second half of a DTO the period of time is determined by the length of bail or the DTO. But the intention of the YJB, in adherence to their desire for ISSP to reduce the number of DTOs, has been for the majority of young people to spend six months on the programme as part of a Supervision Order. It is clear, however, that for these ISSPs to have an impact upon custody rates, they need to target those offenders at genuine risk of custody. In contrast, for those who receive ISSP as a condition of community supervision in the second half of a DTO, the programme can only have an indirect impact upon custody rates by helping to prevent further offending from which a custodial sentence might have resulted.

The final divergence in targeting relates to the offenders' risk of re-offending. While some previous intensive programmes have specifically targeted those offenders deemed to be at low to moderate risk of re-offending, others have targeted those offenders at high risk of re-offending. Importantly, a Canadian study (Bonta, Wallace-Capretta and Rooney 2000) found a reduction in recidivism for the higher-risk offenders only, supporting the 'What Works' principle of 'risk classification', which stipulates that the level and intensity of the intervention should be matched to the risk of re-offending. Adhering to this evidence, and providing support to the YJB claim that the programme is 'evidence-based', ISSP targets the 'top-end' of the offending spectrum; more specifically, it was aimed at 'the small group of prolific young offenders (aged 10 to 17) whom Home Office research suggests commit approximately a quarter of all offences committed by young people' (Youth Justice Board 2002b: 5). The research referred to here was carried out by Graham and Bowling (1995) as the first sweep of the *Youth Lifestyles Survey*, and was analysed further in the Audit Commission's report *Misspent Youth* (1996).

Eligibility criteria were developed to target this 'top-end' group, initially restricting the availability of ISSP to those young persons 'charged or warned for an imprisonable offence on four or more separate occasions within the last 12 months, and who had previously received at least one community or custodial penalty' (Youth Justice Board 2000). More simply, it was commonly stated that offenders required four or more 'charging occasions' in the prior 12 months. The YJB further specified that magistrates should only be advised to consider the option of ISSP where the current offence was of sufficient gravity for the court to be considering a custodial sentence or remand. In addition, ISSP teams were given the flexibility to adopt further suitability criteria, encompassing factors such as the seriousness of offending, the need to target crimes linking to local crime reduction priorities, the motivation of the individual under consideration, and, in DTO cases, the risk of re-offending on return to the community.

In April 2002, only nine months after the launch of the first ISSP schemes, the YJB altered the eligibility criteria. This followed concerns that 'tough' government initiatives on street crime, and robbery in particular, could lead to an increase in the use of custody for first-time serious offenders, while the implementation of Section 30 of the Criminal Justice and Police Act of 2001 could lead to secure or custodial remands for young offenders with a history of offending while on bail. In addition, the term 'charging occasions' was creating difficulties for ISSP teams, some of whom were still struggling to achieve their numerical targets for ISSP referrals (Youth Justice Board 2002c). Practitioners had also expressed concerns that the criteria were preventing them from targeting a number of young people for whom ISSP could be beneficial, and there was a further suggestion that sentencers favoured the wider availability of the programme.

As a result, the Board widened and refined the eligibility criteria to include 'serious' as well as 'persistent' offenders. More specifically, ISSP began targeting those young offenders who:

- had been charged, warned or convicted of offences committed on four or more separate dates within the last 12 months and had received at least one community or custodial disposal, or

- were at risk of custody because the current charge or sentence related to an offence serious enough that an adult could receive a custodial sentence of 14 years or more (the 'serious crime' shortcut), or

- were at risk of custody because they had a history of repeat offending on bail and were at risk of a secure remand (the 'repeat offending on bail' shortcut). (Youth Justice Board 2002b: 5)

One further amendment has since been made, with the serious crime shortcut being amended in 2005 to cover those offences that could attract a custodial sentence of up to ten years, rather than 14 years.

A number of previous intensive programmes have targeted both serious and persistent offenders. Notably, the IT initiatives in the 1980s targeted those who were 'serious or persistent young offenders at real risk of a custodial sentence' (Bottoms 1995: v). While the research evidence suggests a 'considerable overlap between serious, violent and persistent offending' (Whyte 2001: 1), it can also be expected that one-off serious offenders will have differing criminogenic risk factors to the more persistent offenders. Interestingly, the question of whether ISSP was suitable for both groups was not explicitly addressed at the time of the revision. Consideration instead focused upon the likely impact on numbers eligible for the programme, which were expected to rise significantly, although estimates of the exact amount varied.

The structure of the programme

The majority of intensive community programmes in the US have been developed and implemented at the local county or state level, while national standards in England and Wales have maintained a degree of discretion at the local level. A degree of local discretion has also been a feature of the 'new youth justice', contrasting to the more prescriptive nature of the recently established accredited programmes for adult offenders. Local variation is thus a feature of ISSP, with a number of key differences between the 41 schemes that were included in the evaluation. Notably, some ISSP schemes were associated with a single YOT, while others involved a consortium of YOTs. Furthermore, *who* actually delivered ISSP varied between the schemes. In the majority of instances, ISSP was provided predominantly through existing YOT staff and structures. However, four schemes were subcontracted to non-YOT agencies who were responsible for co-ordinating and delivering the programme. In three of these schemes, the non-YOT agency was a nationally based voluntary organisation (NACRO), while in one scheme it was a locally based voluntary organisation (AXIS) which worked in alliance with the YOT, a social work leaving care team and a Christian childcare initiative.

Five of the 41 schemes adopted a specific model of change. Four of these schemes employed the principles of the Youth Advocate Programme (YAP), which was established in the US in 1975. This programme promotes a strength-based, holistic approach, developing problem-solving strategies by focusing upon the young persons' strengths. The fifth scheme employed the principles of Multi-Systemic Therapy (MST), combining family and behavioural therapy strategies with intensive family support services. While MST is well established in the US, its employment within the framework of ISSP represented one of the first trials of the model in the UK.

Reviewing the history of intensive programmes, their only common characteristic is that they involve more supervision than routine community interventions. There is, however, no standard as to how much more supervision is required for a programme to be deemed 'intensive'. In some instances a doubling of the number of contacts from one to two a month seems to have sufficed, whereas in other instances an expectancy of several contacts per day has been established. For ISSP, the YJB has specified that, for those on six-month programmes, the first three months should entail a structured supervision programme of at least five hours a day during the week and access to support during the evenings and weekends. After three months there must be provision for day-to-day contact with the young person for at least one hour each weekday with access to support during the evenings and weekends. Comparing these requirements to those of previous programmes, it is clear that ISSP is much more demanding than many of its predecessors, in both England and Wales and the US. Attention seems, therefore, to have been paid to the 'What Works' evidence that 'programmes must be of sufficient intensity and duration to achieve their aims, especially with those who are chronic or serious offenders' (Utting and Vennard 2000: 22).

Previous intensive programmes have also differed in terms of their programme components. In many of the US programmes, particularly those of the 1980s, supervision has actually taken the form of monitoring, surveillance and control. In England and Wales, in contrast, the need for some form of treatment/rehabilitation has been more consistently applied, and the use of terminology has been more consistent with supervision referring to rehabilitative components, rather than surveillance or monitoring. For ISSP, the YJB has specified that all programmes should contain the following five core supervision modules: (i) education and training; (ii) changing offending behaviour; (iii) interpersonal skills; (iv) family support; and (v) restorative justice (with the exception of recognising that the offending behaviour and restorative elements are not suitable for those on bail who plead not guilty). There is a particular emphasis upon the first of the five core components, recognising the well-established links between educational disaffection and youth crime (Youth Justice Board 2003b).

The YJB also specified that other modules should be provided according to the needs of the individual, encompassing work to address risk factors such as mental health, drug or alcohol misuse, accommodation problems, as well as provision for counselling or mentoring and some form of constructive recreation. ISSP is thus very much a multi-modal intervention with a range of treatment components that can be tailored to the individual offender. In this sense there is adherence to both the 'What Works' principle of 'intervention modality', which identifies multi-modal programmes as the most consistently effective, and the evidence from the US that the greater the emphasis upon treatment within an intensive community programme, the greater the impact upon re-offending rates.

The YJB was keen, however, for ISSP to be perceived as 'tough' and 'stringent', hopefully ensuring its acceptance as a high-tariff alternative to custody. Hence, at the core of ISSP is an attempt to achieve a proper balance between supervision and surveillance, providing reassurance to the community and sentencers that these 'top-end' young offenders will be subject to controls, as well as care. Furthermore, the surveillance components are intended to ensure the young people's engagement with the supervision elements of the programme. It is not, therefore, merely another project with more help, more care and more resources, but is based on the strict enforcement of rules and requirements, and consistent monitoring involving electronic and human tracking whenever possible.

The YJB has prescribed that ISSP teams should carry out surveillance checks at least twice daily, and should have the facility for around-the-clock surveillance for those cases in which it is deemed necessary.

One of the following four forms of surveillance has to be provided in every case: tagging, voice verification, human tracking or Intelligence-Led Policing (ILP). Three private electronic monitoring contractors have had regional responsibilities for the delivery of both tagging and voice verification services. For those who are electronically tagged, monitoring is continuous during the specified period, with the tag acting as a transmitter, sending signals to a monitoring unit that detects whether the tag is in range of the specified location. Voice verification, an alternative form of electronic monitoring, works by checking the voice print of the young persons over the telephone at times specified in a contract schedule. Unlike the electronic tag, monitoring is intermittent rather than continuous. The two main perceived advantages over the tag are reduced stigmatisation, as there is no physical sign of the young person's whereabouts being checked, and greater flexibility, as it is not restricted to a single location. It is not appropriate, however, to monitor a curfew operating through the night as it requires the young person to make or receive phone calls.

Human tracking involves ISSP staff tracking the whereabouts of the young persons throughout the week: accompanying the offenders to appointments, providing support and advice when necessary, and following up any non-attendances. As for ILP, this requires the police to overtly monitor the movements of the young people at key times and to exchange information with ISSP staff. While it has been defined as part of the National Intelligence Model, there has been very little central guidance as to how it can be applied in the context of ISSP, contrasting to its more explicit use within Prolific and other Priority Offender (PPO) projects.

In providing surveillance alongside the supervision components, practitioners are left with the difficult task of trying to reconcile the controlling and rehabilitative aspects of the programme. Furthermore, the YJB has emphasised that strict enforcement is crucial to the success of ISSP, and in providing reassurance to the community (Youth Justice Board 2002d). ISSP teams are required to deal with non-compliances according to National Standards (Youth Justice Board 2004b), but the YJB has stated that the additional resources available for ISSP provides the teams with the opportunity to set even higher standards. Hence, consideration can be given to accelerating the decision to initiate breach proceedings following the wilful missing of an appointment, instead of waiting for two formal warnings. Seemingly, however, in setting out this advice, there was no recognition of the tension between using an intensive programme as an alternative to custodial sentences and increasing the likelihood of custody through a promotion of rigorous enforcement. For practitioners, therefore, a dilemma is clearly raised between the desire to maintain engagement with the offender, ensuring programme completions, and the need to maintain the credibility of the programme itself.

A multi-dimensional evaluation

The YJB commissioned the Probation Studies Unit in the Centre for Criminology, University of Oxford, to evaluate the first 41 ISSP schemes. The study provided a valuable opportunity to examine the potential of an intensive multi-modal programme to address the offending behaviour of a high-risk target group. While the YJB were keen to promote the effectiveness and 'success' of ISSP at a very early stage, the research team aimed to take a longer-term, more measured view. The overall aims of the evaluation were as follows: (i) to produce evidence of the relative value and success of the ISSP schemes; (ii) to provide detailed research evidence of the characteristics of the young offenders on ISSP; and (iii) to identify the extent to which their criminal careers could be truncated by the activities and interventions of the ISSP schemes and associated agencies. The number of ISSP schemes and the variability in their approach made the evaluation a complex and stimulating challenge. Data collection entailed a broad range of quantitative and qualitative techniques, incorporating standardised measures that permitted a comparison of efficacy and impact across the ISSP schemes.

Basic data regarding the ISSP cases were extracted from the core YOT IT systems (e.g. YOIS, Careworks), supplemented by monthly data returns to the YJB. A timetabling software package was created to assist the ISSP teams in planning individual programmes. When used, the timetabler software provided data for the research team regarding the young offenders' timetables, non-compliances with these timetables, and the final outcomes of their cases. However, it was sometimes employed solely as a means of constructing timetables, rather than recording actual delivery. In other words, amendments to the programmes and non-compliances were not systematically recorded. The evaluation thus turned to more general records to supplement the process data, but the quality of these records was again variable.

Extensive information regarding the young persons' needs and circumstances was extracted from *Asset*, the standardised risk/needs assessment tool used in the youth justice system. *Asset* requires practitioners to engage in interviews with the young persons and their families, to obtain information from a range of other sources, and to make a series of judgements about the factors that affect their offending behaviours. Practitioners also have to rate the extent to which identified problems are associated with the risk of re-offending. Further information was obtained from 'What Do YOU Think?', the young persons' self-assessment form which operates as a companion to *Asset*. Individual interventions were observed to assess how well they were being delivered in practice, while case managers were asked to complete case review questionnaires pertaining to the progress of each case. Further quantitative and qualitative data were obtained from a range of young person, parent and staff interviews.

To assess the impact of ISSP upon re-offending, data were obtained from the Police National Computer (PNC). Reconviction within two years has become the convention for studies in England and Wales, and the ISSP evaluation included both a 12- and 24-month follow-up period. Cases also needed to be followed-up *at liberty* following the start of supervision, or release from custody in the case of DTO ISSPs. A quasi-experimental design was adopted in which ISSP outcomes were compared with those for a comparison group not receiving ISSP (Cook and Campbell 1979). There were two main comparisons. First, actual and expected reconviction rates were calculated for both the ISSP and comparison groups. Differences between actual and expected rates were then compared to see whether ISSP outperformed the comparison group. In this way, expected rates were used to control for differences between the groups. Second, the frequency and seriousness of offending in the pre- and post-periods were analysed for both groups. Changes in the frequency and seriousness of offending over time were then examined to see, once again, whether ISSP performed better than the comparison group. In this way, offending data for the first time period were used to control for differences between the groups.

The comparisons were further refined using a form of propensity score matching (Heckman 1979). This statistical procedure is used to narrow the differences between experimental and comparison groups in quasi-experimental designs. It thus ensured that the comparison sample closely matched the ISSP sample across a range of important background characteristics. Referring back to the five-level methodological rigour scale (see p. 32), this approach corresponded to level 4. An RCT, level 5 on the methodological rigour scale, was proposed by the research team at the start of the project but was not considered to be a viable option by the YJB and Home Office.

Analysing the impact of ISSP upon custody utilised the YJB's Themis (The Management Information System) data. Since ISSP was introduced across the country in phases, a multi-wave research design was used, allowing comparisons to be made between ISSP and non-ISSP YOTs over differing time periods. This made it possible to see whether changes in custodial sentencing corresponded to the dates on which ISSP was introduced, with the sentencing data for earlier time periods being used to control for differences between the YOTs. This design again corresponded to level 4 on the methodological rigour scale.

During the course of the study a large amount of rich qualitative data was collected from practitioners, young people and parents. In-depth analysis of over 350 interviews was undertaken, informed by the grounded theory approach (Strauss and Corbin 1998), and tentative themes were coded within each of the interviews using NVIVO software. These themes were then developed to create more concrete theories, representing the views of the respondents. To gauge the views of sentencers, a postal questionnaire was distributed in Spring 2003 to those magistrates who chaired the benches of eight youth courts, and the District Judges (DJs) at those courts. The courts were selected on the basis of their geographic spread, relatively high numbers of ISSP cases, and their willingness to participate in the research. The questionnaires were supplemented in Autumn 2003 by face-to-face interviews with the youth panel chairpersons for each of the eight courts and two DJs.

A partial cost–benefit analysis of ISSP was also included in the evaluation. The cost savings from the use of effective interventions, particularly with persistent and serious young offenders, are potentially substantial. These benefits might apply to both public expenditure and individual citizens who might be the victims of crime. Unfortunately, it was beyond the scope of the study to compare the cost-effectiveness of the ISSP and comparison groups because valid and reliable financial data were not available for the latter. It is important to recognise that due to the numerous services provided by YOTs, young people in the comparison group may have received some similar services, although the package will not have been as intensive as ISSP or involved the same combination of supervision and surveillance.

The broad evaluation ran from the start-up of the initial schemes in July 2001 until April 2003. The main body of the study was published in 2004 and involved an investigation of the implementation, process and outcomes of the ISSP model (Moore *et al.* 2004). The second phase of the work extended the reconviction study from one to two years, explored further the impact of ISSP upon the use of custody, refined the views of staff, young people and their families on the effectiveness of ISSP, and updated the cost–benefit analysis (Gray *et al.* 2005). Through the two phases, it was hoped that the immediate and wider impact of ISSP would be captured.

Summary

The YJB introduced the first fully-fledged ISSP schemes from July 2001. Within six months the first 41 schemes were operational and nationwide roll-out followed in October 2003. ISSP is a highly intensive multi-modal programme, targeting persistent and serious young offenders, with the aims of reducing their re-offending, tackling their underlying problems while ensuring sufficient controls are in place, and making inroads into the levels of custodial sentencing. The key features of the ISSP model can be summarised as follows:

• An intensive programme initially targeted at young people who were persistent offenders and had high criminogenic needs. This was subsequently modified to include serious offenders at risk of a custodial sentence.

• A multi-modal programme tailored to the risk factors facing each young offender, with a strong educational emphasis.

• A disposal seen by sentencers as sufficiently demanding and tough to be used as an alternative to a custodial sentence.

• A combination of intensive help and strict surveillance, with prompt breach procedures in the event of non-compliance.

The programme fits very well into the multi-faceted framework of the 'new youth justice', particularly through its combination of supervision and surveillance. Bearing in mind the complexity of the programme and the range of goals, a multi-dimensional evaluation, with a quasi-experimental design, was established. The evaluation was further complicated by the local variations between the numerous schemes, indicative of the devolved approach favoured by the YJB. Data collection thus involved a broad range of quantitative and qualitative techniques, incorporating standardised measures that permitted a comparison of efficacy and impact across the ISSP schemes. The next three chapters present the findings of the evaluation, beginning with intake (targeting and referrals), then process (implementation and delivery), and finally outcomes (impact).

Chapter 4

Targeting and referrals on to ISSP

This chapter looks at the referral rates on to ISSP and presents a profile of the young people within this population. While the risk factors for youth offending are well recognised and the research into typologies of young offenders has steadily developed, there is still limited understanding of the most persistent and serious young offenders. The following analysis attempts to provide further insight, emphasising how risk factors tend to cluster together and exploring differences between 'individual characteristics' and 'social influences'. The differences between those young offenders who are persistent and those who commit serious offences are also explored, revealing that the tendency for policy-makers to treat them as a homogeneous group is mistaken.

Referral rates

Previous evaluations of intensive programmes indicate that teething problems are common, and a number of initiatives have suffered, for various reasons, from low referral numbers. Perhaps aware of such findings, the YJB employed PA Consulting, a management consultancy firm, as primary facilitator in the project management of ISSP. As part of their role, they monitored referral rates, helped to establish protocols, conducted assurance reviews of the schemes, and attempted to disseminate good practice.

While increasing referrals was earnestly encouraged, various complications meant that it took time for the numbers on ISSP to

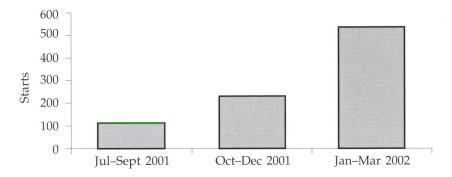

Figure 4.1 ISSP starts July 2001 to March 2002

reach the fairly demanding targets imposed by the YJB. Figure 4.1 shows more precisely the gradual build-up of ISSP starts. Schemes were initially set an annual target of 50 starts, and while some schemes fell short, the overall number of starts in the third quarter (536) was equivalent to the national target. In effect, some schemes took on substantial numbers of young people, while others accepted fewer than they had originally anticipated.

In April 2002, the eligibility criteria changed, with the 'serious crime' shortcut and the 'repeat offending on bail' shortcut being introduced (see pp. 80–81). The impact of these changes, alongside the addition of ten more schemes, was an increase in the number of starts of more than 100 per cent over the following 18 months. The revisions were clearly well accepted by the vast majority of ISSP staff, who felt that they would be able to meet capacity targets and attract further young people who would benefit from ISSP. The few negative responses related to the speed at which the eligibility criteria were amended and the ability of 'on the ground' practitioners to cater for the needs of offenders who had committed serious sexual offences or acts of violence.

> They're definitely an improvement from just charging occasions. We were missing, as a result, some quite persistent young offenders. The seriousness shortcut is again an improvement. They may not be suitable and they might not need ISSP, but generally it's an improvement. (ISSP manager)

Adhering to previous research (Whyte 2001), Figure 4.2 shows that there was a notable crossover between the 'offending episodes'

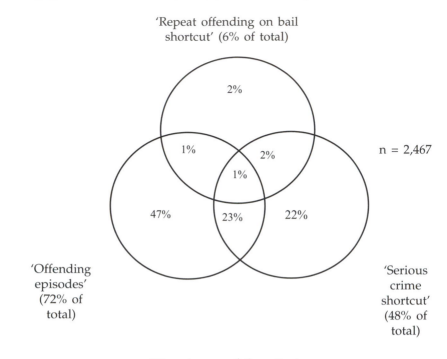

'Repeat offending on bail shortcut' (6% of total)

2%

1%

2%

1%

n = 2,467

47%

23%

22%

'Offending episodes' (72% of total)

'Serious crime shortcut' (48% of total)

2% met none of the criteria

Figure 4.2 Overlaps between the three main qualifying criteria (April 2002 to April 2003)

eligibility criterion and the 'serious crime shortcut' (24 per cent of all cases). Nevertheless, while 72 per cent of the young people still met the persistence criterion, a further 24 per cent met the seriousness criterion. The original conception of an intensive programme targeted at highly persistent young offenders was, therefore, significantly altered by the addition of young people who had committed serious, but less frequent offences.

During the whole period of the evaluation, a sizeable total of 3,990 ISSP cases were recorded, although the numbers at individual scheme level ranged greatly from 32 to 205. Nevertheless, the overall number of cases was impressive, particularly when one recognises that shortfalls in referral rates have been a feature of many previous intensive and non-intensive interventions. The YJB encouraged the use of ISSP as part of a Supervision Order, and 55 per cent were

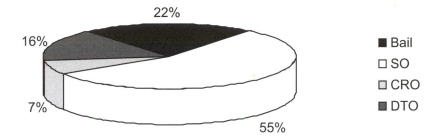

Figure 4.3 ISSP starts by type of ISSP case

attached to such an order. A further 7 per cent of the cases were at the community sentence stage, being incorporated into a CRO. Twenty-two per cent of the cases were pre-sentence at the bail stage, leaving just 16 per cent of cases that were post-custody as a condition of community supervision in the second half of a DTO.

Further analysis revealed that multiple ISSP cases for a single young person were not uncommon. While 75 per cent of the ISSP cases corresponded to the first such case for an individual young person, 19 per cent of cases related to a second ISSP, and 6 per cent related to the third or more ISSP.

Young offender profiles

The vast majority (93 per cent) of the young people on ISSP were male, with a mean age at the start of their programme of 16.4 years. Approximately four in five were of white ethnic origin, but the variability in ethnic background was much more pronounced in certain areas of the country, notably London. As was explained in the previous chapter, the 'offending episodes' eligibility criterion for ISSP required the young person to have been charged, warned or convicted of offences committed on four or more separate dates within the last 12 months. Analysis revealed that the young people on ISSP had a median of five such offending episodes. The mean was slightly higher at nearly six (5.8) as a small number of young people had built up a considerable number of offending episodes within the recent time period. The median number of recorded offences in the prior 12 months was eight, with a mean of nearly nine (8.8).

In the initial eligibility criteria, the YJB specified that magistrates should only be advised to consider the option of ISSP where, in addition to the persistence criterion, the current offence was of sufficient gravity for the court to be considering a custodial sentence or remand. The 'serious crime shortcut' was then introduced in April 2002, specifically targeting those young offenders who were at risk of custody because the current charge or sentence related to an offence serious enough that an adult could have received a custodial sentence of 14 years or more. Looking at the ISSP sample as a whole, the most common current offences were burglary of a dwelling or a robbery, with an offence gravity score of 5 or 6, on the YJB's 8-point seriousness scale in approximately three in five cases (see Figure 4.4). For context, analysis of the YOT sentencing data for 2001 demonstrated that 25 per cent of those young people committing a gravity 5 offence received a custodial sentence, with 65 per cent receiving a community sentence. The corresponding proportions for gravity 6 offences were 43 per cent (custody) and 50 per cent (community).

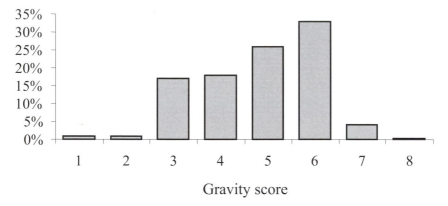

Figure 4.4   Gravity scores of current offence

Recent research on young offender characteristics

Before exploring the criminogenic needs of the young people who were referred on to ISSP, it is worth highlighting some of the important international studies of young offenders from the past half-century. Much of the most valuable research on young adult offenders has been developed around what is now known as the criminal career paradigm. A good deal of the early research on young offenders' criminal careers focused on the prediction of recidivism and typologies of young offenders (Glueck and Glueck 1950; Mannheim and Wilkins 1955). Later, significant use was made of longitudinal studies in the US (Wolfgang, Figlio and Stelim 1972; Blumstein *et al.* 1986), the UK (Farrington and West 1993) and Sweden (Wikström 1990). These important cohort studies have produced theoretical understandings and considerable empirical evidence of how recidivism rates rise quickly for some young offenders, from first convictions or reprimands to persistent and frequent convictions, whereas for other offenders little further offending appears to occur or the patterns are more disrupted.

Gottfredson and Hirschi (1986) in the US and Graham and Bowling (1995) in the UK have added to our understanding of different young offender groupings, some with low probabilities of recidivism and others with high probabilities, distinguished by factors in family dynamics, school experiences, and their individual development and abilities. Further work by Barnett, Blumstein and Farrington (1987; 1989) has identified differences between frequent and occasional chronic young offenders with distinctive long-term criminal career patterns. Nagin and Land (1993) extended this type of analysis by differentiating further sub-groups which distinguished high-level chronic offenders, adolescence-limited offenders, and low-level chronic offenders. Moffitt (1993) presented evidence of two distinct categories of adolescent offenders: adolescence-limited, and life-course persistent. In the latter group, young offenders' neuropsychological problems appeared to interact cumulatively with their criminogenic environments across development, culminating in what was described as 'pathological personalities'. Graham and Bowling (1995) identified not only a wide range of risk factors but also many potential protective factors, with definite gender variations, which help to explain why some young offenders largely desist from offending in later adolescence, while others persist into adulthood. The work of Sampson and Laub (1993) has produced evidence not of fixed individual traits in young offenders, but of different experiences that have accentuating or perpetuating effects via interplay between predisposing individual characteristics and dynamic risk factors.

Despite these developments, Rutter, Giller and Hagell (1998) recognise in their review of the literature and research on anti-social behaviour by young people that there is still only limited understanding and evidence of the most persistent and serious young offenders. In recent years the continuing work of a number of academics (notably Loeber and Farrington 1998; Stouthamer-Loeber, Huizinga and Porter 1997; Wikstrom 2003; Bronfenbrenner 1979; Tolan and Guerra 1994) has examined more closely risk and protective factors, improving our understanding of persistent, prolific and serious offending in young offenders. More generally, the recognised risk factors have been summarised (Youth Justice Board 2001: 8) as follows:

- Family factors (including poor parental supervision and discipline, family conflict, a family history of criminal activity, parental attitudes that condone antisocial and criminal behaviour, low income, poor housing and large family size).

- School factors (including low achievement, beginning in primary school, aggressive behaviour, lack of commitment to school and school disorganisation).

- Community factors (including living in a disadvantaged neighbourhood, community disorganisation and neglect, availability of drugs, and high turnover and lack of neighbourhood attachment).

- Personal or individual factors (including hyperactivity and impulsivity, low intelligence and cognitive impairment, alienation and lack of social commitment, attitudes that condone offending and drug misuse, and early involvement in crime and drug misuse).

The same review also concludes that these risk factors can cluster together, and that the exposure of young people to multiple risk factors from an early age is more likely to lead to persistent, serious and violent offending.

Characteristics of young offenders on ISSP

For those young people referred on to ISSP, Table 4.1 summarises the proportion of 'high-risk' cases for whom there was a quite strong or very strong association between each factor and the risk of re-offending, as recorded by practitioners completing *Asset*, the standardised risk/needs assessment tool used in the youth justice system. As can be seen, the areas with the greatest proportion of high-risk cases were lifestyle (70 per cent), thinking and behaviour (65 per cent), attitudes to offending (53 per cent), and statutory education (48 per cent). These figures are compared to those of a national sample of young people, encompassing a wide range of criminal histories and current offences (Baker *et al.* 2002). The corresponding percentages for lifestyle, thinking and behaviour, attitudes to offending and statutory education are notably lower at 36 per cent, 38 per cent, 25 per cent and 16 per cent respectively.

Table 4.1 Proportions of 'high-risk' cases for ISSP sample and national sample

Asset section	% high risk		
	ISSP sample (max. n=2,131)	National sample (max. n=3,159)	Difference
Attitudes to offending	53%	25%	+28%
Living arrangements	38%	16%	+22%
Family and personal relationships	47%	22%	+25%
Statutory education	48%	16%	+32%
Employment and training	32%	9%	+23%
Lifestyle	70%	36%	+34%
Substance use	37%	18%	+19%
Emotional and mental health	24%	13%	+11%
Thinking and behaviour	65%	38%	+27%
Perception of self and others	35%	16%	+19%
Motivation to change	34%	15%	+19%

Many young people referred on to ISSP had a range of risk factors, demonstrating that they had entrenched multiple problems. The Social Exclusion Unit (2005: 16) uses the terminology of 'complex needs' to refer to those who face particularly severe disadvantage due to interlocking problems, with the total representing more than the sum of the parts. Many offenders on ISSP fell into this category, and their interlocking problems, often associated with their offending behaviour, posed huge challenges to ISSP practitioners.

> One of the lads I've got here at the moment, his mum's a chronic alcoholic and the house was in a state, it really was. There was graffiti all over the wall ... She was epileptic and on medication. Drunk a hell of a lot ... Dad wasn't at home ... So you know, he was in trouble at school ... He rebelled, I did a lot of work with him, it has taken me over a year but we have now turned him ... He is now not drinking ... and now he is going on an electrical installations course in September. (ISSP manager)

Efforts to address the offending behaviour of those with mental health problems or substance misuse problems, for example, could not be effective without fully addressing these wider needs. Many of the young people had serious educational deficits and learning needs, some having been outside the school system for long periods, and many lacked suitable accommodation. Practitioners often felt that these underlying needs had not been addressed by other agencies, and that, in effect, ISSP was being used as a dumping ground for those young people with the most entrenched problems.

> These are the kids that no one else wants to touch. You know, no one in the YOT wants to have to deal with the multiple problems some of these cases present, so ISSP gives us the chance to work with these kids, rather than write them off. (ISSP manager)

> Some of these kids need a lot of different things to help them and we can't do everything, you know. The accommodation problems are the worst ... Schools are not interested in them, social workers have given up on them, mental health services don't want to know ... It's hard to think no one else apart from us are bothered. (ISSP caseworker)

Nearly half the young people on ISSP were recorded as living in a deprived household, 38 per cent absconded or regularly stayed away from home and 36 per cent were recorded as living with known offenders. Previous research has consistently shown that 'poor parenting and lack of parental care and supervision are important influences on youth offending' (Audit Commission 2004: 79), and over half the young people on ISSP were thought to be subject to inconsistent parental supervision, with parents failing to show care in approximately a third of cases. Three in ten were thought to have experienced abuse in the past.

> They tend to come from problematic families and there always tends to be either neglect or abuse and alcohol is always involved, or some sort of substance. They are often termed as being streetwise but they're not wise at all. Most are from single-parent families, often with stepfathers. Often the contact with a responsible adult tends to be a grandparent, not the parents. The grandparent comes to court, to the police station and so on. A lot of parents are unemployed and are often involved in crime as well. (ISSP worker)

> They stay up all night and are in bed all day, they are not encouraged to get up and often run the home. They're like the father figures and it's their household, as the majority are

from one-parent families … That can't be a coincidence. There's a lack of boundaries and positive role models for them. (ISSP manager)

There were additional concerns that, in many cases, family members had significant problems in their own lives, which impacted upon the young person's situation. A quarter of young people were recorded as having a significant person in their life involved in drug/solvent abuse, 22 per cent involved in heavy alcohol abuse, and 45 per cent involved in criminal activity.

Parents are a cause of concern. They sometimes collude with young people, and they are often single parents, or pro-criminal, or have poor boundaries, or mental health problems. There is poor parenting generally. (ISSP manager)

While some families had previously approached other agencies for help, many had been unsuccessful and consequently they felt that they had been let down by statutory agencies.

A lot of the families we work with suffer multiple deprivation and it's something we don't want to ignore. With a lot of families, they've been asking for help for some time, but it's not made available until crisis point … There's a few with mental health problems and drug abuse, domestic abuse in one case. (ISSP manager)

I've been looking for this sort of help for a long time. I mean, I've tried to get help for him in the past, you know the sort of thing – with his education and career and all that. I spoke to the school before. I've been to family support groups and everything … but I was always told, there's nothing we can do. (Parent)

A significant number of young people referred on to ISSP were not living within the family home. Fifteen per cent were classified as having no fixed abode, and this lack of permanency, along with the offenders' general chaotic lifestyles, were reported to cause significant problems for the practitioners. Thirteen per cent were currently accommodated in local authority care with the consent of their parents, 9 per cent were subject to a care order and 6 per cent were placed on the child protection register. A further 12 per cent had previously been listed on the child protection register. Almost three in five of the ISSP sample were currently or had previously been involved with social services departments. Practitioners expressed concerns that young people in care were more likely to be criminalised by typical teenage behaviour.

> They need a stable address. Supported lodgings are particularly useful but there are not enough good ones about. Young people moving around different addresses, living on floors and kipping down in cars is not suitable, and it's no wonder that these young people keep getting breached. (ISSP officer)

> The only trend is that those in looked after care are less likely to succeed. Their behaviour is criminalised very easily, for example making toast without permission or against unit rules and then being charged with theft. (ISSP manager)

Over half the young people on ISSP who were beyond compulsory school attending age were unemployed. Of those young persons of statutory school attending age, less than one in five attended mainstream school, with over a quarter having had no main source of educational provision in the prior six months. Of those not permanently excluded, two out of three reported that their school attendance in the three months prior to their order had been poor or very poor. The links between educational disaffection and youth crime are well established, with previous research finding non-attendees three times as likely to become involved in offending (Graham and Bowling 1995). In this vein, ISSP practitioners indicated that the boredom and lack of structure, which resulted from a lack of regular schooling, was directly linked to many of the young people's offending behaviour. Some young people had been out of education for extended periods and ISSP practitioners were highly critical of the local education authorities' treatment of these young people's cases. As the Audit Commission (2004) has highlighted, it is not exceptional for excluded pupils to have to wait up to a year for alternative provision to be identified, while there are further problems with young people being informally excluded.

> A lot of them are bored, they have too many hours to fill in the day with nothing to occupy them and they get into trouble because they're hanging out on the streets with their mates. (ISSP manager)

The most accurate picture regarding the literacy levels of the young people on ISSP was obtained through a basic skills reading test (a sentence completion form designed by NFER-Nelson). Those completing the test had a mean reading age below that of an 11-year-old (n=1,199), lagging five and a half years behind their mean chronological age at the start of ISSP.

> Some of them are totally illiterate. Can you believe that when we breach them, they can't read it. They haven't been to school for so long. (ISSP caseworker)

According to practitioners, over four-fifths of the ISSP sample were not using their time constructively and were thought to be associating with pro-criminal peers, while approximately three-quarters were thought to be engaged in reckless activities. Almost half were thought to see themselves as offenders, and in around a quarter of cases staff believed that the young person saw further offending as inevitable. Nearly a quarter of the young people were said to show no commitment to dealing with personal problems and no wish to curb their offending.

> Peers are one of the biggest problems. It's the only place they feel they have credibility, they have a reputation they want to keep. They're going to have to be strong enough to resist pressure from their peers. (ISSP project officer)

Use of alcohol and drugs was common according to both the ISSP staff and the young people themselves. Approximately four out of five young people had tried alcohol or cannabis. Of the drugs most commonly associated with acquisitive crime, 14 per cent of the ISSP sample were known to have used heroin, 12 per cent were known to have used cocaine, and 11 per cent were known to have used crack cocaine. There were regional differences, however, with some schemes finding alcohol misuse to be a significant problem, other schemes facing largely cannabis problems, and a few schemes finding considerable problems with the misuse of heroin, cocaine and 'crack'.

> We're working with pretty damaged young people in the majority of cases. Just at the moment we have two young people with difficult alcohol problems and if they come in hung over they're very likely to be quite negative about themselves and others. (ISSP manager)

He'd got into smack and was in a right state ... he looked like a right bag-head. He still had crusty blood up his arms from where he'd fallen asleep with a needle in his arm. He'd probably used dirty needles too ... He was kipping in a car because he hadn't paid his rent. (ISSP co-ordinator)

The Audit Commission (2004) has reported a significant rise in the number of young people with mental health problems in recent years, and ISSP workers found undiagnosed or untreated mental health problems in many cases. A notable number of young people were experiencing emotional difficulties such as phobias, eating disorders or sleeping disorders (12 per cent). Fifteen per cent were said to be deliberately self-harming and 9 per cent were known to have previously attempted suicide.

With a couple of clients, there's real issues of depression, anxiety and psychotic behaviour which will most definitely cause problems later in life. (ISSP case worker)

We assessed a young kid who said he heard voices. He really was very disturbed ... There were a number of school and medical reports stating that he should be assessed by psychiatric services and I couldn't believe nothing was being done, they just thought they would dump him on us. (ISSP officer)

Practitioners also indicated that the general health levels among the young people on ISSP were poor. It is well documented that the general level of health of young people involved in the criminal justice system is below that of the general population (Pitcher *et al.* 2004), and one in ten of the young people on ISSP had a health condition that significantly affected their everyday life functioning and 8 per cent were not registered with a doctor. In some cases staff had needed to intervene to ensure young people received medical treatment.

We had a 15-year-old coughing up blood for days. We asked his mum, who also has ten other children, if he was registered with a doctor. She said he was but wouldn't take him, which makes me think that he isn't registered, so my staff took him to casualty in the end ... We thought it might be TB, but it's still undiagnosed. (ISSP manager)

Individual characteristics vs. social influences

Grouping together the above findings relating to a range of criminogenic needs, it is recognised that, at a very basic level, explanations of offending can be divided into those theories that focus on individual characteristics, in terms of 'internal' disposition, personality, reasoning and temperament; and those theories that focus on 'external' social or societal problems and their influences on the development of criminality. While it is well accepted that there is no clear divide between these two types of theory, with individual variations developing through reciprocal interactions with the social environment (Burnett and Maruna 2004), a distinction can be employed for the purpose of exploring differences between the offenders in the ISSP sample. Accordingly, the sections in *Asset* were grouped into those reflecting 'individual characteristics' and those reflecting 'social influences'. In this instance, the former encompasses values, perceptions, reasoning, beliefs, attitudes and goals, while the latter encompasses the family and home, the school and workplace, and the peer group. It is recognised that these two dimensions, so defined, do not account for wider environmental, community or neighbourhood influences. By using factor analysis, the theoretical groupings were then tested against the ISSP data to see which section scores were most highly correlated. Those sections that were both within the same theoretical groupings and the same factors were added together to produce two composite scores. The composite scores were then divided into high and low by splitting at the median score, providing four groups, as set out in Table 4.2.

As can be seen, those who scored highly in terms of individual and social factors were more likely (i) to be female; (ii) to have received a DTO ISSP; (iii) to have qualified by virtue of their persistence with a greater number of offending episodes in the last 12 months; and (iv) to have higher total *Asset* scores. They also had higher scores on Crime-Pics II, a criminal attitudes scale that has been used in a number of recent studies with adult offenders (e.g. Lewis *et al.* 2003; Rex *et al.* 2004). The profiles of those who scored highly in terms of either individual or social factors alone were fairly similar, although those who scored highly on individual factors tended to have higher total *Asset* scores and higher Crime-Pics II attitudes scores but lower Crime-Pics II problems scores. By way of context, previous research has found that individual characteristics remain 'the most proximal influences on behaviour development' (Stouthamer-Loeber, Huizinga

Table 4.2 Offender typology – individual vs. social characteristics

	Low individual, low social (max. n=599)	Low individual, high social (max. n=275)	High individual, low social (max. n=495)	High individual, high social (max. n=675)
Personal				
Mean age**	16.5	16.4	16.4	16.2
% male*	94%	91%	95%	89%
% white*	81%	86%	87%	86%
ISSP type*				
% bail	12%	13%	14%	13%
% Supervision Order/CRO	75%	69%	70%	67%
% DTO	13%	18%	17%	20%
Eligibility				
% persistent offenders**	75%	86%	87%	88%
% serious offenders**	40%	34%	29%	29%
Mean number of offending episodes in last 12 months**	5.4	5.9	6.3	6.8
Mean offence gravity	4.9	4.8	4.8	4.7
Scores				
Mean *Asset* score**	14.5	21.9	24.8	32.0
Mean Crime-Pics II general attitude to offending score**	4.0	4.8	5.4	5.3
Mean Crime-Pics II perception of current life problems score*	4.2	5.0	4.4	5.0

Asterisks indicate whether groups differ significantly (adjusted confidence levels *<.05, **<.01). Tests of significance used are ANOVA (interval data) and chi-square (nominal data).

and Porter 1997) and on change in young adults who are persistent offenders and occasionally commit serious offences.

Overall risk levels

The total *Asset* score was obtained by adding together the 12 section ratings, providing a score from 0 to 48. The *Asset* validation study (Baker *et al.* 2002) demonstrates that the higher this score, the greater the associated risk of reconviction. The mean rating for the young people coming on to ISSP was 24, which is at the very top-end of the medium–high score band. Figure 4.5 shows the distribution of total *Asset* scores for the ISSP sample. These values are compared to those of the same national sample of young people as used in Table 4.1. As can be seen, nearly half of the ISSP sample fell within the high score band, compared to one-fifth of the national sample. This score band has a corresponding risk of reconviction within 12 months of 76 per cent. Furthermore, one in ten of the ISSP young offenders scored 35 or more on *Asset*, which corresponds to a risk of reconviction within 12 months of 84 per cent.

ISSP was thus successful, on the whole, in targeting high-risk young offenders, adhering to the 'What Works' principle of 'risk classification'. In addition to ensuring that the eligibility criteria

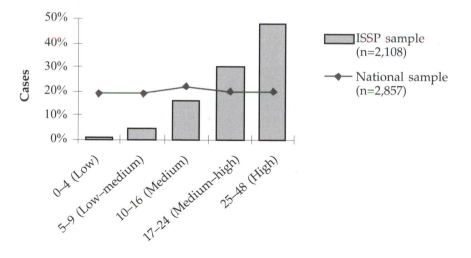

Figure 4.5 Total *Asset* scores for ISSP and national samples

were met, ISSP schemes were given the flexibility to adopt further suitability criteria, and of those schemes that were more selective, practitioners expressed a desire to avoid 'cherry-picking' those young persons with the least pronounced problems who were most likely to complete the programme easily. In fact, some schemes appeared to view suitability as a means of ensuring that only those with the most entrenched problems were referred on to the programme.

> Alongside the eligibility criteria, we have our own suitability criteria. Simply because you're eligible doesn't mean that ISSP is the best option for you. It might be that you don't need the intensive support or the ISSP might not be able to arrange an address or manage particular problems, e.g. mental health or drug and alcohol problems. We have tried to ensure that we don't take all without then 'cherry-picking'. (ISSP manager)

In some cases practitioners felt that the young people might have benefited from receiving the intensity of ISSP earlier in their offending careers. This was indicative of a more welfarist approach in assessing suitability, focusing on young people's needs rather than their offending risk. There were, in fact, instances of schemes using their discretion and lowering the eligibility criteria to allow those offenders with specific underlying needs on to the programme, particularly young female offenders who were often considered more 'needy'.

> There was ... a young girl, only 16 and we'd had her on the programme before, and she got a new offence of affray and although it was only one offence and she's not a persistent or serious offender, she would have got custody. It was a dead cert. So I agreed to offer an ISSP and she came back and did fine ... I think that was a risk worth taking. (ISSP manager)

However, other ISSP managers and co-ordinators were aware of the dangers of net-widening, and were determined to reserve ISSP for the most persistent or serious offenders.

> Oh, there are lots of kids who need quality supervision, who need someone to give a shit, there's lots of kids who need the level of support you can get on ISSP, but if you're name's not a PYO you're not coming in. (ISSP co-ordinator)

Bearing in mind the high-risk nature of the ISSP referrals, the challenge facing practitioners was clear, and it was inevitable that there would be a significant number of cases in which the young person did not successfully engage and continued their offending. Notably, the motivation of the young person to change was considered an important suitability factor by many ISSP teams, and several practitioners commented on the dilemma they faced in deciding whether or not to propose ISSP for a young person who appeared to lack motivation to change.

> You are always going to get young people who don't want to change so we have to be astute about suitability and who will really benefit and whether the community will benefit and therefore whether we're achieving best value. We need to make sure that a young person is motivated and wants to change. There's no point giving them an ISSP if they don't want it. You could put them on anything and throw resources at them but it's not going to work if they fundamentally don't want to change. (ISSP worker)

> If prolific male offenders are going to stop, for whatever reason, it's usually at about 17/18 years old. With young women it's usually about 15 or 16. They can want to stop offending for a number of reasons: pregnancy, a new relationship, a new job, something alters about their mindset that's crucial. It's about catching these young people when they are motivated to stop offending anyway and then we can help them to achieve that. (Senior practitioner)

Persistent vs. serious offenders

There is no commonly accepted definition of persistence, and differing demarcations have been employed (see pp. 202–204). For example, the Government has defined a Persistent Young Offender (PYO) as 'a young person aged 10 to 17 years who has been sentenced by any criminal court in the UK on three or more occasions for one or more recordable offences and within three years of the last sentencing occasion' (Home Office 1997b), while the Youth Lifestyles Survey 1998/99 defined a PYO as 'someone who, in the last year, had committed three or more offences' (Home Office 2000).

The definition of persistence used for the targeting of ISSP was even more discriminating, initially requiring four or more 'charging occasions' in the prior 12 months, and from April 2002, four or more 'offending episodes' in the prior 12 months (see pp. 80–81). The seriousness criterion added in 2002 also ensured that those young people who had committed the most serious offences were eligible for the programme. This criterion was restricted to those who had committed offences that were serious enough that an adult could receive a custodial sentence of 14 years or more (Youth Justice Board 2002c: 5), amended in 2005 to those offences that could attract a sentence of up to ten years for an adult.

Seemingly, the question of whether ISSP was suitable for both persistent and serious offenders was not explicitly addressed at the time of the eligibility revisions. This can be seen as indicative of the tendency for policy-makers to treat persistent and serious offenders as a homogeneous high-risk group, residing at the top-end of the offending spectrum. Consideration instead focused upon the likely impact on numbers eligible for ISSP, which were expected to rise significantly, although estimates of the exact amount varied.

> I think the initial criteria were correct ... We all know that the seriousness criteria came through probably because the numbers weren't looking that great. We get kids who appear for serious offences, but they're one-offs, and probably don't need an ISSP, you know, but they're at risk of custody. They meet the criteria, and also the courts are asking for it, you know, when they see someone up for robbery ... I would say that the change in criteria, although it's really helped everyone meet the targets, it's pulling in kids that you normally would think, well, they could have been dealt with differently. (ISSP manager)

It has already been surmised that one-off serious offenders are likely to have differing profiles from the more persistent offenders, and Table 4.3 reveals that offenders meeting the persistence criterion for ISSP (Groups A and B) had greater criminogenic needs, and therefore a higher risk of re-offending, and more entrenched pro-criminal attitudes than offenders qualifying on grounds of seriousness but not persistence (Group C). The latter group were more likely to be female and from a minority ethnic group. Bearing in mind the 'What Works' principle of 'risk classification' and the evidence from the US that indicates that intensive programmes should target high-risk offenders, these findings suggest that serious offenders may be

Table 4.3 Offender typology – persistent vs. serious offending

	Group A (max. n=2,009) Persistent, not serious	Group B (max. n=607) Persistent and serious	Group C (max. n=583) Serious, not persistent	Group D (max. n=176) Not persistent or serious
Personal				
Mean age	16.4	16.2	16.4	16.4
% female**	6%	6%	11%	6%
% minority ethnic group**	13%	19%	37%	30%
ISSP type				
Bail**	17%	22%	31%	35%
Supervision Order/CRO**	67%	60%	58%	53%
DTO**	16%	18%	12%	12%
Scores				
Mean *Asset* score**	24.6	24.2	19.1	22.2
Mean Crime-Pics II general attitude to offending score*	5.1	4.7	3.8	5.1
Mean Crime-Pics II perception of current life problems score**	4.7	4.2	3.6	4.5

Asterisks indicate whether groups differ significantly (adjusted confidence levels *<.05, **<.01). Tests of significance used are ANOVA (interval data) and chi-square (nominal data).

less suited to an intensive programme such as ISSP than persistent offenders.

Practitioners themselves recognised that those young offenders eligible through the persistence route and those eligible through the seriousness route had quite different profiles. Persistent offenders were generally considered to have greater underlying needs, to be more difficult to engage, and more likely to breach the programme.

> Re-offending [has] been a part of their lives, it's their way of life in most cases, it's a way of them getting stuff. One young person was caught stealing the other day and when I asked him why I got told he needed some breakfast. (ISSP manager)

> It's young people ... who have got into that cycle where they can't see a way out, where their friendships and everything they do revolves around behaviour which is anti-social or committing offences to raise money for their various lifestyles. (Senior YOT officer)

In contrast, staff frequently described young people eligible for ISSP through the seriousness route as having less chaotic lifestyles and fewer ingrained attitudinal and behavioural problems. They were found to be more motivated to comply with the order, and more likely to complete.

> I believe ISSP is a very appropriate scheme for serious crime offenders, in fact they bring something refreshing to us. Take the young man we've just had. He turned up far more motivated than most of the others. It was quite a breath of fresh air to work with him without all the persuading and cajoling we normally have to do. He was in school, turned up for sessions, it was great. (ISSP teacher)

In some areas, staff were apprehensive about mixing serious and persistent offenders, fearing that lower-risk offenders could be contaminated by the exposure to higher-risk peers. The introduction of the seriousness criterion also created delivery challenges for ISSP schemes. Staff were particularly concerned about their ability to work with sex offenders, and some schemes were unwilling to take young people considered to be a risk to the public or members of staff without considerable assistance from specialist agencies.

A one-off sexual offender who might be intelligent, have a good family and home life, be well educated; what does he have in common with a room full of car thieves? (ISSP manager) ·

I think we're taking a massive risk with sex offenders. I don't think I've got the expertise or the staff to co-ordinate that. I would have serious reservations about recommending ISSP, unless I could co-ordinate an outside agency to run the intervention. (ISSP manager)

We have two young people who've come via the serious crime route for committing manslaughter. We've had to change the way we deliver the offending behaviour work with them. We have to work one to one and don't mix them with the persistent young offenders. We have to be very selective about the young people they mix with when doing structured leisure activities. (Assistant team leader)

Summary

New initiatives for offenders are often undermined by delays in implementation and low numbers of referrals. In the case of ISSP, all 41 schemes included in the evaluation were successful in setting up programmes, establishing ISSP teams, and attracting referrals. During the whole period of the evaluation, a sizeable total of 3,990 ISSP cases were recorded. Considering that the programmes had to be set up from scratch, this can be seen as a significant achievement.

Extensive information was collected for profiling the young offenders referred on to ISSP. The Audit Commission (2004: 72) has stated that 'almost all serious and persistent young offenders have complicated lives and most have a variety of problems', and this was certainly true for the young people referred on to the programme, posing a significant challenge for the ISSP practitioners. Many were clearly already damaged and deprived by their early life experiences and a high proportion were firmly engaged in a career of criminal behaviour. Many had developed strong pro-criminal attitudes, a distrust of adults in authority and a resistance to changing behaviour. Particularly high-risk factors were lifestyle, thinking and behaviour, attitudes to offending and lack of statutory education. However, the nature of both the damage and the deprivation they had experienced was not uniform. Some showed evidence of mental health problems and others displayed considerable vulnerability.

The ISSP schemes were largely successful in meeting the YJB's targeting criteria. For example, in the initial period 90 per cent of orders met the persistence criterion. Once the criteria were widened to include serious offenders at risk of custody, it continued to be generally met. The main targeting concern is whether intensive programmes are suitable for both persistent and serious offenders. The 'What Works' principles indicate that intensive interventions are most effective with offenders who have high levels of criminogenic need and a high risk of further offending. Where such risks are low, for example with one-off serious offenders, the research suggests that intensive interventions are likely to be less effective. In our study about 25 per cent of the cases did not meet the persistence criterion. Notably, those who qualified for ISSP through the seriousness of the current offence, rather than through the persistence of their offending, were found to have fewer criminogenic needs, better social problem-solving skills and less entrenched pro-criminal attitudes. The suitability of ISSP for both persistent and serious offenders thus needs further consideration.

Chapter 5

Implementation and delivery of ISSP

Having set out the programme requirements for ISSP, this chapter considers how individual schemes implemented and delivered the programme in practice. When assessing the value and effectiveness of an intervention such as ISSP, one can consider the three threats to programme success as set out by Connell and Kubisch (2002):

- Theory failure: the theoretical grounding of the programme is flawed.
- Implementation failure: the theory is sound but the implementation is flawed.
- Evaluation failure: the theory is sound and the programme is well implemented, but the evaluation is flawed.

The theoretical grounding of ISSP and the evaluation methodology were considered in Chapter 3. As was shown, the programme can be classified as a welfare-based, risk management or authoritarian intervention, building upon the rationales of rehabilitation and deterrence, delivering both care and control, while being supported by potential incapacitation through rigorous enforcement. The main concerns would appear to be the difficulty of reconciling these differing rationales, as well as the differing objectives with which ISSP has been set. As for the evaluation methodology, attempts were made to avoid any 'evaluation failure' through the collection of large amounts of quantitative and qualitative data, providing information regarding intake, process and outcomes, with the analysis of re-offending and custody rates corresponding to Level 4 on the five-level methodological rigour scale (Sherman *et al.* 1997).

While the theoretical concerns will need to be revisited, the three threats outlined above highlight the need to pay equal regard to the implementation and delivery of the programme in order to ensure that the programme is 'conducted in practice as intended in theory and design' (Hollin 1995: 196). The following aspects of implementation and delivery are considered below: (i) management and organisation; (ii) accommodation and staffing; (iii) programme model; (iv) multi-modal supervision; (v) surveillance; (vi) compliance and breach; (vii) completion rates; and (viii) costs of ISSP.

Management and organisation

ISSP was launched by the YJB in Spring 2001, and the evaluation encompassed the first 41 ISSP schemes rolled-out in the first two phases between July 2001 and February 2002. While this implementation timetable was not imposed on YOTs, who were invited to participate when they felt ready, there were financial advantages in early participation. It is important to bear in mind that much had to be achieved by the early schemes in a relatively short time. ISSP represented a completely new form of intervention in England and Wales in numerous ways: highly intensive, requiring 25 hours per week of organised activity for each young offender; combining surveillance and supervision; requiring an ISSP team to be set up within the YOT; needing referral/assessment procedures to be established; requiring service level agreements with several external providers; and needing to be 'sold' to sentencers. In addition, the vast majority of schemes had to develop the programme from scratch. Whereas the National Probation Directorate (NPD) had opted for a more centralised procedure for programme development, accreditation and roll-out, the YJB decided to fund YOTs to develop their own programmes around a set of basic principles and requirements.

A consequence of this model was that the quality of local management, leadership and organisation was critically important. Such quality varied from area to area, and some schemes experienced delays and morale problems because of difficulties in securing suitable managers. In the absence of an ISSP manager, the YOT manager was usually expected to cover both roles. A further layer of complication was caused by the fact that some YOTs decided to form consortia because they were unable to provide enough cases individually to be viable (the YJB specified a minimum of 50 starts per year). Steering groups were set up for all schemes, but in the case of some consortia, these did not result in successful co-operation. By the end of the evaluation, the research team judged leadership quality to be good in approximately seven out of every ten schemes.

> Some of the staff have been very unhappy about aspects of the management of ISSP, for example the rotas and some of the philosophies behind ISSP. They've ended up complaining to me about it, but I've not been able to offload that. Formal complaints were made against the ISSP manager; I ended up making a formal complaint as well. It's been very difficult and very stressful ... I think the way the team was set up in the first place has caused a lot of these problems. The ISSP workers started first, then myself and then the ISSP manager. The YOT managers had control for so long that when it came to hand over to [the ISSP manager] it was difficult. (Senior practitioner)

> We're supposed to operate as a consortium but that hasn't happened either ... I just don't know how they saw it working really. I mean [one YOT] is too far away to share resources, and to be honest they can be a little possessive of the centre, so we can't really access that. And [another YOT] were meant to be leading the consortium, but haven't had nearly half the cases they were predicted to have, but then they have all the staff ... Apart from that there's the cultural barriers: you couldn't mix our kids with those from the city. Our kids are very different, there's a big cultural gap, I mean you must see it yourself over the whole area ... In [the first YOT] the kids are really turned on, they'd have our lot for breakfast. (ISSP co-ordinator)

Communication between ISSP staff and the core YOT staff was positive and productive in over half the schemes. In the remaining schemes, some problems were created by a 'them and us' mentality. In some instances, there were tensions between the ISSP and YOT managers, with confusion about their respective roles. In other schemes, YOT staff had doubts about the value of ISSP, particularly as part of a DTO, but also in relation to the electronic tag. These were largely resolved by the end of the evaluation period.

> We're not working as a unified scheme but three separate teams and I think some of the staff feel very isolated, more than they

expected to anyway. It would be nice to see a more co-ordinated service. There's definitely a need to share resources ... It's not to do with ISSP staff but tensions between the three [YOT] managers. I mean, we just haven't got our act together yet, there's a lot of resistance to us working more closely higher up. (ISSP co-ordinator)

PA Consultants were contracted by the YJB to provide project management support for ISSP, and in the early stages of implementation they provided invaluable help to schemes in organising themselves and starting operations. Their assistance included organising seminars for staff, developing tools and guidance materials, visiting YOTs and developing systems for quality assurance and management information. The consultants also provided help and advice to the YJB.

Accommodation and staffing

The 'What Works' principle of 'programme integrity' emphasises that adequate resources need to be available for a programme to meet its aims (McGuire 1995). In terms of fundamental resources, the Home Office (2002) has highlighted the need for appropriate accommodation, and the Feragarrach project (Lobley, Smith and Stern 2001: 79–80) for persistent juvenile offenders in Scotland concluded that a 'reasonable physical environment' was essential. In the case of ISSP, there were two main issues surrounding accommodation: establishing adequate accommodation for the ISSP team, and accessing suitable accommodation in which to deliver the programme to young people. In most cases, the ISSP staff occupied the same offices as the rest of the YOT. Such co-ordination was useful for ensuring good communication, but sometimes led to cramped office space for staff, limited space for working with the young people, and a lack of a separate ISSP identity. In some cases, the ISSP team was located in separate premises, and this usually had the advantage of enabling the programme to be delivered on-site, ensuring closer relationships with the young people and a clearer sense of ISSP identity.

You need a place where kids can go at all times of day: if they're in school, then it's after 4 pm, but for others you need a place where they can go during the day too ... Getting some premises that are child-friendly, appropriate and adequate. Usually the premises that we give them is the one that nobody else wants, and then we're giving them the message that they're down there. (ISSP sessional worker)

Overall, evaluators judged accommodation to be adequate in about three in five schemes. Consortium schemes spread over several YOTs sometimes had little space in any single location. In one instance, sessions were conducted in corridors of leisure centres or community centres, and even sometimes in the cars of ISSP workers. One ISSP was located in a police station, which had an intimidating effect on some of the young people.

Other evaluations of intensive programmes have highlighted the need for adequate numbers of skilled, well-trained and motivated staff (e.g. Goodstein and Sontheimer 1997). For individual ISSP schemes, the staff numbers and individual skills required depended upon which services were commissioned and which were provided in-house. Generally, however, staffing was a prominent issue throughout the period of the evaluation. In most schemes, it took time to identify and appoint suitable practitioners and, in some instances, there were long periods in which posts were unfilled. Bearing in mind that ISSP deals with high-risk offenders, often with multiple problems, the intensity of the programme was clearly very demanding upon workers both physically and psychologically, with some practitioners suffering work-related stress or taking prolonged periods of sick leave. Over half the schemes experienced staffing difficulties, such as absence or high turnover, at some point in the evaluation. More positively, training for practitioners was generally considered satisfactory.

Staffing is still a problem. We're a small team having to provide 24-hour cover seven days a week. We've accumulated a lot of toil but have no time to take it. There's no cover for sickness or holidays either. There's a high rate of staff absence/sickness. (ISSP case manager)

Recruitment has been very difficult. There's problems with getting supply teachers, I mean it's taken almost 12 months to get a teaching assistant on the team. The police checks on staff can take months too, even if I try and speed things along with some old colleagues ... There's been a lot of sickness too. (ISSP manager)

Programme model

The devolved model employed by the YJB permitted YOTs to choose between providing elements of the programme themselves or buying them in from other agencies. The ease with which services could be commissioned differed greatly, and approximately four out of five schemes organised their programmes in-house, even if specific components were commissioned.

> We do the in-house stuff because you can't always rely upon other people. But we have got other options as well ... If there is an agency, you can feed into it, but if there's nothing available, we can fill the gaps. We've got the six months really sorted. But it does depend upon the individuals. At the moment it's going quite smoothly because most are looking for work and nobody is excluded. (ISSP support worker)

> [Another scheme] has got absolutely everything, whereas in some cases we've had to deliver the whole 25 hours. And I'm talking about statutory provision. When you try to find the services, they're not there. There's nothing more frustrating than that. (ISSP manager)

A few schemes contracted out the delivery of ISSP to a non-YOT agency, which was responsible for co-ordinating the whole programme. In three cases the agency was a nationally based voluntary organisation (NACRO), and in another it was a locally based voluntary organisation (AXIS). The qualitative data indicated that the working relationship with these agencies was good and did not lead to specific implementation problems. While most schemes used the YJB's specification to develop their own supervision programme, a few schemes used pre-existing models of change, which had already been tested with young offenders. These models had the advantage of an established theory-base, materials and training resources, which meant the programme could be implemented quickly and efficiently.

Three schemes adopted the American Youth Advocate Programme (YAP). This programme aims to provide a 'wraparound' service that looks at the whole needs of the young person and their family, and then attempts to address these needs through the involvement of official agencies, school, neighbours, local business and families. It also uses a strengths-based approach that builds upon a person's positive qualities. YAP advisers provided initial training for staff in the three ISSP schemes and retained close links for consultancy and further training. Advocates were recruited from local communities to work mainly one-to-one with the young people, but also with their families and in other group settings, with community reintegration being an important aspect of the model. The relationship between the advocates and the individual young people was of key importance, and YAP helped to promote a positive, pro-social model of working.

One scheme used Multi-Systemic Therapy (MST), also an American programme. MST combines family and behavioural therapy with intensive family support services, and its aims are to empower parents with the skills and resources needed to address the difficulties they face in raising their children and to empower the young people to be able to cope with family, peer, school and neighbourhood problems. For the ISSP scheme, therapists were required to be qualified as clinical psychologists, and they received training and ongoing supervision from MST advisers. The main thrust of the model is family work, and it had to be adapted to accommodate the emphasis of ISSP upon education. A further problem was that the scheme had low numbers of offenders eligible for ISSP, with not all of these offenders being considered suitable, leading to an under-employment of the therapists. Comparing the YAP and MST models, the latter fitted less easily within the structure and demands of ISSP.

Multi-modal supervision

The YJB specified that all programmes should contain the following five core supervision modules: (i) education and training; (ii) changing offending behaviour; (iii) interpersonal skills; (iv) family support; and (v) restorative justice (RJ), with the exception of recognising that the offending behaviour and restorative elements were not suitable for those on bail who pleaded not guilty. There was a particular emphasis upon the first of the listed components, and Figure 5.1 indicates that nearly all (97 per cent) young people were recorded as being involved in some form of education or training. Offending behaviour work (95 per cent) was the second most prevalent intervention, while RJ was the least prevalent of the core components, although it was still provided in seven out of ten cases.

The YJB further specified that other modules should be provided according to the needs of the individual, encompassing work to address risk factors such as mental health, drug or alcohol misuse, accommodation problems, as well as provision for counselling or

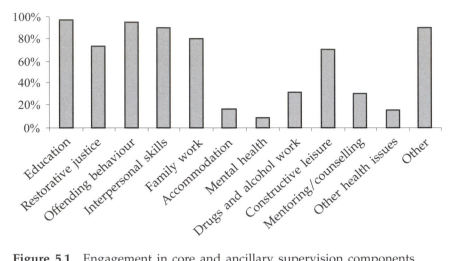

Figure 5.1 Engagement in core and ancillary supervision components

mentoring, and engagement in some form of constructive recreation. Approximately one in three of the offenders were recorded as engaged in drug/alcohol work, while seven out of ten were engaged in constructive leisure activities. Nine out of ten were engaged in 'other' activities, which did not fall easily within any of the substantive categories. Mental health was the least utilised element, with provision in place for just 8 per cent of the sample.

Core supervision components

While staff recognised that it was important to re-engage a young person with mainstream providers, they often found such re-engagement difficult to achieve in practice. Despite the YJB's target of ensuring that 90 per cent of young offenders were in suitable full-time education or training (2002a), a recent Audit Commission report (2004) found that only one-third of YOTs had good access to education. Perhaps not surprisingly, therefore, ISSP staff reported problems arranging suitable provision in over half of all ISSP cases. Where it was not possible to access statutory services, some schemes developed their own in-house educational programmes to meet the individual needs of the client group. Other schemes employed in-house educational specialists who worked on developing links with the local education authorities. Bearing in mind the ages of the young people, many of them were more interested in gaining employment, and ISSP teams made positive efforts to engage them in training courses or assisted them in their job searches.

It is the education authorities who are directly contributing to the amount of young people on the street during the day … They don't seem to care about their responsibilities to provide some education, as long as they've got a kid listed at the school they get money, but they don't want to do anything with that kid and they don't want to release the funds either. (Operations manager)

There are huge gaps in education, both pre- and post-16, because the funding isn't there to deliver it. Training providers aren't geared up to deal with our sort of kids because of their behaviour. (ISSP manager)

Things have improved since the education worker joined the team. He's our first point of contact for schools, he knows the legislation and what schools have to provide for the young people. He's set up literacy and numeracy workshops in-house. (ISSP case manager)

A wide range of offending behaviour sessions were delivered across the ISSP schemes. Perhaps because much of the offence-based work was conducted in-house, 'few' obstacles were reported in providing this service in approximately two-thirds of cases. Participatory activities, such as group discussions and drama workshops, were regarded highly by many staff members and some of the young people. However, some practitioners expressed a lack of confidence in the delivery of some aspects of 'off-the-shelf' offence-focused packages, mainly due to their inflexibility in dealing with those offenders with short attention spans or learning difficulties. In addition, many of the young people had experienced the sessions during previous orders, and consequently found them 'boring' and repetitive.

The drama workshop has had a big impact, the young people are able to express themselves in a different way through drama. This is a popular session. The sessions have also had an impact on self-confidence. (ISSP deputy manager)

They're not very suitable or flexible for young people, especially not the ones who can't sit still for five minutes. (ISSP manager)

They're just a waste of time, just questionnaires, sheets I've filled out before. (Young person, male, 17 years old)

Nine out of ten young people participated in interpersonal skills sessions, which again were mainly delivered in-house. Encouragingly, such sessions were comparatively accessible, with two-thirds of practitioners, at the end of the young persons' programmes, reporting 'few' difficulties in delivering this component. These sessions could be more accurately described, however, as 'life skills', encompassing modules as diverse as independent living skills, budgeting, cooking, first aid, health and safety, DIY and communication skills.

As advocated by the desistance research literature (e.g. Graham and Bowling 1995; Utting and Vennard 2000), staff also spent a significant amount of time working with young people's families. This enabled practitioners to undertake assessments of the influences affecting the young person, while extending the 'intensity' of the programme into the home environment and allowing them to offer parenting advice, to act as mediators, and to undertake preventative work to dissuade other siblings from becoming involved in offending. In this sense, ISSP practitioners were adhering to the desire of the YJB to reinforce parental responsibility.

> You see them in their home, as it is, every day and then you can start to piece together what is going on for them. If I were in that position I'd probably offend as well. A lot of it is survival really, and you can't take away their ability to survive without replacing it with something else. (ISSP worker)

> Maybe there's another child, normally a sibling, who is on the brink of becoming involved in crime, following in their older sibling's footsteps so to speak. If you do work with that individual you can then reduce the likelihood of that young person offending and reduce risk of harm for them. Normally by channelling them into community programmes and so on. (ISSP manager)

The majority of schemes favoured indirect reparation through work in the community, rather than direct reparation work with victims, which was reported to be difficult to organise and deliver. Young people undertook a range of projects including gardening, recycling and environmental improvements, such as removing graffiti, and outdoor projects. Young people preferred being involved in constructive activities through which they developed new skills, and were less able to relate to activities such as litter picking and leafleting, calling them 'pointless' and a 'waste of time'. Wilcox and Hoyle (2002: 11) recommend that reparation should be 'more than just a punishment'. More specifically, it should relate closely to the offence, be matched to the young person's skills and interests, enable the development of new skills where possible, and encourage the young people to consider the consequences of their actions on the victims and the community and to accept responsibility. In contrast, the direct reparation delivered through ISSP tended to be less well developed.

Ancillary supervision components

Of the ancillary supervision components, perhaps the easiest to provide were the constructive leisure activities. Common activities for the young people included playing football, joining a local gym, playing games of pool and visiting commercial leisure facilities and high street fast-food outlets. However, the young people were also introduced to activities they would not usually have been able to access, such as outward-bound weekends, go-karting and the Duke of Edinburgh Awards scheme. These activities were hugely popular with the young people. Nevertheless, staff were aware of the necessity to not overuse leisure activities. Interestingly, the provision of leisure pursuits was sometimes questioned by the parents of the young people, who did not see the relevance of 'rewarding' their children. Moreover, parents felt it set a bad example to siblings.

> I never normally go out and do things like rock climbing. It's fun! (Young person, male, 17 years old)

> The only thing that I don't agree with ISSP, I've got to admit, is when they first go out on treats. You shouldn't need to treat a child of 14 or 15. They should know better. (Parent)

A number of the other ancillary supervision elements proved more difficult to provide, as they depended on access to statutory services, including accommodation, mental health and drugs services. Practitioners noted that social services seemed to lose interest in the young people once the ISSP team had assumed responsibility. Accommodation was often particularly difficult to locate for the client group as their status as offenders, or their more specific substance misuse or mental health needs, made them ineligible for the majority of beds available.

> Social workers are passing their responsibilities on to us and expect us to address all the young person's issues. (ISSP case manager)

> Finding accommodation, suitable accommodation for young people who are homeless for one reason or another, is a real problem ... It's got to be planned usually and if it's not planned because our young people live in crisis situations, you're into things like bed and breakfasts, and they're not conducive for young people who are already being sucked into the criminal arena ... Sometimes you can make a bad situation worse by what's available, so I think accommodation's another area that drastically needs more resources, something specifically for young people. (Senior YOT officer)

Mental health provision was reported to be variable in both quality and coverage. The Audit Commission (1999) has detailed the extreme regional variability of Child and Adolescent Mental Health Services (CAMHS) provision, and ISSP staff reported some or many difficulties accessing provision in about half their cases. Staff had particular concerns regarding those cases in which they needed to access tier three and four services, for those offenders who were severely mental ill, at suicidal risk or who had the more severe, complex and persistent disorders, and when the offenders' mental health needs were linked to serious offending, especially of a sexual nature.

> Mental health assessments are done when requested, but intervention packages are not put in place. Basic services are available, but the more in-depth interventions are not available – for example those who need residential rehabilitation, there's just no funding. (ISSP manager)

Substance misuse resources were also reported to be limited in some areas. The Audit Commission (2004) has reported that fewer than 20 per cent of YOT managers are able to access suitable substance misuse services, and in some instances young people were rejected by the ISSP schemes because their substance misuse needs could not be met.

> We don't have the resources to work with hard drug users. You know we had those three cases a while ago, they were heroin and crack users. We fought to get them on the programme.

But in the end we didn't do them any favours to be honest, because no one wanted to cough up the resources to help them get clean. No one's going to pay for proper residential rehab or specialised care, so what are we meant to do with them when they're strung out? (ISSP manager)

Taken together, these findings regarding the ancillary supervision components of ISSP clearly support the conclusions of the National Audit Office (2004) that there is a need to: (i) convince mental health services of the crucial role that they have to play; (ii) develop more accessible, child-centred substance misuse services; and (iii) provide a wider range of appropriate, supported accommodation. The Carter Report (2003) also recommended that persistent offenders should have priority access to interventions to help reduce their offending, which would have further assisted the ISSP teams.

Tailoring of supervision

In designing young people's timetables, staff attempted to tailor provision according to individual needs, meeting the 'What Works' principle that interventions should focus on criminogenic needs (McGuire 1995). Many schemes adopted a 'holistic' approach, matching interventions to each young person's strengths, while also involving the young person in the decision-making process in order to encourage their continued engagement. However, there remained large numbers of young people on ISSP whose full range of needs were not being met. The difficulties accessing education and training providers, alongside other statutory services, meant that staff often had to deliver large proportions of the programme in-house. In addition, staff reported that, in some cases, the underlying needs and chaotic lifestyles of the young people meant that they had difficulties delivering all the core elements. Staff indicated that sometimes they had to adopt a more flexible approach.

We have to conduct ongoing assessments to ensure we are giving the young people what they particularly need. It's an individual approach, you've got to do it on a one-to-one basis. (ISSP manager)

We look at the more holistic approach of working with the young people, and keeping them in the middle of all the work that we do. I think that and the commitment of the staff as well … is what makes our programme successful. (ISSP manager)

I know the YJB outlined the core elements, but what needs to be acknowledged is that you need to deal with what turns up on the doorstep. Sometimes you can spend a whole week dealing with one problem. You tend to end up doing a lot of work in the area of family support. Basically, it's not always possible to focus on the core elements because you have to meet the welfare needs. (ISSP manager)

Quantity and quality of supervision

As an average, the young people typically received 22 hours per week of supervision in the intensive period, falling just short of the 25 hours stipulated by the YJB. In contrast, as shown by Table 5.1, supervision tended to far exceed the recommended five hours per week in the less intensive period, with an average of 16 hours provided for each young person. The distinction between the intensive and less intensive periods was not as marked, therefore, as had been prescribed by the YJB guidance, with practitioners themselves favouring a tapering-off of the intensity of contact in the last three months of supervision. This difference between the prescribed and actual amounts of provision can be seen as a good example of how practitioners reformulate policy 'at the coalface' (Young and Sanders 2003: 342). It should also be recognised, however, that the average contact time in the less intensive period will have been raised by the removal from the scheme of the least compliant offenders during the intensive period.

Table 5.1 Mean weekly provision by module and period of intensity

	Mean weekly provision (hours)	
	Intensive period (max. n=894)	Less intensive period (max. n=394)
Education and training	9.3	7.7
Restorative justice	1.3	0.7
Offending behaviour	2.0	1.2
Interpersonal skills	2.6	1.3
Family support work	1.7	1.5
Other ancillary modules	5.0	3.1
Total	21.8	15.5

The National Audit Office (2004) has recognised that public services and relevant agencies often find it challenging to provide holistic support to young offenders who frequently have chaotic lifestyles and face numerous problems. Bearing in mind the profiles of the young people on ISSP, creating full and varied timetables was particularly challenging, and the skills, knowledge-base and commitment of ISSP staff proved important. Notably, a multi-modal programme was successfully delivered in most locations, and, as Table 5.2 shows, about three-quarters of practitioners were satisfied with the adequacy of the supervision arrangements. In many cases, ISSP served as a catalyst to urge other agencies into action, and was able to provide opportunities for the young people to address their problems and offending behaviours. In this sense, ISSP was adhering to a welfare-based model. One of the successful case studies was as follows:

> Stuart, 15, is sentenced to ISSP for domestic burglary. His offending is classified as both persistent and serious, but all his offences have been committed during a brief friendship with a group of other offenders. He appears to have few underlying problems: his usual peer group are not involved in offending or substance misuse; he is in full-time education and he comes from a supportive family background. He does, however, have anger management issues and has received fixed-term exclusions from school for fighting. While on ISSP Stuart is able to write an apology letter to his victim, and is involved in face-to-face victim mediation. Both Stuart and his family also benefit from family support sessions. Stuart successfully completes his ISSP, despite eight surveillance non-compliances, and his mother provides positive feedback about the programme, noting positive changes in Stuart's behaviour.

Table 5.2 Staff views of adequacy of supervision arrangements

	n	Inadequate	Not sure	Adequate
Early exit questionnaire	345	13%	8%	80%
End of intensive period	300	20%	5%	74%
Completion of ISSP	401	16%	6%	78%

Surveillance

Alongside the supervision components, the YJB specified that, in each case, one of the following four forms of surveillance had to be provided (see p. 84): tagging, voice verification, human tracking and Intelligence-Led Policing (ILP). Analysis revealed that voice verification was used in less than one in five ISSP cases during the evaluation period. This was largely due to initial technical and installation difficulties, causing many schemes to lose faith with the equipment. This loss of confidence can be illustrated by looking at the proportionate use of voice verification over time: it was used in 26 per cent of those cases commencing prior to May 2002, but only 13 per cent of those cases commencing thereafter.

> We thought it was just teething problems, but it's just a nightmare. I've been there with a family and a young person trying to get it to work, and the lad's giving his name and password and it's recording a missed call. It's too complicated for our kids. (ISSP deputy manager)

With regard to ILP, there were clear examples of aspects of such a model, with police involvement in some ISSP schemes, (i) being focused upon specific individuals; (ii) involving police intelligence units; (iii) being underpinned by the need for enforcement; and (iv) being based upon close liaison and communication between ISSP staff and the police. However, a fully developed and integrated model of ILP had not at the time been consistently delivered within the context of ISSP. More specifically, structures were still developing, processes were yet to be fully clarified and understood by concerned parties, and the commonly desired product was not yet fully identified. There was a strong belief among some ISSP practitioners that much more education and awareness of ISSP was required among local police officers. Importantly, a significant number of practitioners commented on the need to have officers dedicated to the programme, working within the ISSP team. More generally, ISSP practitioners believed there was a need for greater liaison and communication between themselves and local police officers.

Some of the most important skills or factors that police officers were seen as able to bring to ISSP were (i) a 'street-wise' knowledge of offenders and offending; (ii) access to police intelligence systems; (iii) a counter-balance to the 'softer' service-oriented values of other practitioners; and (iv) a measure of 'seriousness' and authority in the eyes of offenders. In this sense, greater involvement of police officers in ISSP can be seen to affect the balance between control and care, strengthening the first of these two dimensions.

As voice verification was little used and a model of ILP had yet to be consistently delivered, surveillance for young people on ISSP was mainly delivered through the use of electronic tagging and human tracking.

Electronic tagging

Under the Criminal Justice and Court Services Act 2000 and the Criminal Justice and Police Act 2001, electronic tagging was available as a condition of a Curfew Order, CRO, Supervision Order, bail conditions and the community part of a DTO. These statutory provisions made it an option for all forms of ISSP, and it was found to have been used in 70 per cent of ISSP cases, making it the most commonly used form of surveillance. Indeed many young people referred to ISSP as 'the tag', supporting the argument of Roger Smith (2003) that as surveillance becomes more central to youth justice practice, the young people will perceive it as the 'most significant' aspect of intervention. In this sense, ISSP was clearly seen as a very controlling intervention.

Turning to the practitioner perspective, previous research has reported some ethical concerns among probation officers regarding tagging, but also that these concerns can be alleviated with greater awareness (Boswell, Davies and Wright 1993; Nellis and Lilly 2001). Similarly, during the ISSP evaluation, such concerns were initially evident among some practitioners, often core YOT staff, but their uneasiness dissipated as the value of the tag in providing structure and discipline, and securing a period of calm, became more widely recognised. Practitioners clearly believed that control and care could be successfully combined, with the tag providing the surveillance context within which the more rehabilitative components could be delivered.

> The main thing is that it's imposing some kind of order as they're expected to stay in their own homes. You might say that the tag is inappropriate if all the offences have been committed during the daytime, but it's still instilling some sort of order. It's a punishment as well, and I'm sure society likes the message it gives them. (ISSP sessional worker)

> I think the tag is one of the biggest stabilising factors for young people ... because it gets them out of the habit of waking up at two in the afternoon and coming home at four o'clock in the morning. They know they have to be in ... and that's the best way to get them up to go to college ... It's regulating their body clock. (ISSP co-ordinator)

Some ISSP staff also believed that the tag enabled a number of young people to avoid peer pressure, hopefully disrupting contacts with pro-criminal associates.

> I think it needs to be with a tag, for it to work really. A lot of young people are used to friends saying to them, 'Look it doesn't really matter if you're seen by the police and you're on a curfew. You're not a well-known young person. You're not one of the police's key targets. The chances of you being stopped just because you're on a curfew are fairly limited.' But to actually be able to say to friends, 'I can't come out, I've got this on my ankle', it actually does work, and some young people seem to respond well to it. I'll put my hands up and say that wasn't what I totally expected at the beginning. (ISSP manager)

> Staying in was like, the hard bit, but it did help me stay out of trouble, I haven't got into half as much trouble as I used to. (Young person, female, 17 years old)

A further perceived benefit of the tag was an improvement in family relationships, due to the stability brought to the young people's lives and the increased amounts of time spent in the home. The evaluation of the national roll-out of Curfew Orders (Walter 2002) reported similar benefits, while noting that the presence of the offender in the home can sometimes cause friction.

> Problems at home can be exacerbated by the curfew if you're not careful. It can also help as well, though, as the responsibility for them being there is out of the hands of the carers. They don't have to keep them in any more as there's a tag on their leg doing it for them. One particular young person's family and home life improved dramatically because of his curfew. Because he was in every night, his mum stopped drinking every night. Previously he had been going out because of her drinking and

she had been drinking because he was going out and getting into trouble. (Senior practitioner)

However, in some instances, the use of the tag led parents to feel that they were required to adopt a role of policing or challenging behaviour, rather than simply supporting their children.

The tag meant most of the time I knew where he was and I had something to threaten him with. I told him if he broke his curfew I would not be lying to anyone for him and he had to be in on time. (Parent)

At times there's been no one policing it apart from me. A while ago, he kept coming in late, and then it got later and later and I think he realised he could probably bend the rules ... We didn't know what to do about it and I just didn't want to see him in any more trouble so I called the office and told them he was getting in late. I felt terrible about it afterwards, it's not something I wanted to do, but I had the feeling no one cared. (Parent)

A higher proportion of males on ISSP were tagged than females (71 per cent compared to 58 per cent). This adheres to previous research findings which have detected concerns regarding the tagging of females on the grounds of (i) the greater visibility of the tag due to dress; (ii) potential domestic violence; and (iii) greater childcare responsibilities (Walter, Sugg and Moore 2001). Logistic regression confirmed that use of the tag was more common for those with fewer criminogenic risk factors and a lower risk of reconviction, as measured by *Asset*. This would suggest that, despite the perceived benefits of the tag, there was some reluctance among ISSP managers and practitioners to tag the highest-risk young offenders.

Anita Gibbs and Denise King (2003) have previously reported 'problems with technology, particularly monitoring and equipment – technical faults, poor monitoring coverage, equipment failure and uncomfortable tags'. There were similar complaints from the ISSP schemes in the early stages of the evaluation, encompassing both technical problems and failures to install equipment on time or at appropriate times. Another problem concerned breaching for non-compliance. At the time of the evaluation, the three electronic monitoring contractors had responsibility for breaches of stand-alone Curfew Orders, and there were complaints from ISSP practitioners regarding failures to breach, inappropriate breaching, and failures to inform the ISSP teams of breach actions. The shifting of responsibility for breach has since shifted from the contractors to supervising officers under Schedule 2 of the Anti-Social Behaviour Act 2003, hopefully alleviating these problems.

> There are ongoing problems with [the contractor] which every scheme seems to be experiencing. They jump on young people and breach them when there's a valid reason for them breaking their curfew, but when they should be breached it's very difficult to get them to move. Also, we're not being told when young people are failing to comply, which is affecting our credibility as a scheme. (ISSP practitioner)

Relations with the providers improved over time, however, particularly when schemes were provided with designated persons as their local points of contact. In consequence, the proportionate use of the tag increased during the period of the evaluation. A further reason for the increased use is likely to have been the popularity of the tag among sentencers. When asked to rank the four types of surveillance in order of preference, about half the sentencers ranked the tag as their preferred option. Furthermore, some sentencers viewed the tag as an indispensable part of ISSP.

> I very much agree with the tag and the curfew while they settle down ... I've been told that not everybody on ISSP is tagged. That's no good to me. They've got to be tagged. It gives them the structure that they need. Otherwise it's a watering down of the order. (Sentencer)

Human tracking

An alternative form of 'surveillance' for ISSP, as outlined by the YJB, involved designated practitioners tracking the whereabouts of the young people throughout the week, requiring them to accompany the young people to appointments, providing support and advice when necessary, and following up any non-attendances. Such trackers were employed in about two-thirds of the ISSP cases, with the flexibility of tracking perceived by ISSP staff as particularly valuable.

> Young people know we are talking to other agencies and they know it's not just 'Okay, off you go, and all the best' ... We

are keeping an eye on them ... Some days the workers will go out, and be around there, some days sessional workers will be doing that, other times it's about telephone contact, about having arrangements set up where there is a daily phone call to somebody within the school or the project, or wherever it might be. (ISSP manager)

A further perceived benefit was the ability for those staff designated as 'trackers' to develop positive relations with the young people. Reviewing the English literature on tracking, Mike Nellis (2004a: 90) concludes that 'it was rarely undertaken *merely* to know where young offenders were at particular times', and he argues that the emphasis of tracking has changed 'from something primarily surveillant to something primarily supportive' (*ibid.*: 77). Similarly, during the ISSP evaluation, there was often a clear overlap between 'tracking' and the role of 'mentoring', which the YJB has defined as 'more than befriending', with the aim of 'making constructive changes in the life and behaviour of the young person' (Youth Justice Board 2003c: 6). As with the Intermediate Treatment (IT) initiatives in the 1980s, ISSP trackers were used to assist the young people to gain understanding of their offending, and to encourage them to develop a more constructive lifestyle (Errington 1985). Thus, while the YJB's requirements for ISSP suggested a clear demarcation between supervision and surveillance, the use of human trackers brought about a merging of the two concepts, perhaps helping to overcome any potential tensions between control and care.

I would have to say our tracking [has had the greatest impact] to be honest, and that's for two reasons really. It's not just about, 'Are you in, what are you doing?' but we've also developed that into a youth work role which is not just about tracking but putting them into positive leisure activities as well ... and I think it's also been positive for parents. (ISSP manager)

Combining surveillance methods

More than one surveillance method could be used with the young people, and trackers were used in conjunction with a tag in 42 per cent of cases (see Figure 5.2). The combination of these two methods was more common than the use of either method on its own. The YJB's effective practice guide for ISSP (Youth Justice Board 2003d) states that 'surveillance should exploit the most appropriate mix of electronic and human monitoring', and the combination of the tag and trackers was viewed by practitioners as a particularly effective form of surveillance.

> The curfew on its own is a temptation for a lot of young people. The tag gives it authority and takes the temptation away from them to an extent. That's if they don't cut it off. We use a lot of trackers too, to give it a face, and so we can keep on top of any little tricks with the tag. (ISSP manager)

Compliance and breach

Non-compliances by the young people on ISSP were common, particularly in the early stages of their programmes. Around three in five did not fully comply with the conditions of supervision in the first and second months of their programme, and one in five clocked up five or more non-compliances. Such non-compliances also tended

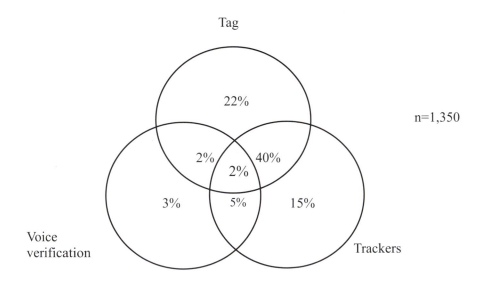

There was no tag, voice verification or tracking in 11% of cases.

Figure 5.2 Overlaps between use of surveillance methods

to cluster around the end of the intensive period, when there was a significant reduction in supervision and surveillance. Some young people were reported to view this as a 'liberation point'. By the sixth month of ISSP, 70 per cent of those still on the programme were complying fully.

> When they come off the tag at the end of the intensive period they go off the rails a bit. (ISSP support worker)

> When I went down to one hour a day I didn't like it as much and I started missing appointments. I got breached for not going, but it wasn't one thing I missed, it was just anything. (Young person, female, 16 years old)

Schemes were required to deal with non-compliances according to National Standards. These standards specify that formal warnings must be issued on failure to comply without acceptable reason, with breach proceedings usually being required following two such warnings. The data indicated that formal warnings were issued to 84 per cent of the young people who had not complied, and this was followed up by breach action in 78 per cent of cases where there had been two or more formal warnings. Although this falls short of the intended 100 per cent, it is similar to the performance levels found in studies of adult offenders supervised by the probation service (e.g. Hedderman and Hough 2004). Nevertheless, enforcement procedures were not applied with consistency across all the schemes, and in some instances enforcement was not as 'tough' and 'stringent' as prescribed by the YJB.

> Some ISSP support workers are too lenient. Our structure and guidelines have evolved and we're much firmer now. Some case-holders are reluctant to breach. The caseworker isn't communicating with the ISSP support worker as to whether or not the young person is being breached. The young people need to know what's happening. (ISSP support worker)

The overall breach rate was high, with nearly three in five of the young people being breached at some stage. Such a high rate is partly a result of the profile of the ISSP group, and recent research findings, particularly in the US, indicate that high levels of breach tend to be a feature of intensive community programmes. Similar breach rates have also been recorded for adults attending Drug Treatment and

Testing Orders (Hough *et al.* 2003). But the high breach rate on ISSP is also a result of the YJB's promotion of strict enforcement. When breaches were taken to court, sentencers had the option of allowing ISSP to continue or to revoke and make an alternative sentence. As Table 5.3 shows, almost half the offenders were permitted to continue at their first breach, indicating a level of confidence among sentencers in the programme. This option remained popular even on a second or third breach, but by the third breach custody had become the most common outcome.

Table 5.3 Result of breach

Result of breach	Breach 1 (n=896)	Breach 2 (n=237)	Breach 3 (n=52)
Allowed to continue on ISSP	46%	41%	34%
DTO/custody	31%	41%	44%
New ISSP order	6%	4%	6%
Alternative community disposal (non-ISSP)	6%	7%	10%
Other	11%	7%	6%

Table 5.3 illustrates that breach is not necessarily an indication that the young people will not complete their ISSP. In fact, 35 per cent of successful completers had been breached at some stage. Nevertheless, it is clear that more rigorous monitoring of compliance, alongside the high demands of ISSP, is likely to lead to non-compliance, breach and a custodial sentence for a significant proportion of the target group. This unintended consequence will to some extent undermine the objective of using ISSP to divert young people from a custodial sentence.

Completion rates

Completion is clearly important because people who do not remain on a programme to its conclusion cannot be expected to benefit from all it has to offer. In fact, the less time an offender spends on a programme, the less treatment effect he or she can be expected to gain. From a sentencers' viewpoint, compliance with the courts' requirements is paramount, while for policy-makers and researchers, completion is a valuable early outcome measure. As Hedderman and Hough (2004: 153) highlight, 'a consistent finding from the What

Works literature is that those who fail to complete programmes have worse reconviction results than those who complete'. This is often taken as evidence of the impact of completion, but it must also be borne in mind that people who fail to complete are also likely to be those who re-offend, regardless of the efficacy of the programme (Roberts 2004).

The YJB consistently monitored the completion rate for ISSP, and the research team did likewise. As shown by Figure 5.3, approximately half the ISSP cases completed successfully (n=3,248). The level of termination for breach was high – 34 per cent including those who committed further offences as well. Early termination for a further offence was also high – 29 per cent including those who also breached. There were variations between the types of ISSP, however, with bail cases much more likely to complete (65 per cent). This is to be largely expected as these cases tended to be significantly shorter in length, and compliance may have been motivated by a desire to influence the court sentence.

There are very few recorded statistics as to the completion rates of earlier intensive programmes. The comparative value of such data is, in any case, limited by the differing targeting groups and programme structure of these earlier interventions. For example, in the Michigan programme for juvenile delinquents set out in Chapter 2, the completion rate was 46 per cent, but these young people had an average of just 3.2 prior charges, and the average number of contacts per month was less than 15 (Barton and Butts 1990). For further context, the annual probation statistics for 2002 show that for Community Punishment and Rehabilitation Orders, 52 per cent of under 18-year-olds completed the specified hours of community punishment, while 22 per cent failed to comply with its requirements and 17 per cent were convicted of an offence (Home Office 2004a). The completion rate for those schemes piloting the Drug Treatment

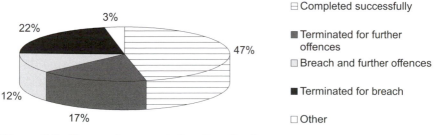

Figure 5.3 Reason for completion/termination

and Testing Orders was just 30 per cent, with 67 per cent having had their orders revoked (Hough *et al.* 2003), while Rumgay (2004: 132) comments that the drop-out rates for adult pathfinder programmes have been 'worryingly high, ranging upwards from 24 per cent and achieving 100 per cent at one programme'. Bearing in mind the risk profiles of the young people on ISSP, the intensity of the programme and the promotion of strict enforcement, a completion rate of almost 50 per cent thus seems encouraging.

> I think the reason why some young people have not completed ISSP is because it's a very tough order and it requires a lot of hours and a lot of commitment from them, and that, for some young people, is just too much. They're expected to work, or try to complete 25 hours a week, to turn up at a training scheme, or alternative education … Some of those young people have problems with what's going on in their lives, like being in the care system. In terms of the chaotic lifestyle they have, like mothers who are on drugs, fathers who, you know, those kind of things. (ISSP manager)

There were differences between the completion rates of the individual schemes. Sixteen schemes had a completion rate of 50 per cent or more, 18 schemes had a completion rate from 40 to 49 per cent, and seven schemes had a completion rate of less than 40 per cent. Importantly, a number of the schemes employed wider definitions of success. In some of the more difficult cases, any form of engagement with the young person was judged a success, as were any resulting changes in attitude or behaviour, criminal or otherwise.

> It depends how you measure success. To me, for the kid I was talking about before, I would classify him as a success, [if he was] on the programme for two months. He's still with us, he's on a work programme, and attending his appointments. Some of them are going out and committing offences, but you have to measure what they'd done before. My own personal view is that the scheme is needed. (ISSP worker)

Factors associated with completion

The 'What Works' principle of 'risk classification' and the evidence from the US suggests that intensive programmes should target high-risk offenders, but those young people with less pronounced criminal histories, fewer offending-related problems and attitudes less predisposed towards involvement in crime were found to be more likely to complete ISSP successfully. As Table 5.4 demonstrates, the completion rates were highest for those offenders with lower scores on *Asset*, indicating that they were at relatively low risk of re-offending. But while this clearly demonstrates the difficulty of engaging with high-risk offenders, it does not necessarily indicate that ISSP was more appropriate for lower-risk offenders. In fact, this latter group may not have required such an intensive intervention as ISSP, and may have benefited from other less demanding and restrictive forms of community supervision.

Table 5.4 Completion rate by *Asset* score

Asset score band	n	Completion rate
0–4 (low)	19	68%
5–9 (low–medium)	90	70%
10–16 (medium)	294	58%
17–24 (medium–high)	587	52%
25–48 (high)	946	41%

As shown in Table 5.5, there was a notably higher completion rate for those young people who qualified through the seriousness of their current offence (Group B) rather than the persistence of their offending (Group A). This is consistent with the finding that the former group tended to be of lower risk (see pp. 108–109). The introduction of the 'serious crime shortcut' in April 2002 thus helped

Table 5.5 Reason for completion/termination by persistent vs. serious offending typology

	Group A (n=1,737) Persistent, not serious	Group B (n=420) Serious, not persistent	Group C (n=509) Persistent and serious	Group D (n=150) Not persistent or serious
Completed successfully	44%	70%	45%	54%
Terminated for further offences	19%	8%	19%	13%
Terminated for breach	23%	16%	20%	23%
Breach and further offences	14%	5%	17%	10%

to raise the overall completion rate for ISSP, encouraging the YJB to view the expansion of eligibility in a positive light.

The ISSP offenders can also be distinguished according to their particular risk factors. Employing a distinction between individual characteristics and social influences (see pp. 103–105), Table 5.6 demonstrates that the lowest completion rates were for those groups with high individual scores. While scoring highly on this dimension was most indicative of poor compliance and completion, the highest completion rate was for those with low scores on both dimensions.

Table 5.6 Reason for completion/termination by individual vs. social characteristics typology

	Low individual, low social (n=544)	Low individual, high social (n=256)	High individual, low social (n=463)	High individual, high social (n=617)
Completed successfully	58%	52%	43%	42%
Terminated for further offences	14%	21%	23%	18%
Terminated for breach	15%	18%	19%	22%
Breach and further offences	13%	10%	14%	18%

The two commonly used methods of surveillance for young people on ISSP were electronic tagging and human tracking. Comparing the two methods reveals that the young people were more likely to violate 'tracking' obligations. As was explained above, this method of surveillance had the advantage of great flexibility, and it appears to have been relatively effective in detecting non-compliances. Nevertheless, analysis revealed a positive correlation between successful completion of the programme and the use of trackers. In contrast, there was a negative correlation between successful completion and use of the tag. Table 5.7 provides a further breakdown of the outcome of ISSP by use of the two methods, demonstrating clearly that the lower completion rate for those young people who were tagged was due to a higher proportion of terminations for further offences, rather than solely breaches of the programme.

One possible explanation for the differing outcomes is that the sub-samples were different in terms of their risk profiles. However, the mean *Asset* scores revealed that the 'tag only' sub-sample had

Table 5.7 Reason for completion/termination by surveillance methods used

	Tag, no trackers (n=293)	Trackers, no tag (n=241)	Tag and trackers (n=539)
Completed successfully	42%	56%	49%
Terminated for further offences	27%	14%	21%
Terminated for breach	18%	21%	17%
Breach and further offences	12%	9%	13%

a slightly lower risk of reconviction than the 'trackers only' group. It would thus appear that while the tag proved popular with ISSP practitioners and sentencers, many of the young people were undeterred from committing further offences while on ISSP. In these cases, the tag seemingly reinforced pro-criminal attitudes and behaviours. Applying labelling theory, it is possible that wearing the tag contributed to an internalisation and/or reinforcement of the young person's deviant self-image.

> Oh, well, some of them really hate the idea of the tag and the curfew, they really can't hack it and you know they would prefer a month inside ... They think, 'So what?' – there has been a couple who've just point blank refused to comply. (ISSP manager)

The negative impact of the tag clearly contradicts the recent Canadian study by Bonta, Rooney and Wallace-Capretta (1999), which suggested that completion rates for intensive programmes could be aided by the use of electronic monitoring. The conflicting results could be explained by differences in targeting and programme content/intensity between ISSP and the Learning Resources Program (LRP), which was the subject of the Canadian study. Unlike ISSP, LRP targeted adult offenders who were 'drawn from the local prison and placed on temporary absences'. The maturity levels of these older offenders will have been more advanced than those on ISSP, and most were found to be at moderate to high risk of re-offending. LRP was also less intensive than ISSP, offering nine hours per week of group, cognitive-behavioural programming, with a particular emphasis upon substance abuse and anger management. A further possible explanation for the differing results is that the probationer comparison group sample in the Canadian study was very small with just 17 cases, severely weakening the study's reliability and external validity.

In contrast to the tag, the use of trackers appeared to aid completion on ISSP with fewer terminations for further offences. There was often a clear overlap between 'tracking' and 'mentoring', with the trackers seeking to create positive relations with the young people and hoping to assist them to develop more constructive lifestyles. In this sense, there was a narrowing of the gap between the supervisory and surveillant aspects of the programme. Applying social learning theory, it can be argued that the trackers provided the young people with valuable pro-social role models. Furthermore, Nellis (2004b) has developed a typology of enforcement in community supervision, distinguishing between incentive-based, trust-based, threat-based, surveillance-based and incapacitation-based enforcement. Trackers can be viewed as flexible in their approach as they can use incentives and/or threats, and/or seek to establish a degree of trust, depending upon which tactic seems most appropriate at any given time.

> I would say the trackers have the greatest impact because they are spending the most time with the young people. I think it's more about giving young people a positive role model, in order to give them the support that they need and the understanding. I think the one thing you don't get on a traditional Supervision Order is someone to spend that time with you, and give you that guidance and understanding. All they've got is a figure of authority telling them what they should or shouldn't do. Whereas I think with our trackers it's very much a more of a relationship that's based around trust and respect. (ISSP manager)

Costs of ISSP

At the start-up of ISSP, individual YOTs, or a consortium of YOTs, submitted their proposals for establishing schemes to the YJB, and, once these proposals were approved, funds were released on an annual basis. While there were no apparent problems regarding the releasing of these funds, there were some difficulties regarding financial accountability within the YOTs. Some YOTs were slow in establishing separate accounts for ISSP expenditure, and where there were delays in setting up the schemes, there were some concerns that ISSP funds were being used for general YOT expenditure. These teething problems were overcome in due course, but the regional evaluators had great difficulty, even as late as 2003, in extracting ISSP expenditure data from schemes.

Both set-up and running costs, such as staff, accommodation, equipment, management and other ongoing costs, were eventually calculated for 36 of the 41 ISSP schemes included in the evaluation. The costs of supervision were estimated through self-reports on expenditure from the schemes, while the private costs of surveillance were estimated from average figures made available by the Home Office and the number of young people per ISSP scheme. Non-financial costs (i.e. resources that were deployed in the schemes but were donated or otherwise not paid for, such as voluntary work) were also requested from the ISSP teams, but it was recognised that where apparently cost-free resources were utilised and not accounted for, the unit cost estimates would be somewhat undervalued.

Overall, the total costs of ISSP were found to vary greatly across schemes and regions. The average cost of supervision across schemes was nearly £850,000 over a 21-month period, while the average cost of surveillance was about £250,000 for the same period. Therefore, the total cost of ISSP in the evaluation period amounted to an average of just over £1 million per scheme. It was found that costs per start were significantly associated with total costs, with larger schemes, in terms of the number of ISSP starts, tending to have lower costs per unit. Schemes that made greater use of electronic monitoring through tagging reduced the cost of supervision per start, perhaps indicative of lower staffing levels.

A breakdown of supervision related costs for 2002/03 is presented in Table 5.8. It is apparent from the table that the variation of costs across schemes was very large, with substantial standard deviations for all costs. Nevertheless, by far the most substantial cost was staffing. Looking at the average expenditure, about two-thirds of the total went towards staff costs. A further 26 per cent went towards 'other' costs, including the costs of contracted-out supervision element. Just 4 per cent of the average expenditure went towards accommodation costs, and only 3 per cent was spent upon equipment and central management fees.

Compared to these total costs, the costs per start and per completion have the advantage of taking into account the numbers of young people who were potentially benefiting from the programme. For the ISSP sample, the average cost of supervision per start was just below £10,000, while including surveillance brought the average to just over £12,000 (see Table 5.9). Costs per successful completion were

Table 5.8 Costs of supervision (2002/03)

	Mean	Standard deviation	Minimum	Maximum
Accommodation	£20,126	17651.30	£0	£57,392
Equipment	£12,404	13745.87	£0	£53,289
Management fee	£13,100	16649.93	£0	£60,000
Other	£125,146	86721.77	£17,779	£372,920
Staff	£309,550	132816.90	£84,202	£596,084
Total cost	£480,325	215408.10	£149,102	£940,710

much higher than these amounts, reflecting the levels of attrition and its associated financial consequences. The overall cost of ISSP per successful completion, including both supervision and surveillance, was almost £32,000, but this ranged at scheme level from £12,000 to £81,000. As can be seen, therefore, attrition can undoubtedly render a project like ISSP substantially more expensive.

Table 5.9 Unit costs per start and completion

(36 schemes)	Mean	Standard deviation	Minimum	Maximum
Supervision cost per start	£9,686	5233.91	£3,042	£27,990
Overall cost ISSP	£1,097,064	452984.60	£342,812	£2,038,647
Overall cost per start	£12,274	5313.05	£5,529	£29,790
Overall cost per completion	£31,865	14734.15	£11,782	£80,609

'Overall' includes supervision and surveillance.

Summary

This chapter has examined the extent to which the ISSP model, as set out by the YJB, was implemented in practice. Requiring a multi-modal approach with appropriate surveillance, and a process for case management, heightened the challenges schemes faced. A range of implementation difficulties were encountered by the ISSP schemes, but in a relatively short period of time most schemes were able to establish viable programmes. However, the schemes were not equally successful. For example, approximately two-thirds were judged to have adequate accommodation and a similar proportion had good quality leadership. About half had staff recruitment problems at some stage during the study period.

Creating full and varied timetables was particularly challenging, and the skills, knowledge-base and commitment of ISSP staff proved paramount. Analysis revealed considerable variation in the style and quantity of intervention provided, and, in accordance with recent Audit Commission (2004) findings, practitioners reported particular difficulties in accessing education, accommodation, mental health and drugs services. Nevertheless, schemes were imaginative in providing suitable alternatives, and a multi-modal programme was successfully delivered in the vast majority of instances, with the desired emphasis upon education and training. Further analysis revealed a gradual 'tapering-off' of provision, with schemes almost achieving the target of 25 hours in the intensive phase and providing well in excess of the minimum five hours in the less intensive phase. While it appeared that services were not always tailored to individual needs, practitioners remained confident that ISSP was able to provide the chances and opportunities for the young people to address their problems and offending behaviours.

The tag was the most commonly utilised form of ISSP surveillance. There were some initial ethical and moral concerns regarding the use of the tag, but this apprehension dissipated as the value of the tag in providing structure and discipline became more widely recognised. It was also thought that the tag could enable young people to avoid peer pressure, and assist in improving family relationships. Tracking the young people also proved popular due to its flexibility, and the ability of the 'trackers' to develop positive relations with the young persons, narrowing the gap between the supervisory and surveillant aspects of the programme. Combining trackers with the tag was the most common arrangement in ISSP, and was perceived by the staff to be a particularly stringent and effective form of surveillance. Less positively, voice verification was dogged with technical problems and schemes tended to switch to tagging, while Intelligence-Led Policing suffered somewhat due to the lack of a consistent model of practice.

Maintaining engagement with the young offenders, as well as resolving the tension with the desire for rigorous enforcement, was far from straightforward. Only 47 per cent of cases completed the programme, reducing the potential of ISSP to instil change in the young people. Non-compliance was highest in the early stages of ISSP, with 60 per cent not complying fully in the first and second months of their programme. Enforcement of non-compliance appeared to be fairly strict, with formal warnings being issued to 84 per cent of young people who failed to comply, and breach action being taken in 78 per cent of cases where there had been two formal warnings. While the use of trackers appeared to assist completion, in some cases the tag seemingly reinforced pro-criminal attitudes and behaviours. Further analysis revealed that the highest-risk offenders were least likely to comply, and that many of those cases that completed successfully had been breached at some stage. While the average cost of per start, including both supervision and surveillance, was just over £12,000, the average cost per successful completion was almost £32,000, indicating how attrition can render a project like ISSP substantially more expensive.

From this analysis it is clear that, although the national ISSP model was largely implemented as intended, there was considerable variation between schemes and the majority faced a number of practical problems and issues. These have to be borne in mind when judging the success of ISSP outcomes in the next chapter. In particular, the suitability of an intensive programme for offenders who are persistent and have high needs, as well as those who are not persistent and do not have such high needs, remains in question. A further issue concerns the ability to provide services, notably education and training, to a particularly difficult client group. The third issue relates to the low completion rates, and the consequent failure to expose some of the young people to the levels of intervention planned. Despite these potential problems, the strength of ISSP was to set up an intensive and multi-modal programme, including surveillance, in a short period of time, and to achieve a high level of referrals from the courts meeting the YJB's targeting criteria.

Chapter 6

The impact of ISSP

The 24-month reconviction study provided the opportunity to monitor the longer-term influence of ISSP in reducing the frequency and gravity of re-offending among programme participants. In the course of the ISSP evaluation, it was also possible to explore and update additional outcomes. The value of broadening the scope of evaluative frameworks has become progressively recognised (e.g. Hedderman 2004; Farrall 2003). Indeed, in the field of youth justice, Smith (2005) suggests the term 'effectiveness' might legitimately encompass singular results such as behaviour change, crime reduction and/or victim satisfaction. The ISSP evaluation thus included a broad range of 'outcome' measures to explore more revealingly the impact of ISSP, as well as combining quantitative and qualitative data to provide a more complete picture of the processes involved (see pp. 85–88). Specifically, the impact of ISSP was considered in terms of satisfying sentencers, reducing custody rates, addressing underlying problems as well as reducing re-offending.

Impact upon re-offending

The impact of ISSP upon re-offending was measured in three ways:

- **Method 1**: By comparing actual and expected reconviction rates (although it was not possible to compare these rates over two years, since at the time of the analysis *Asset* was only validated to predict 12-month reconviction rates) (Baker *et al.* 2002).

- **Method 2**: By comparing frequency and seriousness of recorded offending before and after the start of ISSP in contrast to a well-matched comparison group.

- **Method 3**: In addition, it was considered worthwhile to explore, within the ISSP group, where and with whom the programme was having a greater or lesser impact.

Reconviction rates are generally used as key indicators of performance (Carter, Klein and Day 1992). Notably, the Home Office's Public Service Agreement specifies its re-offending targets in terms of reductions in reconviction rates. However, the shortcomings of these figures are well known (Harper and Chitty 2004). The limitations include: being an undercount of actual re-offending since only recorded offences are included; being an 'all or nothing' measure; and being affected by changes in police recording practices (see pp. 215–216 for further discussion).

In addition, persistent offending is, by definition, resistant to change (Little *et al.* 2004). For this reason, the primary objective for ISSP, as set out by the YJB, was to achieve a 5 per cent reduction in offending frequency and seriousness. Measuring such an impact was thus the focus of the ISSP reconviction study. However, there are further methodological concerns with pre-test/post-test research designs that are relevant to the ISSP study. Cook and Campbell (1979: 99–103) discuss the possible threats to the validity of findings, which include:

- history (possible influence of changes occurring outside the programme)
- maturation (behaviours change as a result of subjects maturing, rather than because of the programme)
- testing (subjects learn how to perform tests better by the post-test stage)
- instrumentation (e.g. measures of change are prone to subjective bias)
- statistical regression (tendency for extreme scores at pre-test stage to move towards the average at post-test stage).

The latter threat of statistical regression recognises that people recording an extreme number of offences in the first time period (high or low) will tend to revert to a more average number in the next time period. This commonly occurs when a programme is targeted at people with extreme scores at the pre-test stage. Given the targeting and aims of ISSP, it was not possible to avoid this problem of 'regression to the mean'. The use of a comparison group with similar characteristics was thus crucial, enabling the impact of ISSP to be measured through an assessment of whether the ISSP group outperformed the comparison group in terms of reductions in offending frequency and seriousness.

In addition to ensuring that all comparison cases were eligible for ISSP, disposal differences were controlled for by separating the analysis into two parts: (i) Supervision Order/CRO with ISSP and without ISSP; and (ii) DTO with ISSP and without ISSP. The following analysis was further refined using the Heckman two-step statistical method (Heckman 1979), narrowing the differences between the experimental and comparison groups. The method operates by using logistic regression to identify factors that are significantly different in both samples. These factors are then used to produce a propensity score for each case, which is included in the subsequent multiple regression analysis to reduce the selection bias. This research design equated to Level 4 on the five-level scientific methodological rigour scale (see p. 32).

Table 6.1 shows the number of cases used in the reconviction study. Of the 3,884 ISSP cases submitted to the Police National Computer (PNC) for reconviction data, reliable matches were obtained for 3,264 (84 per cent). Cases also needed to be followed up for 12 and 24 months at liberty following the start of supervision, or release from custody in the case of DTO ISSPs. Reconviction within 24 months has now become the convention for reconviction studies in England and Wales, and in the ISSP study 29 per cent of the ISSP group did not start the programme early enough to be followed up for this period. In addition, some cases could not be followed up because of further periods spent in custody; 10 per cent were dropped from the

Table 6.1 Sample sizes for reconviction study

	12-month sample		24-month sample	
	ISSP	Comparison	ISSP	Comparison
SO/CRO	1,840	586	685	327
DTO	433	526	109	183
Bail	570	–	149	–
Total	2,873	1,112	943	510

12-month sample and 28 per cent from the 24-month sample. These attrition rates are likely to have introduced some bias into the sample by removing some of the most prolific and troublesome offenders, but the treatment was applied to the ISSP and comparison cases alike, so they remain comparable.

Table 6.1 reveals that the 12- and 24-month samples were markedly different in size due to the follow-up problems outlined above. The following results are quoted for both 12- and 24-month samples, but because of the reduced size of the latter, the 24-month findings must be regarded as less robust. Furthermore, the findings at 12 and 24 months cannot be directly compared as the samples were different.

Impact upon reconviction

The percentage of the ISSP sample reconvicted at least once in the 12-month follow-up period was very high at 89 per cent. However, this was not seen as surprising given that the ISSP sample had committed an average of 8.6 offences in the previous 12 months. Perhaps more worryingly, the 89 per cent compared to an expected rate of 79 per cent derived from the revised *Asset* scores. The results are broken down further and contrasted to their respective comparison groups in Figure 6.1. To summarise, 12 months after intervention,

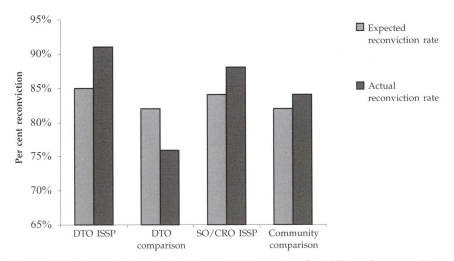

Figure 6.1 Expected and actual reconviction rates for ISSP and comparison groups

the reconviction rates of the ISSP groups were higher than would be expected. Furthermore, when differences between the actual and expected rates were compared, and using logistic regression to control for profile differences, the DTO comparisons achieved significantly lower reconviction rates. However, it is important to bear in mind that by virtue of being on ISSP, the young people were very likely to be subject to greater levels of surveillance by the police, which may in turn have increased the levels of reconviction. Interestingly, the most recent reconviction data available from the Offender Management Caseload Statistics 2003 (Home Office 2004b) indicate higher rates of reconviction for offenders of a similar age and risk profile upon leaving custody or after starting community sentences. For example, there were 24-month reconviction rates of 96 per cent (custody) and 97 per cent (community sentence) for young males with seven to ten previous convictions.

Impact upon the frequency of recorded offending

Compared to the equivalent periods pre-ISSP, the reductions in the frequency of offending at 12 and 24 months after ISSP were 40 per cent and 39 per cent respectively. These reductions exceeded the 5 per cent target by a substantial margin. However, as noted above, 'regression to the mean' may have accounted for these large reductions, since all groups had high initial scores. Table 6.2 separates the results by type of ISSP, indicating that all ISSP types had similar significant reductions in offending frequency. When controlling for

Table 6.2 Change in offending frequency by type of ISSP

	Mean number offences pre	Mean number offences post	% change
12 months			
Bail ISSP (n=570)	7.8	4.9	–37%
Community ISSP (n=1,840)	8.5	5.1	–40%
DTO ISSP (n=433)	10.2	5.6	–45%
All ISSPs (n=2,843)	8.6	5.1	–40%
24 months			
Bail ISSP (n=149)	10.2	7.0	–32%
Community ISSP (n=683)	11.7	6.9	–42%
DTO ISSP (n=109)	13.0	8.5	–35%
All ISSPs (n=941)	11.6	7.1	–39%

the differences between the groups using multivariate analysis, no significant differences emerged.

Table 6.3 compares the results for the community (Supervision Order and CRO) ISSP group with those for the community comparison group. While there was a steep fall in the frequency of subsequent offending, it was apparent for both the ISSP and comparison groups. Indeed, when multiple regression was used to control for variations in key characteristics, there were no significant differences between the groups.

Table 6.4 provides a similar analysis for the DTO ISSP group and the DTO comparison group. Looking at the 12- and 24-month figures together, both ISSP and comparison groups showed a strong reduction in offending frequency, but it appears that the comparison group outperformed ISSP in percentage terms. This result was confirmed through multiple regression; when *Asset* scores and other key characteristics were held constant, the comparison group performed significantly better than the ISSP group over both time periods.

It is difficult to assess exactly why the DTO ISSP group performed less well than the comparison sample, but it may be that the perceived high demands of DTO ISSP were counter-productive. Interviews with practitioners suggested that there was considerable resistance to the application of DTO ISSPs in some schemes, with staff feeling that it was sometimes perceived as a 'double punishment' that young people reacted to negatively.

We haven't had a DTO finish and while everyone says 'DTO ISSP is not double punishment, it's just another part of the

Table 6.3 Change in offending frequency by community groups

	Mean number offences pre	Mean number offences post	% change
12 months			
Community ISSP (n=1,840)	8.5	5.1	–40%
Community comparison (n=586)	8.5	4.9	–42%
24 months			
Community ISSP (n=683)	11.7	6.9	–42%
Community comparison (n=327)	10.4	6.4	–39%

Table 6.4 Change in offending frequency by custodial groups

	Mean number offences pre	Mean number offences post	% change
12 months			
DTO ISSP (n=433)	10.2	5.6	–45%
DTO comparison (n=526)	8.6	4.6	–47%
24 months			
DTO ISSP (n=109)	13.0	8.5	–35%
DTO comparison (n=183)	11.6	7.0	–40%

order', the point is, the young people see it as punishment. They're eager to get out [of custody] so they say yes to it, but they don't really understand it as something to help them. They see it as punishment, they see the tag as punishment, and they think, 'Sod this, I might as well be in prison', and they've all breached. (ISSP manager)

Don't see why I should do it [ISSP] at all. I've done time already so don't see why I should have to do this as well. It's a right piss-take. (Young person, male, 17 years old)

Impact upon the seriousness of recorded offending

A similar method was used to assess the reduction in offending seriousness. As shown by Table 6.5, there was a 13 per cent reduction in the mean offending gravity score for all ISSP cases at both 12 and 24 months. While there was a slightly greater reduction for the community group in both periods, regression analysis confirmed the differences between ISSP types were not statistically significant.

Most importantly, when considering the results for the ISSP groups against their respective comparison groups, the reductions were very similar. For example, there was an identical reduction in offending seriousness for the community comparison group of 15 per cent over 24 months, and a reduction for the custodial group of 10 per cent in the same period. Furthermore, applying regression analysis revealed no statistical differences in the reductions between the ISSP and comparison groups.

In summary, ISSP failed to outperform the comparison groups in terms of reducing both offending frequency and seriousness. Further

Table 6.5 Change in offending gravity by type of ISSP

	Mean gravity score pre	Mean gravity score post	% change
12 months			
Bail ISSP (n=483)	5.2	4.6	–12%
Community ISSP (n=1,586)	5.2	4.5	–13%
DTO ISSP (n=384)	5.5	4.9	–11%
All ISSPs (n=2,453)	5.3	4.6	–13%
24 months			
Bail ISSP (n=122)	5.2	4.6	–12%
Community ISSP (n=554)	5.4	4.6	–15%
DTO ISSP (n=92)	5.4	4.8	–12%
All ISSPs (n=769)	5.4	4.7	–13%

analysis showed that the significant reductions for all groups was at least partly attributable to 'regression to the mean', the statistical phenomenon that causes extreme scores at pre-test stage to move closer to the average at post-test stage. It is very apparent, therefore, that the phenomenon of peaks and troughs in the offending patterns of prolific offenders (Loeber and Farrington 1998) is critical to our increased knowledge and understanding of how best to achieve further reductions with this group of offenders.

These results replicate those of a number of the earlier studies on intensive community programmes (see Chapter 2). More generally, assessment of the research evidence on 'What Works' has shown that flagship programmes often have a modest effect over and above generic supervision in changing the future behaviour of young offenders (Smith 2005). It is often not clear, however, whether the results of 'no difference' for intensive programmes are due to (i) the theoretical tensions that arise from a programme with multiple aims; (ii) the practical difficulties in implementing the programme; or (iii) the research methodology that has been employed.

Factors associated with re-offending

As ISSP was employed with different types of offenders, its effectiveness was further explored to see if certain groups responded more positively to the programme than others. In terms of reductions in both offending frequency and gravity, it was found that young women performed significantly better than young men. There was a significantly greater reduction in offending frequency for those offenders who were both persistent and serious, compared to those young people who did not meet the eligibility criteria for the programme. Such evidence that ISSP may be achieving its best results with the most difficult young offenders clearly needs to be recognised in the future development and use of intensive community programmes.

As expected, completers of ISSP showed statistically significant gains in reducing the rate and gravity of their offending when compared to non-completers, though this may be due to pre-existing differences between the groups rather than the impact of ISSP. There was also evidence, consistent with previous research findings (Raynor and Vanstone 1997; Merrington and Stanley 2004), that the impact of ISSP upon all sub-samples reduced over time. In many instances, statistically significant differences at 12 months had disappeared at 24 months.

In many multi-site evaluations, such as ISSP, the more successful results for some sites are offset by the poorer results for others, potentially leading to misleading conclusions. In fact, there was considerable variation in the performance of individual ISSP schemes in relation to their impact upon the frequency and seriousness of further offending, with some schemes performing well on both measures and some poorly on both. Those schemes that were managed by non-YOT providers and which did not employ a 'specific model of change' such as MST or YAP (see p. 82) made lesser inroads into reducing offending frequency when compared to other models of ISSP provision. Overall, the more successful schemes seemed to be able to engage the young people for longer periods. All these factors may, in combination, have been representative of the quality of staff on the schemes and the rapport they established with the young people.

Bearing in mind that ISSP is a multi-modal intervention, it was also assessed whether the differing supervision components were associated with more successful outcomes. When controlling for offender characteristics and other key factors, two elements of the programme appeared to bring about greater reductions in the frequency of offending: (i) restorative justice (12 months only); and (ii) constructive leisure (12 and 24 months). Leisure activities were in fact identified by ISSP staff as a valuable motivational resource, increasing compliance with all elements of the programme, as well as potentially reducing the negative influence of peer group relationships.

The impact of employing differing forms of surveillance was also assessed. It was indicated in the last chapter (see pp. 140–141) that there was a lower programme completion rate for those young people who were tagged, with a higher proportion of terminations for further offences in these cases. Nevertheless, differing surveillance methods, on their own or in combination, were not found to be associated with significantly different reductions in offending frequency or seriousness over the 12- or 24-month time periods, perhaps indicative of how initial differences dissipate over time.

Impact upon underlying problems

> Mark, 15, is sentenced to a series of ISSPs for driving-related offences. He is a highly persistent offender, having committed 18 offences in the prior 12 months and has a medium-to-high risk of reconviction. Mark successfully completes his fourth and fifth ISSPs and there are optimistic signs that the programme has had a positive impact upon his attitudes and behaviour, and that he is ready to make changes to his lifestyle. Many of the risk factors in his life have been addressed: despite his poor attendance record and a history of fixed-term exclusions from school he has gone on to enrol at college; he has the stabilising influence of a girlfriend; his substance misuse has reduced; and the family support sessions have improved family relations. Mark is optimistic that he will not re-offend. 'My girlfriend was getting naggy with me, she doesn't want to have her boyfriend inside, so I decided to calm it down.' Despite these improvements, there is no change in Mark's risk of reconviction, and in the following year he does continue offending, albeit at a lower rate. He is later sentenced to a DTO for fresh offences of shoplifting and assaulting a police officer.

While the majority of young people on ISSP were reconvicted, the programme often made clear inroads into tackling their underlying problems. Not surprisingly, greater progress was made with those who completed the programme successfully and had thus received its full 'dosage'. The changes in the proportions of 'high-risk' cases for this sub-sample, according to the practitioner ratings from *Asset*, are set out in Table 6.6. As can be seen, the programme brought about statistically significant levels of positive change across all risk factors except substance use and emotional and mental health. It is possible, of course, that these two areas were particularly susceptible to 'disclosure effects'. This phenomenon recognises that in some problem areas practitioners are over-reliant upon the views

Table 6.6 Change in percentages of 'high-risk' young people (ISSP completions)

	% 'high-risk' young people		
	Start of ISSP	End of ISSP	% change
Attitudes to offending	43%	34%	–9%
Living arrangements	32%	23%	–9%
Family and personal relationships	42%	34%	–8%
Statutory education	44%	33%	–11%
Employment, training and further education	23%	14%	–9%
Lifestyle	60%	48%	–12%
Substance use	31%	30%	–1%
Emotional and mental health	22%	21%	–1%
Perception of self and others	31%	25%	–6%
Thinking and behaviour	58%	45%	–13%
Motivation to change	27%	23%	–4%

and opinions of offenders themselves at the commencement of an intervention. In fact, various studies of structured assessments have found that in areas such as substance use offenders may under-report problems at the commencement of an intervention that later they disclose more readily (Raynor *et al.* 2000).

For those young people who engaged with ISSP and spent a significant amount of time on the programme, practitioners noted a number of positive changes in attitude, thinking skills, constructive decision-making, social skills and general demeanour.

> To see the difference in the young people's social skills, from their body language to the way they actually can articulate. Some of the artwork. We have one young person here who has done some artwork on their life and their message to other young people is that it is not big and it is not clever. Another young person who has been both sexually and physically abused in their life, we found out they are actually good at poetry. So I said, let's take him to poetry clubs and through the poetry they are able to share their feelings. (ISSP manager)

> I went to Pizza Hut with a client. He engaged me, was confident, he held eye contact throughout the conversation, he started

conversations with me. The complete opposite from when he started. (ISSP manager)

They feel able to be open and it's given them a voice. Some of them have even started complaining in a constructive manner. A group of them were unhappy about an unavoidable change in their timetables for some group work. They got hold of some complaint forms and have filled them in, making an official complaint. I'm so pleased! It's far better than kicking the door in and shows that they have come a long way. (ISSP manager)

The importance of intensive contact

A significant proportion of the young offenders indicated in their exit interviews that they welcomed the high and consistent levels of contact with ISSP staff. Similarly, the intensity and flexibility of the supervision was valued by the practitioners themselves, recognising that in many cases there was a need for a round-the-clock service. In many instances, the programme provided the first form of daily structure the young people had encountered for a long time, having an immediate and dramatic impact upon their lifestyles.

I think the fact that the young people have a requirement to complete 25 hours Monday to Friday and weekends ... and subsequently we can be flexible with those hours I think is very, very good, because ... in ISSP we don't just knock off at 4:30pm on Friday, we're a 24-hour service. (Senior YOT officer)

The first thing the young person realises when they're on the programme is there's a structure to it. They can't stay in bed all day and they have to go to bed at night at a reasonable time to be able to get up for their appointments the next day. They are entering the real world and they have to do things that adults have to do. (ISSP worker)

Further analysis revealed that no individual supervision component was associated with greater improvements in risk scores, suggesting that it was their combination as part of a multi-modal package that was most important. Notably, ISSP managers emphasised the quality of the relationships developed between the young people and individual ISSP staff, rather than any particular component of the programme. Developing a trusting relationship, empathy and the ability to listen have been found to be key factors in engagement and the desistance process (Burnett 2004; Rex 1999) and ISSP staff had to demonstrate commitment before the young people were receptive to their supervision. In addition, staff utilised pro-social modelling techniques, acting as positive role models for the young people, and encouraging pro-social actions (Trotter 1999).

> I think it's good for them to see people who are committing to them, prepared to support them, prepared to put time and effort into them, which I don't think all of them have had in the past. It's good for them to see they can't always shake those people off. (ISSP manager)

> I think it's more about giving young people a positive role model, in order to ... give them the support that they need and the understanding. (ISSP manager)

> It keeps me out of trouble. It's sorted out my temper problems. Now I can call Steve or Phil [ISSP workers] and talk to them about it. It's brilliant. I'm much better at talking with adults. (Young person, male, 17 years old)

The supervision elements of ISSP aimed to impact upon the community, social and personal contexts faced by offenders, as advocated by the desistance literature (Farrall 2002). The holistic and integrative approach of the programme went some way towards establishing 'a new set of pro-social linkages, resources and opportunities' (Raynor 2001: 92), with staff emphasising the importance of using locally available provision where possible, rather than providing activities in-house, in order to re-engage young people with local services.

> I see the effect, especially after the six months, with the services and community links that we've made. If those young people are plugged into the colleges and are plugged into the community centres or the youth centres, and they are still able to make links with the advocates that are with them as youth workers after the six months has finished, that's how you follow that work, because you're still plugging them in. (ISSP manager)

> I don't think there's any doubt that we will have a positive and valuable impact on the young people's lives. We'll impact on some young people more than others, of course, and hopefully

we'll have shaken up a lot of those statutory services that should have pulled their fingers out some time ago. If we've done a good job we'll have frightened quite a few heads of service into improving what they have to offer these young people. (ISSP development officer)

Practitioners reported that re-engagement with either education or employment further assisted in creating a new daily structure for young people. It was considered to increase young people's confidence, motivating them to complete the programme, and raising their long-term opportunities.

By improving their educational attainment, we can give them the confidence to continue their learning and maybe go on to college. This can also continue on when the programme has finished. It's part of my job to give them the self-belief that they can achieve whatever they set their mind to if they work at it. (ISSP project officer/manager)

They got me on a training course to help me because I want to be a forklift truck driver. I'm going to see someone next week about getting my forklift licence. (Young person, male, 17 years old)

It's just great he's in college three days a week now. Really I'm so proud of him. We're glad he went on the ISSP. It showed him how to get out and do things, going to college and talking and meeting new people ... They sent him off to so many other places, like college, the sports centre and places in town with his mentor. It was just really good for him. (Parent)

Leisure sessions introduced young people to new activities and motivated them to use their time more constructively in the future, rather than associating with offending peers. The sessions were also important in building self-esteem. As noted in the previous section, these sessions were associated with reductions in the frequency of offending.

About six weeks ago we took him down to the gym and there's a really good youth worker down there. He's big and tough and has great rapport and he's devised a workout for him. He's just starting to see the difference, you know, getting muscles and tone. For a guy who's had problems with drink, that's been great for him, because he's getting some respect for his body. It's building his self-esteem. He's really proud of himself. You can see it and he talks about it a lot. He's cut the drinking right down. That sort of stuff can make a quick difference. (ISSP officer)

The family support element gave practitioners a platform to promote positive change within the home environment. In many cases young people and their parents welcomed the assistance, and staff were able to offer general parenting advice, improving family relations and benefiting other siblings.

Family support has been crucial. We've made some real positive changes to the lives of young people and their relationships with their families. I think being able to work with the whole environment of the young people is one of the big advantages of ISSP. (Senior practitioner)

It's helped my mum to have someone to talk to. I go and look after the other kids now sometimes, so my mum can have some time off. It's made things better at home than they were before I was on this. (Young person, male, 17 years old)

Differing degrees of impact

However, while the intensity of the 25 hours a week supervision provided practitioners with the time to address many underlying problems, they distinguished between the impact they were likely to have upon those who had few underlying needs and those who had more complex, entrenched needs. They found it particularly difficult to make substantial progress with those young people who had a combination of mental health needs, substance misuse issues or unstable accommodation. As discussed in the previous chapter, staff often had difficulties accessing suitable provision for these young people.

Thinking about somebody who essentially is getting into trouble because they haven't got anywhere decent to live, and if you could resolve that issue, or if they've got problems with their family, you can resolve the problem with the family, then I think that those kinds of definable problems are amenable to intervention. I think potentially we could make quite a difference. Where somebody has, as one or two of ours have had, a kind of cocktail of long-standing problems and comparably bad personality disorder, I think it would be very difficult to say how that would be successful. (YOT manager)

Where we've struggled: we've had some accommodation problems and also mental health. We had one young lad whose mental health was such that he wasn't suitable for ISSP. Another lad, the hostels wouldn't take him because of an arson offence. General needs we're able to cater for very well, but sometimes we have somebody with very specific issues. And that's difficult to deal with. (ISSP manager)

The ones we've failed with have been heroin users. The other one that springs to mind, you could say that one member of the family was not prepared to co-operate with us. That young man was very much influenced by his father. So drug addiction and inability to form relationships due to the family background. (ISSP sessional worker)

Practitioners also struggled to have an impact upon those young people who lacked any motivation to change and who failed to engage with the ISSP team. Whether these young people should have been deemed suitable for ISSP was a difficult issue to resolve (see p. 107).

Well, of course, there's a whole range of reasons, but one of the major themes has been disengagement. Where young people have no trust or cannot engage with the service at all. In some cases they walk away from the court with ISSP and we don't see them again. There's not a whole lot you can do about that. (ISSP development officer)

We're meeting kids who just refuse to change their attitudes. Whether that attitude is formed because of problems at school or family problems or lack of family. It's just like hitting your head against a brick wall. Some kids just aren't ready to change. (ISSP manager)

The response of sentencers and the impact upon custodial sentencing

The widespread use of ISSP by the courts provided perhaps the clearest evidence of the acceptability of the programme to sentencers. Further insights into their views were sought in a postal questionnaire distributed in Spring 2003 to those magistrates who were able to chair the bench of eight youth courts, and the District Judges (DJs) at those courts. The courts were selected on the basis of their geographic spread, relatively high numbers of ISSP cases, and their willingness to participate in the research. A total of 256 questionnaires were distributed; and 109 were returned, a response rate of 43 per cent. The questionnaires were supplemented in Autumn 2003 by face-to-face interviews with the youth panel chairpersons for each of the eight courts and two DJs.

Crucially, when asked about the usefulness of ISSP as an option for the courts, taking into account the full range of sentencing options, seven out of ten responded that it was 'very useful' and a further 28 per cent that it was 'quite useful', leaving just 2 per cent who thought it was 'not useful'.

> Extremely useful. Absolutely no doubt about that. As far as the magistrates are concerned, they see it as a very sound and supportive sentence. It assists them in thinking that they are going to keep the young person out of custody, but still infringe upon their liberty. It is rigorous, there's no doubt about that. It's very heavy stuff. (Sentencer)

> I'm very keen on it as it's a whole support package. I'm very keen on it as part of bail as well. Most of the clients we see are illiterate and have been out of school for some time. A short custodial sentence doesn't enable them to get back into education, so a stringent community sentence with a strong education element is something that the magistrates welcome. Some of them have other problems, people with epilepsy, people who are on drugs, and the magistrates don't really like sending them to custody. (Sentencer)

As has been emphasised, ISSP attempts to provide a balance between supervision and surveillance, with the aim of delivering both control and care. In their evaluation of an Intermediate Treatment (IT) project in the 1980s, Ely, Swift and Sutherland (1987: 156) found that magistrates did not see any 'contradiction between rehabilitative intentions and the exercise of adequate control'. Similarly, in their more general examination of sentencing practice in the mid-1990s, Flood-Page and Mackie (1998) reported that the majority of respondents did not see the aims of helping and punishment as 'mutually exclusive'. Adhering to these findings, 79 per cent of sentencers responded that supervision and surveillance were equally important components of ISSP, with just 17 per cent responding that supervision was the more important and only 4 per cent that surveillance was the more important.

> Supervision is required to challenge behaviour and help develop an alternative lifestyle. Surveillance is a necessary deterrent. Without it, many magistrates would be reluctant to make an ISSP order as an alternative to prison. (Sentencer)

> Both supervision and surveillance should reduce offending. Supervision – addressing needs of offenders, through education and training should give confidence, which many offenders lack. The intensity of the supervision should make offenders aware of their damaging effects on their communities. Surveillance – both reassures the community and monitors the offender. (Sentencer)

Interestingly, there was some disagreement among sentencers regarding the appropriate place for ISSP in the sentencing tariff and whether it should be confined to an alternative to custody. A MORI survey of magistrates' perceptions (2003) found that 31 per cent of respondents agreed that community sentences were soft options, and those sentencers who favoured a wider use for ISSP were clearly concerned about the effectiveness of other non-custodial alternatives.

> I, for a long time, have felt that the Supervision Order, on its own, is not altogether useful. It needs something attached to it, geared towards the initial period of the order. ISSP is a natural follow-on to this, and if you look at it that way, then every form of Supervision Order should be some form of intensive programme. The idea of a Supervision Order without any strength to it is, frankly, a waste of breath. This would place ISSP in the middle to the top range of penalties. But if you're saying it is an alternative to custody, then you're looking at it above everything else. (Sentencer)

To assess the impact of ISSP upon the use of custody, the YJB's sentencing data were analysed for the period April 2000 to December 2004. The analysis revealed that there had been a 2.1 per cent reduction in the use of custody nationally during this period. The data were split into the phases of the ISSP roll-out so that the pilot schemes in the evaluation (phases 1 and 2) were compared to the phase 3 and 4 schemes that did not receive ISSP until one and two years later respectively. This made it possible to see whether changes in custodial sentencing corresponded to the dates on which ISSP was introduced, with the sentencing data for earlier time periods being used to control for differences between the YOTs. This design again corresponded to level 4 on the methodological rigour scale (see p. 32).

It was found that similar reductions took place in both ISSP and non-ISSP areas, indicating that the fall in custodial sentences was not related to whether ISSP was in place or not. The Audit Commission (2004) produced similar findings when comparing the use of both custody and remand in ISSP and non-ISSP areas. This suggests that the drop in the use of custody was probably influenced by a range of national policies and initiatives to reduce the levels of juvenile imprisonment, as well as local factors, including the sentencing practices of individual youth courts. Notably, the YJB set a corporate target to reduce the use of custody for juvenile offenders by 10 per cent between October 2002 and March 2005 and adopted a series of measures at a national level in order to enable this target to be met (Youth Justice Board 2002a). A more detailed analysis at the level of ISSP area showed that there had been some diversion from custodial disposals to ISSP, but that the programme had also replaced some less intensive community disposals as well. Consequently, concerns about 'net-widening' remain relevant.

Similarly to the ISSP findings, closer analysis of the impact of IT in the 1980s led Tony Bottoms (1995: 34) to conclude that there was no 'automatic or necessary relationship' between its introduction and custodial sentencing levels. Previous research has also found that sentencers see custody as inevitable once a certain threshold is reached (NACRO 2000). Similarly, in the 2003 MORI study, 52 per cent of magistrates agreed that custodial sentences were generally more effective for persistent offenders, with 23 per cent disagreeing. Adhering to these findings, there was a strong consensus among sentencers interviewed that, whatever the intensity of ISSP and its appropriate place in the sentencing tariff, custody remained the only option in certain instances.

It's when matters are so serious that a custodial sentence is the only option. What makes that up is very difficult. It's obviously protection of the public. It's the severity of the offending. The frequency of the offending. One has to make the decision in the individual circumstances. There is no doubt that there are situations where custody is the only way forward. (Sentencer)

It is thus useful to compare the profiles of the young people who received a community ISSP with those who were sentenced to a DTO and received an ISSP upon release. The analysis reveals that while young people on a SO/CRO ISSP were generally towards the 'top-end' of the offending spectrum, they were not equivalent to the custody group. As Table 6.7 demonstrates, the custody group had a higher average number of offences in the prior 12 months, a higher average gravity score for the current offence, and a higher average *Asset* score. These offenders were also more likely to have received a previous custodial sentence. The corresponding figures for those who received the equivalent community sentence (SO or CRO) without ISSP are also set out in Table 6.7. As shown, these values were less than those for both the community ISSP and DTO groups. This would suggest that, in practice, sentencers were placing the community sentence ISSP between conventional community sentences and custodial sentences in the sentencing tariff, with custody remaining the only option for some young offenders.

In assessing the relationship between ISSP and custody rates, one also needs to take into account the impact of breach. Bearing in mind that a potential consequence of breach is imprisonment, there is a

Table 6.7 Risk levels of ISSP cases and comparison cases

	Community comparison (max. n=590)	Community ISSP (max. n=1955)	DTO ISSP (max. n=493)
Mean number of offences in prior 12 months	8.5	8.6	10.3
% received previous custodial sentence	11%	28%	48%
Mean offence gravity score	4.3	4.8	5.1
Mean *Asset* score	23.0	23.4	25.4

clear tension between the objective of reducing the use of custody and providing a community penalty that is rigorously enforced. Notably, the YJB has emphasised that strict enforcement is crucial to the success of ISSP, and in providing reassurance to the community. A consequence of such an approach is that even if ISSP successfully targets 'high-risk' cases, many initial diversions from custody will reappear in the custody figures following breach. Furthermore, many of the young people on ISSP were likely to be the subject of greater police monitoring and attention, increasing the likelihood of any further offending being detected.

When considering breach proceedings, the court can allow the young person to continue on the programme if it feels that the structured approach of ISSP represents the most constructive option for engaging with him or her. Notably, many of those who were breached on ISSP were allowed to continue on their programme (see p. 136). When the sentencers were asked about the appropriateness of a custodial sentence for breach of ISSP, their responses indicated that there was a need for some discretion. It was also noted that, in certain instances, breach could be a useful tactic to try to ensure future compliance. There was, nevertheless, an overriding desire to maintain the credibility of ISSP as a tough, rigorous programme.

> A comprehensive report usually accompanies the breach. I think that very often they conclude that given the opportunity to continue the order, Jimmy Smith will go along with it, and we tend to go along with that. But if there has been a complete and utter rejection of the programme, then they set their own stall out. (Sentencer)

It is also worth considering the impact of having received an ISSP on subsequent sentencing. From a limited analysis of subsequent sentences on first reconviction, it would appear that young offenders in the community ISSP group were consequently receiving significantly more custodial orders then their community counterparts. The reasons behind this are not fully known, and it was shown in Table 6.7 that there were some small but potentially important differences between profiles of the two community groups. Nevertheless, it can be hypothesised that, in some instances, the courts perceived ISSP to be a clear and unambiguous opportunity for the young person, leaving custody as the only appropriate remaining sanction for subsequent convictions.

Summary

It would appear from the 'What Works' principles that an intensive programme such as ISSP should be effective in reducing the offending levels of high-risk young offenders. In fact, all forms of ISSP demonstrated a large reduction in offending frequency, with an overall reduction of 40 per cent using one-year data and 39 per cent using two-year data. The seriousness of any further offending fell by 13 per cent in both time periods. The evaluation further revealed that the programme was intensive, and that the offenders were generally high risk. Nevertheless, a convincing causal link between ISSP and reduced offending could not be established. Using a quasi-experimental design with reasonably well-matched comparison groups, these comparators performed at least as well, and even slightly better when one considers the custodial group. A probable explanation for the considerable reductions in offending for both ISSP and comparison groups is the statistical phenomenon known as 'regression to the mean', with the perceived high demands of DTO ISSP perhaps also being counter-productive.

While ISSP cannot claim to have been responsible for the large reductions in the frequency and seriousness of offending, it is important to remember that offenders in the comparison groups received 'normal' treatments rather than no treatment. Although not so intensive as ISSP, these treatments may have included interventions of a similar kind to those provided in ISSP schemes. This study does not demonstrate, therefore, that 'nothing works'. There are also some weaknesses in the research design. For example, it is well known that reconviction is a gross underestimate of actual offending. A Random Control Trial (RCT) would have been more rigorous than a quasi-experimental design, but was not available as an option. Yet even where it has been used, treatment effects have often still been lacking (see Chapter 2). It thus remains questionable whether well-designed evaluations of intensive community programmes will consistently demonstrate reductions in the levels of re-offending.

The young offenders on ISSP had higher than average personal and social problems, many of which were related to their offending, and in only six months of intensive provision it was clearly not possible to change dramatically all their circumstances, experiences, attitudes and pro-criminal associations. Nevertheless, the various components of ISSP attempted to address directly the young people's problems, and the evidence indicates that real improvements were made in a significant number of cases, with the young people and their families appreciating the support provided. The ethos of ISSP emphasised community, social and personal considerations, and it was evident that, despite some implementation difficulties, the content of the supervision had enabled practitioners to meet many of the young offenders' needs. The intensity of the programme provided staff with the time to address a wide range of underlying problems, while the structure provided by the intensive supervision, alongside re-engagement with local services and the work undertaken within the family, provided young people with a strong basis from which to progress.

However, staff reported having less success with those young people with the most complex interlinked needs and those who showed little motivation to change, while further analysis confirmed that less progress had been made with those who failed to complete the programme. The evidence regarding improvements is also not conclusive. For example, it is unknown whether problems returned after ISSP had finished or whether similar improvements could have been achieved without ISSP. With regard to the latter, it is rare, in fact, for studies of this kind to collect intermediate outcome data for the comparison group.

Sentencers welcomed the introduction of ISSP, with the programme providing an appropriate balance of supervision and surveillance to satisfy their desire for a high-tariff sentencing option that delivered control as well as care. In consequence, the programme was widely used. However, despite adhering to the eligibility criteria and successfully targeting those young people towards the 'top-end' of the offending spectrum, it did not have the clear impact upon custody rates desired by the YJB. Most notably, a survey of sentencing in ISSP and non-ISSP areas suggested that similar reductions in the use of custody occurred in both. Consequently, the introduction of ISSP was not responsible, at a national level, for a reduction in the levels of custodial sentencing.

A common research finding is that sentences introduced as 'high-tariff' alternatives to custody start off as such, but over time sentencers are tempted to use them for less serious offenders and they slip down tariff, having to be replaced by other, new alternatives. For example, it now seems surprising that in the late 1970s Pease, Billingham and Earnshaw (1977) found that 45 to 50 per cent of CSOs were diversions from custody. The ISSP study found that sentencers were keen to emphasise that custody remained the only option in certain instances, and those sentenced to custody appeared to have been slightly higher risk than the ISSP cases. Furthermore, some sentencers favoured a wider use for ISSP, indicating that if their views were to hold precedence, the expansion of the programme to lower-risk young offenders, as a more standardised form of community supervision, would be the likely result. During the evaluation of the six-month ISSP, the YJB also decided to pilot a 12-month version of the programme, only to be used when custody was the single remaining alternative. The obvious danger is that the introduction of a more demanding option will undermine the status of the current ISSP as an alternative to custody.

Yet even if ISSP was to consistently target only those offenders at genuine risk of custody, any impact upon custody rates will be lessened by the use of custody for breach of the programme. A high level of breach is inevitable when dealing with 'high-risk' offenders, and while sentencers emphasised the need for some discretion and proved willing to allow young people to continue on the programme, they also recognised the need to maintain the credibility of ISSP as a tough and rigorous intervention.

Overall, the ISSP evaluation provided a valuable perspective on the complexity and multi-faceted objectives of intensive supervision programmes. The mixed results indicate that great care and prior thought needs to be given to the development of any type of intensive programme, and that the decisions made by policy-makers, practitioners, sentencers, and all those involved in programme delivery, need to take into account the potentially conflicting aims and objectives. Positive ways of safely supervising young offenders in the community should, however, remain one of our major objectives, but not in ways that accelerate such young people into more prolific criminality and which result in the even greater use of custody. The concern remains that disposals like ISSP may have a diversionary effect that is short-lived or non-existent, and whose main impact is to increase the severity of sentencing generally.

Part III
Looking forward

Chapter 7

Emerging lessons

Having set out the political and theoretical foundations of intensive community programmes and presented empirical findings from the ISSP study and a range of other evaluations, the focus in the final two chapters is upon future developments. While the final chapter will address the outstanding critical concerns, re-engaging with the more theoretical considerations, this chapter presents some of the emerging lessons for intensive community programmes, helping to aid design, implementation and delivery. It is submitted that long-term success is dependent upon (i) setting realistic aims and objectives; (ii) employing a clear theoretical model; (iii) applying precise targeting criteria; (iv) tackling implementation and delivery difficulties; (v) adopting a pragmatic enforcement policy; (vi) maintaining the confidence of staff, local police officers, sentencers and local communities; and (vii) continuing to monitor programme integrity and impact, while contributing to the development of the evidence-base.

Setting realistic aims and objectives

It was shown at the outset of this book (see pp. 12–17) that there has been a strong political impetus behind the introduction of intensive community programmes in both the US and England and Wales. The danger, however, as with most new criminal justice initiatives, is that expectations are set unrealistically high, and that intensive programmes are unreasonably promoted as panaceas or 'magic bullets' capable of meeting a wide range of aims and objectives. David Garland (2001: 131–2) has highlighted the tendency for the political machine to indulge in forms of 'evasion' and 'denial', with the imperative tending to be 'the re-imposition of control, usually by punitive means'. This is clearly reflected in some of the rhetoric that has accompanied the introduction of various intensive programmes. Garland continues his analysis by describing certain measures as a form of 'acting out':

> they engage in a form of impulsive and unreflective action, avoiding realistic recognition of underlying problems, the very fact of acting providing its own form of relief and gratification ... Their capacity to control future crime, though always loudly asserted, is often doubtful and in any case is less important than their immediate ability to enact public sentiment, to provide an instant response, to function as a retaliatory measure that can stand as an achievement in itself. (Garland 2001: 132–3)

Put simply, extravagant claims are often indicative of short-termism. Furthermore, such claims are often not conducive to longer-term credibility, and it can be argued that, in effect, some programmes are being set up to fail: 'Intensive supervision, electronic monitoring and home confinement are not panaceas, and they should not be idealized as such, making them vulnerable to any reports of negative or conflicting outcome' (McCarthy 1987: 11). At this point, it is worth remembering that many of the intensive programmes in England and Wales have been short-lived, including the most recent ICCP pilots for young adult offenders (Partridge *et al.* 2005), with the evaluation findings presumably having failed to match the hopes of those less enlightened policy-makers.

It is clearly important, therefore, that achievable and realistic aims and expectations are established from the outset, and that these are not modified according to any changes in the political climate. Crucially, when targeting high-risk offenders, it is essential that their prior behaviour is taken into account, recognising that improvements are likely to be gradual. More specifically, for those who have committed numerous offences in the period prior to their referral on to a programme, some further offending is often likely. The national evaluation of ISSP confirmed this hypothesis: while there were reductions in the frequency and seriousness of the young people's offending, 89 per cent were reconvicted at least once during the following 12 months. Thus, while intensive programmes can provide an important first step towards positive maturation and development, longer-term reinforcements will still be needed for the vast majority of these offenders. It is also important to bear in mind the more general research findings, confirmed by the ISSP study, which indicate that short-term reductions in re-offending are not necessarily translated to longer-term gains (Raynor and Vanstone 1997; Farrington *et al.* 2002).

Realism is also needed when considering the potential impact of intensive programmes upon levels of custodial sentencing. The problems of net-widening and increased levels of breach are well recognised, and it should be acknowledged that intensive programmes do not exist within a vacuum and that custody rates are likely to be affected by a range of other factors. During the ISSP evaluation, for example, the 'Street Crime Initiative' was launched, bringing together ten police areas with government and criminal justice agencies to combat a rising trend in street crime. Analysis by the Home Office and the YJB in early 2002 suggested that a likely consequence was a significant increase in the prison population (Youth Justice Board 2002e). In both the US and England and Wales, there have been a number of other similar political interventions and pronouncements that have had the effect of driving up custody rates. Recognising this similarity between the two jurisdictions, Tonry (2004: 64) argues that they can be distinguished from other jurisdictions by their 'deeper strain of moralistic self-righteousness and punitiveness towards deviance'.

Further empirical findings indicate that the individual aims and objectives of intensive community programmes may not be fully compatible. A potential consequence of breach is imprisonment, resulting in a clear tension between the desire to reduce the levels of custodial sentencing, while also providing tough, stringent community interventions that are rigorously enforced. During the ISSP evaluation, practitioners expressed their desire to continue working with offenders while at the same time recognising the need to maintain the credibility of the programme. Furthermore, the optimum target group for reducing custody rates is likely to be different from that for reducing re-offending rates. Attempting to achieve a multitude of objectives, as was the case with ISSP, would thus appear to carry the risk of diluting the inroads that are made into achieving each objective individually.

Employing a clear theoretical model

When designing an intensive community programme, careful thought needs to be given to the theoretical model employed. Unfortunately, such attention has often been lacking in the formulation of criminal justice interventions, with Francis Cullen and Paul Gendreau (2000: 130) noting that 'many programs fail to work because they either are ill-conceived (not based on sound criminological theory) and/or have no therapeutic integrity'. The importance of programme design is further emphasised by James McGuire (2002: 25) in his review of the developing 'What Works' literature. He concludes that 'there appears to be a strong relationship between the clarity of objectives, theoretical base and methods employed within a programme and its overall effects'. As for which theoretical models appear most effective, Cullen and Gendreau (2000: 157–8) conclude as follows: '(1) across all interventions, rehabilitation is more effective in reducing recidivism than alternative criminal justice sanctions; (2) programs that conform to the principles of effective intervention achieve meaningful, and possibly substantial, reductions in recidivism; and (3) numerous individual programs – such as multisystemic therapy – have been notably efficacious and offer the potential to serve as model interventions in other jurisdictions.'

Applying these three points to the more specific evidence-base for intensive community programmes, the US evaluations indicate that the programmes must have a rehabilitative component to have a successful impact upon re-offending rates. On this basis, Gendreau, Cullen and Bonta (1994: 74) conclude that, 'A persuasive case can be made for abandoning intensive supervision programs that seek only to control and punish offenders in favor of programs that give equal primacy to changing offenders.' In other words, while intensive interventions can incorporate elements of risk management or a more authoritarian approach, a strong welfare-base would appear essential.

With regard to the second point concerning the principles of effective intervention, the ability to tailor individual programmes to individual needs, targeting offenders' criminogenic risk factors, would appear particularly important. For example, evidence from ISSP indicates that for those offenders with entrenched drug misuse problems, it is vital that appropriate treatment is in place before inroads can be made into dealing with other aspects of the offenders' lives. It would also appear important that the range of interventions sufficiently cater for female offenders and for minority ethnic offenders.

As for the third point outlined by Cullen and Gendreau above, differing forms of treatment/rehabilitation can be incorporated within the structure of a multi-modal intensive community programme, and the ISSP evaluation found that those schemes that did not employ a 'specific model of change', such as MST or YAP, had less of an impact upon offending frequency than other models of ISSP provision. In England and Wales, the potential to employ differing models of change and to utilise the skills of public, commercial and not-for-profit/voluntary providers is likely to increase through the proposed introduction of commissioning and contestability into the provision of probation services (Home Office 2005). Those research findings that indicate the types of intervention that have proven most effective will be of particular interest to the Regional Offender Managers (ROMs), who, it is proposed, will have responsibility for such commissioning. Reviewing the evidence-base relating to serious and persistent young offenders, McGuire concludes as follows:

> interventions in the most consistently effective category have been shown to have an average impact in reducing recidivism by 40% in community settings and 30% in custodial settings ... Programmes in this category for the most part employ the following types of methods: interpersonal skills training; behavioural interventions such as modelling, graduated practice and role-playing; cognitive skills training; mentoring linked to individual counselling with close matching of young people and mentors on key background variables; structured individual counselling within a reality therapy or problem-solving framework; and teaching family homes which involve specially trained staff acting in a parental role. (McGuire 2002: 23–5)

The ISSP evaluation suggests that it is the complementary combination of supervisory components, and the way in which they are provided as part of a multi-modal package, that is important in bringing about improvements in offending attitudes and behaviours. Interestingly, there is now a growing movement towards viewing one-to-one work as 'an important component of structured programmes' (Burnett 2004: 191), and at ISSP management level there was a perception that it was often the quality and consistency of the relationship between the young person and the individual ISSP worker, rather than any particular aspect of supervision, that was most crucial.

There is also a growing recognition of the need to pay attention to the sequencing of interventions, as demonstrated by the guidance for delivering intensive community orders under the CJA 2003 (National Probation Service 2005a), and more generally by the Offender Management Model for NOMS (National Offender Management Service). This model states as follows:

> Several factors weigh in the balance to determine the precise sequencing in each case:
> • the sequence needs to map onto and support the change process
> • there are some natural sequences to some interventions e.g. detoxification before relapse prevention
> • the complexity of the sentence
> • the capabilities of the offender and his/her ability to cope with multiple, concurrent demands. (NOMS 2005: 10)

These factors can be seen as particularly relevant to intensive programmes that are multi-modal. As they demonstrate, while sequencing can be incorporated into the theoretical model, there will remain a need for some discretion at individual case level. It is also important to recognise that while the sequencing of interventions within a sentence can help to bring about short-term improvements, the achievement of longer-term gains will often depend upon continued support through mainstream services in the community. Accordingly, accessing such services needs to be built into the theoretical model. It is important that statutory services fulfil their obligations, and that intensive programmes are not expected to remedy their inefficiencies.

Applying precise targeting criteria

The importance of targeting cannot be underestimated, with Carol Hedderman (2005: 7) stating that, 'targeting is key to effectiveness and ability to target is in its infancy'. In terms of intensive community programmes, it is vital that there is a link between offender referrals and the aims of the programme. More specifically, if the primary aim is to reduce re-offending, then some research studies, although not all, support the 'What Works' principle of 'risk classification', which stipulates that the level and intensity of the intervention should be matched to the offender's risk of re-offending. As Cullen and Gendreau (2000: 147) recognise, '"less hardened" or lower risk offenders generally do not require intervention because they are unlikely to recidivate. Subjecting them to structured, intrusive interventions is an imprudent use of scarce resources and, under certain circumstances, may increase recidivism.'

Returning to the ISSP findings, the views among practitioners regarding targeting were mixed. While some believed that ISSP should be reserved for the most persistent and serious offenders, others felt that a number of the young people could have benefited from receiving the intensity of ISSP earlier in their offending careers. The analysis revealed, however, that the greatest reductions in the frequency of offending were achieved when there was suitable matching between eligibility and the use of the programme: while those young people who were both 'persistent and serious' experienced a significant reduction in offending frequency, there was less benefit for those young people who were not eligible for the programme. Despite this finding, the urge to widen the eligibility criteria appears strong, with the Prolific and other Priority Offender (PPO) Premium Service Strategy advising that PPOs who are not eligible for ISSP should receive a programme of 'equivalent rigour and intensity' (Lee and Wildgoose 2005: 31). Furthermore, in a recent consultation document (January 2006), the YJB has asked ISSP managers to consider using their dedicated teams to provide intensive supervision to other less persistent and less serious offenders on account of their individual risk factors or the likelihood of a future custodial sentence. Unfortunately, the suitability of these offenders, in terms of reducing re-offending, does not appear to have been examined.

It was also very clear from the ISSP evaluation that attitudes to offending and their lifestyles were inextricably linked to the progress of young people on the programme. Further research findings indicate that the motivation of the offender and his/her willingness to change are crucial factors towards successful engagement (Folkard *et al.* 1974; Lobley, Smith and Stern 2001). However, deeming a person to be unsuitable on the basis of a lack of motivation is clearly controversial. After all, motivation can be seen as both 'modifiable' and an 'interpersonal phenomenon', which can be developed and sustained during the course of the programme (López Viets, Walker and Miller 2002: 17). Nevertheless, the motivation of the offender could be considered to some extent when assessing suitability. The following comments by ISSP practitioners support such an approach.

They themselves have to have the maturity and the ability to see that they have a problem, they have to want to address it and they have to want us to help them. They will still blip, but they then come back to the general upward trend of wanting to do something about it. (ISSP education officer)

There has to be some initial motivation there and a willingness to respond. What we've seen as essential are some stable foundations to build upon. Family support has been crucial. Where there is some ambivalence, a lack of motivation, no stable accommodation or where parents have not been supportive, we've found it difficult to move forward. (ISSP manager)

Some intensive programmes have developed more elaborate forms of targeting criteria than others. In the development of Prolific Offender Projects (POPs), one of the primary concerns was the reduction in volume of serious property crime, predominantly burglary, theft of and from vehicles and street robberies. For example, the original Dordrecht/Burnley project arose directly from the Safer Cities Partnership in Burnley and the key objective was to reduce the amount of serious acquisitive crime in the target area (Chenery and Pease 2000). The broad targeting criteria were determined by police information and intelligence on such crimes, followed by the police identification of local offenders who were known to be responsible for large numbers of such offences. The majority of POPs have in fact designed two-staged offender selection procedures, involving (i) the generation of lists of potential offenders who have known convictions for the targeted offence types; and (ii) applying a scoring matrix, prioritising the offenders through the generation of scores based on the number, frequency, seriousness and known type of offending (often weighted to reflect the local policing concerns), and in some schemes including intelligence information on suspected offences (Dawson 2005). This approach to targeting can take account of local definitions of the type of offences of greatest concern to the public and the police, and can be easily modified over time.

Already, however, there are concerns that some matrices and identification systems could be in breach of the European Human Rights principles of legality, necessity, relevance and proportionality with regards to (i) the right to a fair trial (Article 6); (ii) respect for private and family life (Article 8); and (iii) the right to liberty (Article 5). Worrall and Mawby (2004: 280–1) have also warned that 'as such projects are implemented more widely, care must be taken that they target offenders who are genuinely high-risk and persistent so that the effect of the project is not diluted, and less persistent or low-risk offenders are not caught inappropriately in the net as it widens'.

Somewhat worryingly, however, the PPO Strategy, launched in 2004, provides that PPOs should be locally defined, leaving much room for discretion and disparity.

The considerations are somewhat different if the dominant aim of the intensive programme is to have an impact upon custody rates. Avoiding net-widening, ensuring that the programme does not amount to a further 'dispersal of discipline', becomes crucial. Consequently, the overriding criterion needs to be a high likelihood of a custodial sentence. While there is likely to be a sizeable overlap between those offenders at high risk of re-offending and those at genuine risk of a custodial sentence, it needs to be recognised that the two groups are not identical. In particular, as was shown by the ISSP evaluation, offenders who commit serious one-off offences, and are thus in danger of receiving a custodial sentence, are not necessarily at high risk of re-offending.

While many ISSP managers and co-ordinators were aware of the dangers of net-widening, there were instances of schemes using their discretion and lowering the eligibility criteria to allow those considered to have specific underlying needs onto ISSP. To ensure that a programme successfully targets those at genuine risk of a custodial sentence, it would thus appear that strict eligibility criteria need to be devised and enforced. Net-widening is not easily avoided, as illustrated by recent history, with Michael Tonry (1998) recognising that its likelihood is increased when the judges control the referrals. A number of empirical studies, including the ISSP evaluation, provide support to this contention with sentencers indicating their preference for a wider use of intensive community programmes. Accordingly, limiting judicial discretion in relation to the targeting criteria would appear essential.

As was indicated in Chapter 1, the targeting of intensive community programmes has also varied in terms of 'stage in process', with some programmes having targeted offenders pre-custody, sometimes even pre-sentence at the bail stage, and others having sought referrals at the post-custody stage. Those programmes that are post-custody can obviously have no direct impact upon custody rates unless through the prevention of further offending, and the ISSP study found that DTO ISSPs performed significantly worse than the comparison sample in terms of reducing both reconvictions and the frequency of recorded offending. It is thought that the perceived high demands of DTO ISSP may have been counter-productive, with some practitioners feeling that it constituted a 'double punishment' that young people reacted to negatively. The value of post-custodial intensive programmes thus remains questionable, as also demonstrated by the most recent US research (Wiebush *et al.* 2005).

Tackling implementation and delivery difficulties

While the initial design of an intensive community programme needs to be carefully considered, equal regard must be paid to the implementation and delivery of the programme in order to ensure that the programme is 'conducted in practice as intended in theory and design' (Hollin 1995: 196). As Roberts (1995: 221) has previously stated, 'I take the view that however good and appropriate are the programmes you are using, or are planning to use, with offenders, they will have little chance of success unless particular attention is given to all aspects of the delivery and organisation of such programmes.' This statement is particularly relevant to intensive community programmes, as the implementation and delivery of a multi-modal programme, which combines supervision and surveillance, is far from straightforward. In their evaluation of the Intensive Aftercare Program (IAP) in the US, Wiebush and colleagues (2005: 90) proclaim that there is a need to 'Take a long-term, multiyear perspective on program implementation that takes into account the complexity of the model and that allows for an incremental approach to implementation.'

The importance of continually monitoring implementation and delivery was highlighted by the ISSP evaluation, and was later brought to light by the serious and disturbing case of Peter Williams. This particular young offender was involved in an armed robbery of a jewellers in Nottingham in September 2003, during which he assaulted one of the proprietors with a crowbar and his accomplice fatally shot another of the proprietors. The case generated much media attention, and it was soon discovered that Peter Williams had been released from custody 20 days previously. As part of his DTO licence, he was subject to an ISSP with a curfew supported by electronic monitoring. This was his second DTO ISSP, and he had previously had a Supervision Order ISSP, both of which he had breached. A subsequent inquiry into the supervision of the young offender revealed a number of instances of implementation failure: there was a lack of suitable accommodation to meet the needs of the offender; there was insufficient formal induction or training for new staff and a lack of regular staff supervision; case records were not being sufficiently maintained; the conditions of the licence had not been managed sufficiently stringently; and the electronic monitoring contractor had not notified the YOT of a number of violations of the curfew (HM Inspectorate of Probation 2005). The case thus provides a good example of how a combination of implementation failures can debilitate a programme, leaving it ineffectual.

Maintaining a balance between control and care

A welfarist agenda and a more punitive, authoritarian approach are clearly uncomfortable bedfellows for intensive community programmes, and in practice maintaining a balance between supervision and surveillance has proved difficult: 'if, as some claim, intermediate sanctions provide in concept a means by which punishment – expressed through intensive surveillance and control – can be reasonably balanced and reconciled with treatment and rehabilitation, the question remains as to whether it is possible, in practice, to implement such a balance' (Altschuler 1998: 372–3). Notably, tensions can arise between the caring and controlling aims; between the benefits from ensuring, on the one hand, that offenders complete their programmes and receive the full 'dosage', and, on the other hand, ensuring credibility with sentencers and the wider public by breaching for non-compliance (Hedderman and Hough 2004). The US evidence demonstrates that the latter controlling aims often assume predominance: 'Even juvenile intensive probation programs, which at least in theory, emerge from a model in which counseling and rehabilitation are at least on an equal footing with control and punishment, succumb to surveillance-orientated intermediate sanctions' (Altschuler 1998: 370–1). As indicated above, however, a strong welfare-base appears essential for reducing levels of re-offending.

The growth in POPs has brought together the politically attractive combination of improved 'Catch and Convict' strategies with improved take-up of 'Rehabilitation and Resettlement' through voluntary involvement or as a requirement in a community sentence or custodial licence (Dawson 2005). Most of the projects have emphasised that their first objective is to reduce the number of mainly acquisitive crimes committed in the area and to help protect the public by limiting the harm to victims of such crimes. The projects have also promoted a swift response to any non-compliance or re-offending. At the same time, however, there is still a focus upon helping individual offenders to improve their life chances and encouraging them to change their attitudes to crime and to be more responsible for their actions.

The police have played a critical role in the development of these types of schemes, strongly supporting them due to their potential to combine high-quality Intelligence-Led Policing practices and targeted policing initiatives with strong inter-agency partnerships, all focused upon a core of the most prolific and problematic local offenders. Police involvement means that offenders on these schemes are aware from the outset that (i) police surveillance will be increased; (ii) their identities and prolific offender status will be communicated to all police personnel including custody staff; and (iii) if they are identified as having re-offended they will be arrested, not bailed (in most circumstances), swiftly prosecuted and recalled to prison if on licence. Active local police involvement also means swift responses to breaches of community sentence requirements or bail conditions. A strong police presence can thus have beneficial consequences, but once again care needs to be taken to maintain the balance between supervision and surveillance.

Worrall and colleagues (2003: 20) describe how the initial choice of a police station as the location for the Stoke-on-Trent POP seemed problematic, but once the project was well established this location became 'one of its strengths, particularly in respect of intelligence links, its access to police intelligence systems and the ease with which it could liaise with the different police sections. It was a safe meeting place and secure project base and symbolically the police station location reinforced the crime reduction objective.' Less positively, one of the ISSP schemes was located in a police station, and this was found to have an intimidating effect on some young people, upsetting the balance between control and care.

During the ISSP evaluation, it was evident that the ISSP teams, alongside the electronic monitoring providers, found it difficult at times to achieve a proper balance between the caring and controlling aims of the programme. The ISSP staff rightly placed considerable emphasis on achieving and maintaining good and positive engagement with the young people. This was demanding in itself, without the problems arising from regular surveillance and the rigorous enforcement of rules and court requirements. Nevertheless, practitioners were very aware of the importance of maintaining a balance, and they believed that resolving these tensions was an important factor in terms of ensuring effective delivery. Developing clear channels of communication with the electronic monitoring contractors proved particularly important.

Other factors

Reviewing the evidence-base for intensive community programmes, a range of factors would appear to underpin successful implementation and delivery. One of the most obvious factors is the provision of appropriate budget levels and resources. The need for intensive programmes to deliver quality contact, rather than simply more contact, has also been emphasised. This can be seen as indicative of the wider requirement, appropriate to all forms of intervention, to assess not only 'what' is being delivered but also 'how' it is being delivered. With regard to the 'how', Holt (2001) has highlighted the important ingredients of consistency, continuity, commitment and consolidation.

Bearing in mind the 'multi-modal' nature of most intensive programmes, establishing close liaisons and clear lines of communication and information-sharing with a range of departments and organisations appears both difficult to achieve in practice and of critical importance for real changes to be achieved. For the ISSP schemes, establishing a broad and influential steering group proved particularly useful in securing service level agreements with outside agencies. Such agreements should set out clear lines of responsibility and accountability, as well as common objectives. Furthermore, there is the potential to move from 'multi-agency' working to 'inter-agency' working, Adam Crawford (1997: 119) defining the former as 'the coming together of various agencies to address a problem', with the latter involving 'some degree of fusion and melding of relations between agencies'. The advantages of the latter include 'speed of access to information, advice and specialist attention' (Burnett and Appleton 2004: 38). There have been some notable successes in this regard, as demonstrated by the following commentary regarding the Stoke-on-Trent POP:

> The development of constructive relations between agencies, particularly police, probation and health, contributed to the operation of the project. The benefits were tangible at a managerial level in terms of strategic integration and policy-making, and also at the operational level where the different team roles of the police officer, crime analyst and probation officer complemented each other in the intensive supervision and monitoring of the participants. The sharing of information between team members from different agencies worked well and

contributed to the ability of the project to monitor and manage offenders. (Worrall and Mawby 2004: 281)

There is much overlap here with other research findings, as reflected in the developing 'What Works' principles. Summarising these principles, Peter Raynor sets out the following factors, all of which can be seen as very much relevant to intensive community programmes

- adapting services to difference and diversity, and recognizing participants' strengths;
- monitoring continuity of services and care, including relapse prevention;
- giving staff clear guidance on principles and on where they can use discretion;
- monitoring and maintaining programme integrity, i.e. that services are delivered as intended;
- developing staff skills, including the capacity to maintain high-quality interpersonal relationships;
- ensuring good knowledgeable management;
- adapting services to local context, client groups and services. (Raynor 2004: 200–1)

The fourth of these points refers to the need for 'programme integrity' which Clive Hollin (1995: 196) states is 'characterized by sound management, tight design and skilled practitioners'. The need for a well-trained and cohesive staff team, supported by strong managerial and operational leadership, has been highlighted by many reports (Goodstein and Sontheimer 1997; Lobley, Smith and Stern 2001; Key 2001). Those in management need to adopt a pro-social approach to leadership, modelling enthusiasm and commitment, while also ensuring that all staff fully understand the aims of the programme and how these aims are to be achieved. While attempts should be made to appoint 'energetic, flexible and creative staff' from the outset and to ensure that their training and supervision needs are met, there is a further need to try to minimise staff turnover and to ensure that vacancies are rapidly filled (Wiebush et al. 2005). It has been further suggested that there is a need for a degree of 'openness, creativity and flexibility' (Altschuler 1998: 383).

A review of management styles has promoted an integrated rather than a fragmented approach, concluding that 'continuity of contact with the same case manager and other staff was essential to building confidence and rapport with the offender' (Partridge 2004: 5). Such continuity has since become a central component of the NOMS offender management model, with an Offender Manager 'binding issue-specific interventions into a coherent whole' (NOMS 2005: 13). Further 'best practice themes' are set out as follows:

- all team members believe in the value of teamwork and are committed to making it work …
- team members share a vision about what has to be achieved
- the Project Manager provides visible, enthusiastic, interested leadership …
- everyone in the team has a good understanding of the overall plan
- there is clarity between team members about who's doing what and by when *and* how each relates to the others
- there is good day-to-day communication between team members. (NOMS 2005: 15)

Bearing in mind the multi-modal nature of intensive programmes, potentially involving a range of agencies, the need for some form of continuity of contact and adherence to these best practice themes would appear particularly strong.

Adopting a pragmatic enforcement policy

The recent policy trend in England and Wales has been towards tougher enforcement of community penalties, indicative of a more general 'low-tolerance' agenda. This can be traced back to 1989, which saw the introduction of National Standards for Community Service Orders (CSOs). Three years later, further standards were introduced, encompassing Probation Orders, CSOs, Combination Orders, Supervision Orders and supervision on licence. These standards were revised and toughened in 1995, curtailing practitioners' discretion regarding their responses to first and second failures to attend and their implementation of breach proceedings. A further toughening occurred in 2000, and each probation area has now been set targets for dealing with failures to comply. Carol Hedderman and Mike Hough (2004: 152) thus conclude that 'as a result there are now very few circumstances in which an absence may be regarded as acceptable and virtually every case in which more than one unacceptable absence occurs will go to court for a breach hearing'. The Criminal Justice Act 2003 further provides that it is a statutory duty for the 'responsible officer' to instigate breach proceedings if there is a second unacceptable failure within 12 months. For young offenders, breach proceedings should commence after a third unacceptable failure to comply with a community penalty (HM Court Service 2005).

The drawbacks of a hard-line approach

In considering the reasons behind the toughening of enforcement, Lucia Zedner (2004: 202) argues that 'National Standards are a covert means both of extending juridicial power and of strengthening the punitive quality of penalties. The presumption behind these standards appears to be that rigorous enforcement is an unequivocal good and that departure from the penalty laid down by the court is generally unwarranted and undesirable.' Yet while tough enforcement can clearly be supported on the grounds of deterrence, adhering to an authoritarian approach, it needs to be recognised that this rationale has limited empirical support (see pp. 28–29). Furthermore, Roger Smith (2003: 115) argues, with regard to young offenders, that 'the threat of further penalties for non-compliance will almost inevitably compromise young people's motivation, commitment and sense of personal responsibility'. Research on intensive programmes indicates that the greater the level of intensity, the more likely it is that offenders will breach its requirements, particularly if the programme is dealing with high-risk offenders. This is not greatly surprising: 'Given that probationers typically have very long histories of non-compliance with parents, teachers, police and courts, it seems especially optimistic that probation officers will succeed in securing compliance where all others have failed' (Hedderman and Hough 2004: 163). Furthermore, the greater the emphasis upon surveillance, the more likely it is that such non-compliances and/or further offending will be detected (Goodstein and Sontheimer 1997).

A potential consequence of non-compliance is the use of custody for breach, which prevents the practitioner from continuing any rehabilitative work with the offender, disrupting any continuity in provision, while lessening any inroads that are made into reducing the levels of custodial sentencing. These drawbacks have become increasingly apparent, no more so than in a report by the Prison Reform Trust (2005) that found, in the preceding five years, the number of prisoners recalled to custody had more than trebled. Furthermore, the majority of offenders were being recalled for technical breaches rather than for further offending. Alarmed by such figures, there are growing calls for a move away from an authoritarian approach: 'The argument against tough enforcement is that it imposes a needlessly high drop-out (or throw-out) rate from treatment, and that a more pragmatic style of enforcement could result in higher retention rates, higher dosage and greater effectiveness' (Hedderman and Hough 2004: 158). Hedderman (2005: 6) further recognises that, somewhat perversely, 'Ever toughening enforcement will ultimately lead to supervision being limited to those who don't need it because they are the only ones who never miss an appointment.'

There is also a danger of programmes losing credibility among sentencers if the courts become overwhelmed with breaches. Strong support can, therefore, be given to a policy of graduated responses to non-compliances, encompassing both reminders and warnings, with a favouring of continuation on the programme when this represents the most constructive option for engaging with the offender. Such a 'minimalist approach' was earlier suggested by Mark Drakeford (1993: 229), through which he advocated the use of breach as a response of last resort.

Notably, a less hard-line approach appears to have been adopted in practice, if not the rhetoric, of some of those intensive programmes that have been the subject of empirical study. For example, Goodstein and Sontheimer (1997: 353–4) found that practitioners 'attempted to differentiate among the various violations and their assessment of the client's likely future behaviour', while Blomberg and Lucken (1994: 73) reported that 'some officers do realize that, on occasion, rigid enforcement may need to be relaxed for practical purposes in order to offset some of the impractical aspects associated with an ideology of "more is better".'

In England and Wales, recent high-level support for graduated responses and a less stringent approach towards enforcement has not been confined to intensive community programmes. The Coulsfield Inquiry (2004: 63), for example, recommended that, 'The Government should legislate to prevent courts imposing custody following breach of a community order, where the original offence did not merit it', while the Audit Commission (2004: 43) has concluded that 'persistent or major breaches should be brought to court but dealt with in proportion to the behaviour, making sure that custody is used only as a last resort'. Similarly, the Sentencing Advisory Panel (2004), in its advice to the Sentencing Guidelines Council, has advised that the 'primary objective' of the court should be to ensure that previously imposed requirements are completed, with custody representing 'the last resort, reserved for those cases of deliberate and repeated breach where all reasonable efforts to ensure that the offender complies have failed'. The Sentencing Guidelines Council (2004: 18) has, in turn, recognised the need to try to avoid further breach: 'When increasing the onerousness of requirements, the court must consider the impact on the offender's ability to comply and the possibility of precipitating a custodial sentence for further breach.'

Supporting a carrot and stick approach

It is notable that the current National Standards in England and Wales concentrate upon the punishment of non-compliances, and have little to say about encouraging and rewarding compliance. This has led a number of critics to argue that 'instead of asking "what works?" in enforcement, we ought to be devoting more attention to the question of "what works?" in encouraging compliance' (Robinson and Dignan 2004: 327). A more balanced carrot and stick approach has been promoted by Altschuler (1998: 382) who argues that it is 'imperative to build into intermediate sanction correctional policy and program design a structured system of both graduated consequences for technical violators and incentives to prevent technical violations from occurring in the first place'. With regard to the latter incentives, Hedderman and Hough (2004: 164) propose a 'graduated system of positive rewards', encompassing attendance certificates, reduced restrictions and perhaps early termination. More generally, incorporation of 'pro-social modelling' principles (Trotter 1999) would have the advantage of requiring practitioners to actively model appropriate behaviour and to ensure that demonstrations of positive, pro-social behaviour are praised and rewarded. Such pro-social modelling has now been encouraged by the National Probation Directorate (NPD) alongside 'a variety of motivational techniques ... to ensure that the offender is engaged and to maintain momentum' (Home Office 2004c: 3).

In their desire to encourage efforts to 'design out' non-attendance, Hedderman and Hough (2004: 165) further argue that there should be 'organisational' rewards for securing compliance, while McGuire (2002: 27–8) lists the following 'strategies' for improving programme attendance: (i) offering inducements to attend by linking participation to other benefits; (ii) providing transport and arrangements for ensuring arrival at the programme site; and (iii) delivering programmes at accessible locations. Further 'innovative approaches', including the use of technology such as e-mailing and/or texting appointment reminders, have been set out by the NPD (Home Office 2004c: 3). Nevertheless, it remains inevitable that some offenders will breach the requirements of their programme at some stage. Positively, however, the ISSP evaluation recognised that a return to court could be viewed purposefully and it was often used as a deliberate tactic in an attempt to ensure future compliance. The emphasis was thus upon enabling behaviour change rather than imposing further sanctions. But for those for whom custody was required, the message to others on the programme was clear. Perhaps most importantly, particularly in terms of sending out a clear message, a number of ISSP managers highlighted the need for consistency.

Maintaining confidence

Dealing intensively with high-risk offenders can be physically and emotionally draining for practitioners, and it is inevitable that some offenders will fail to engage and comply. Consequently, strong managerial leadership is needed to maintain the confidence and enthusiasm of front-line staff. Local police support is vital for long-term credibility, particularly for those programmes that have close links with the police, and efforts need to be made to ensure that local police officers have confidence in the ability of the programme to tackle the offending behaviours of the target group. Some of those officers interviewed during the ISSP study believed that many of their colleagues remained sceptical and held generally pro-custody views, becoming frustrated when individual offenders, who had been subject to community sentences (including ISSP), were seen repeatedly in the system. However, there was also a perception that their levels of confidence in the programme increased as they became more acquainted with it, and how it related to their role and function.

It is important for programmes to engage with local communities in order to raise public awareness and maintain public confidence. The extent to which the ISSP schemes had attempted to forge contacts with their local communities varied greatly, but many schemes had held 'launch' events or sent press releases to local papers to promote positive coverage of the programme. Those schemes that had pursued more direct links with the community had attempted a range of methods, including reparation work within the local communities; ISSP representation on anti-crime partnerships, interactions with volunteers and presentations to neighbourhood organisations and residents' associations. Such efforts can be particularly useful in counteracting some of the more negative press headlines that can accompany high-profile 'failures'.

Intensive community programmes are largely dependent upon the courts for their referrals. It is thus crucial that sentencers have confidence in the programme. Regularly dealing with breaches can give an impression of overall programme failure, but such a perception can be avoided by ensuring that courts receive feedback regarding the progress of the programme and individual cases. Recent research on ICCP (Partridge *et al.* 2005) and the Drug Treatment and Testing Order (Hough *et al.*, 2003) has found support among sentencers for improved feedback, and there was much room for improvement in relation to ISSP; nearly two-thirds of sentencers said that the amount of feedback they had received about individual ISSP cases was 'not satisfactory' or 'poor'. Holding regular reviews can be particularly beneficial, helping to reassure sentencers about the progress in individual cases, as well as providing some context regarding the complexity of offenders' lives. At the same time, the offenders themselves can potentially benefit from the increased interaction with the courts, sometimes from sentencers giving praise and on other occasions from sentencers making more critical comments. Recognising these advantages, the Audit Commission (2004) has recommended that such reviews should be used with all persistent young offenders.

Developing the evidence-base

Monitoring and evaluation at the national level is essential for validation, assessing whether an individual programme works and whether individual aims and objectives are being achieved. Local programme monitoring is equally important, helping to take account of the 'many different features of implementation that can influence overall programme effects, such as characteristics of implementer, environment and the target population' (Debidin and Lovbakke 2004: 48). This is highlighted by the ISSP evaluation, with many differences between the 41 schemes included in the study. While such monitoring is important for evaluators and the wider research community, collecting systematic evidence and information on individual cases, as well as at aggregate level, should be viewed as an integral process for practitioners and managers. After all, only through adopting an evidence-based approach to decision-making, identifying suitable offenders and selecting the most appropriate types of interventions, can successful outcomes be justifiably expected: 'It has generally been found that the extent of monitoring of a programme to ensure integrity of delivery is correlated with higher effect sizes' (McGuire 2002: 28). One suggestion is that quality checklists should be adopted, helping to ensure that good research practice is followed (McDougall, Perry and Farrington 2006).

Further empirical analysis is also needed to contribute to the growing evidence-base for intensive community programmes, as well as the wider 'What Works' literature, both of which require further support and refinement. Despite the claims of some policy-makers, the foundations for the 'What Works' agenda are far from solid: 'Most of us would agree that we are in fact at the earliest stages of the What Works agenda and that we are making our first tentative steps in producing evidence of the effects of these types of programmes, and in identifying the wide range of factors that can affect outcomes' (Roberts 2004: 135). Notably, there has so far been a lack of high-quality research studies in England and Wales:

> While there is a growing evidence base in Britain, much of the evidence on 'what works' with offenders to reduce re-offending comes from the United States and Canada. There are difficulties in generalizing from these studies because it cannot be assumed that their conclusions automatically apply to the British context. In addition, the methods employed by studies vary considerably, which may in part explain differences in the reported effectiveness of programmes. Furthermore, weak research design has contributed to the lack of knowledge about 'what works'. For example, reconviction studies in Britain have met standards one to four of the Scientific Methods Scale but they have rarely achieved standard five, a randomized control trial (RCT) ... Moreover, few studies in Britain have achieved sufficient sample sizes. (Harper and Chitty 2004: viii)

Raising methodological standards

Having set out these limitations, the Home Office report advocates the use of RCTs to 'ensure that knowledge of "what works" is improved and the existing equivocal evidence is replaced with greater certainty and greater confidence' (Harper and Chitty 2004: xx). Future evaluations of intensive community programmes would benefit from the establishment of such trials, provided that sufficient attention is also paid to issues of programme integrity and context (Wilcox 2005). Where randomised studies are not permitted, as was the case with the ISSP evaluation, or practicable, greater efforts need to be made to ensure that comparison groups are well matched. Indeed, some evaluations have not used comparison groups at all, making it extremely difficult to draw any causal conclusions whatsoever. Achieving well-matched comparison groups involves selecting them in such a way as to avoid selection bias. For example, some studies use as a comparison group people who were considered suitable for the disposal being studied, but instead received an alternative disposal. If the alternative disposal is custody, and it can be shown that the profile of people who receive it is different from the treatment group, then selection bias has occurred. In such a case, a difference in outcomes of the two groups is not necessarily attributable to the difference in disposals.

Various methods can be used to minimise selection bias. The best is to select a comparison group that is similar to the treatment group in all respects likely to affect differences in outcome. If this is not possible, various statistical methods can be used to reduce the effect of, or 'control for', selection bias. The most commonly used method in reconviction outcome studies is logistic regression. However, the Government Social Research Unit has also encouraged the use of propensity score matching and regression discontinuity to control for selction bias, as these methods have proven to be most effective in replicating results from evaluations where random assignment has been adopted (Heckman, Ichimura and Todd 1997; Laird and Mosteller 1990). The problem with the regression discontinuity method is that it requires control over the process of allocation to treatment and comparison groups, in the same way as RCT, and this is often not possible in research into alternative court disposals.

Less positively, studies that use an integrated model often have surprisingly little information about the comparison group that receives the 'normal' intervention. It can be argued that in theory as much information is needed about the comparison group as the treatment group. Usually, comparison group data are limited to a 'risk profile', which can be compared with that of the treatment group. But an important consideration is the nature of the intervention received by the comparison group. For example, when Wiebush and colleagues (2005) evaluated three Intensive Aftercare Programmes (IAPs), they found that in one of the sites there was no significant difference between the services received by the intervention and comparison groups. As such, there was no theoretical reason to expect a difference in outcomes. In the ISSP evaluation, much attention was paid to assessing the nature of the ISSP intervention, but little data were collected on the nature of the 'normal' intervention received by the comparison group. While this can be seen as a weakness of the study, it seemed safe to assume in this instance that the 'normal' intervention did not combine supervision and surveillance, or involve an intensity of supervision anywhere close to 25 hours per week.

Details of both the compliance and the completion rates, as well as qualitative information regarding the personal and wider social context of the comparison group, would provide an invaluable point of reference with which to assess the relative value of an intervention. Offender and practitioner views regarding the comparison interventions are also often neglected. It is common for such views to be examined in the treatment group, and for the results to be encouraging. But what if the results for the comparison group are just as encouraging? This would again indicate that significant differences in outcomes might be unlikely to occur.

Adopting broader research designs

The Home Office review of 'What Works' further emphasises the need to employ an 'integrated model of evaluation', combining quantitative and qualitative methods to ensure a sufficient assessment of programme design, process and outcome (Friendship *et al*. 2004: 14). It is clearly important, as shown by the ISSP study, that evaluations should examine offender profile data, implementation process data, and short- and longer-term outcome data (Roberts 2004). Such models are increasingly being used in good-quality offender treatment evaluations (e.g. Raynor and Vanstone 1997), developing understanding as to how programmes work, and allowing more accurate and subtle measurements of effectiveness to be identified.

The value of multiple methods, or a triangulation of techniques, as utilised in the ISSP study, should not be underestimated as this strategy enables the 'advantages of each method to be harnessed, whilst addressing and counteracting their disadvantages, and enhancing the reliability and validity of research evidence' (Torrance 2000: 17). The benefits that can be gained from combining quantitative and qualitative data, exploiting the strengths of each, are now well known. Bryman (1988), for example, indicates that qualitative data can be used to support or illuminate the findings emerging from the quantitative data or to produce further hypotheses that can be checked using the quantitative data. More generally, the two types of data can together produce a more complete picture of the group being studied and the processes involved. Roger Hood thus suggests that 'one cannot convincingly be done without the other' (2002: 159).

One of the key research findings from the ISSP study was the qualitative evidence that suggested that the intensity of ISSP supervision provided a holistic and reintegrative package that went some way towards establishing a new set of pro-social opportunities for the young offenders. Specifically, it was the quality of the relationships developed between staff and young people that was seen as essential in establishing trust and a creating a basis from which to work.

> I think the staff have the greatest impact, the relationships they build up with the young people, they give them someone to talk to, to help solve their problems and listen to them. A lot of them have never had that before. (ISSP manager)

> [The ISSP officer] was just great. He put so much time into my son, really, it was beyond the call of duty. So I really supported him in his role and we tried to work together so when he said 'You've got to do it', or 'Where were you last night?', or 'That's no excuse', I totally backed him up. And he obviously included me in decisions too. (Parent)

In contrast, media interest in the ISSP final report centred almost exclusively on the reconviction rate, despite the fact that this occupied just one paragraph in a 16-page research summary, rendering the other more substantial outcomes effectively irrelevant. The opening paragraph from the *Guardian* article stated: 'The government's community punishment programme [ISSP] to tackle the most hardcore teenage criminals has a failure rate of 91%' (Travis 2005). Similarly, *The Times* opened: 'Nine out of ten persistent young offenders on the Government's £100 million flagship programme to tackle youth crime re-offended within two years. The damning findings are a huge blow to the credibility of a four-year-old scheme hailed by the Home Office as a hands-on way of curbing offending by teenagers' (Gibb and Ford 2005). Regrettably, if such simplistic headlines are the only outcomes to emerge into the wider domain then the considerable resources that are invested in building an evidence-base will be wasted, and other important findings, which are useful to professionals and policy-makers, will perish. Furthermore, the theoretical base from which intensive community programmes gain legitimacy and support will be increasingly questioned, with the programmes remaining vulnerable to shifting political views and their perceptions of public sentiment.

In developing the evidence-base and raising understanding, the use of dynamic variables, which can track changes over time, alongside open-ended interviews can help to uncover the nature and nuances of the supervision process and the course of desistance (or persistence). Dynamic variables in areas such as employment, family relationships or drug dependency are likely to have direct relevance to intervention outcomes. However, by their very nature, dynamic variables require time in which to change and demand a suitably long study period in which to explore the types of problems offenders face, how these have changed from the previous assessments/interviews, how they might change again in the future, and how these issues 'fit' in the context of both the disposal and the wider social environment. There are clear advantages, therefore, to longitudinal designs that follow offenders through the criminal justice system and track changes in their personal and social characteristics (Hedderman 2004; Farrall 2003).

To measure changes in criminogenic needs, as well as ensuring the appropriate targeting and tailoring of programmes to individual needs, requires the standardised use of risk/needs assessment tools. Such third-generation tools have evolved from the first-generation clinical assessments, which are based on traditional interview and assessment processes, and the second-generation actuarial assessments (e.g. the Offender Group Reconviction Scale (OGRS) in England and Wales), which use static factors, such as age and criminal history, to predict the risk of re-offending (Bonta 1996). The third-generation risk/needs tools (e.g. OASys for adult offenders and *Asset* for young offenders) differ in the sense that they combine static and dynamic risk factors. This enables the assessments to achieve the following:

1 estimate a risk of reconviction for an offender based on static and dynamic risk factors;
2 produce a profile of where to target interventions to achieve greatest impact on recidivism;
3 measure changes in risk and need during a period of supervision. (Merrington 2004: 48)

The advantage of measuring change in this context is that it should enable practitioners to deliver improved interventions and become more confident in the approaches they adopt. Even more importantly, the wider public can become more assured that the types of approaches being used are increasing public safety. It was evident from the ISSP study that practitioners were not always aware of the benefits of updating offenders' assessments. Further efforts could be made, therefore, to ensure that they are used to their full potential. Yet further improvements could result from the development of fourth-generation risk assessment tools that 'include the identification and measurement of key responsivity characteristics for treatment matching' (Hannah-Moffat 2004: 33), recognising that the type and style of treatment should be tailored according to the offender's individual cognitive, personality and socio-personal factors, irrespective of whether they amount to risk factors or individual needs.

The need for cost–benefit analyses

A further important concern is whether or not the costs of interventions can be justified relative to their achieved and measurable benefits. Cohen (2001) and Swaray (2006) have both emphasised the importance of developing a financial perspective on the relative merits of different forms of intervention, and they argue that cost–benefit analyses can no longer be avoided. In fact, since the 1998 Comprehensive Spending Review the Home Office has been required by HM Treasury to ensure that any new initiatives are not only adequately assessed as to their effectiveness but also their cost-effectiveness. As part of the Crime Reduction Programme (1999–2002), the Home Office produced a guidance document entitled *Analysis of Costs and Benefits: Guidance for Evaluators* (Dhiri and Brand 1999), and they have since published two research reports that provide well-documented and empirically derived estimates of the economic and social costs of crime (Brand and Price 2000; Dubourg, Hamed and Thorns 2005). These two reports not only provide accurate estimates of the full economic costs of many common criminal offences, but also the contribution different 'cost categories' make to each of these offences.

Cost–benefit analyses would appear particularly important for intensive community programmes, as these tend to have high resource demands and require high levels of staffing and increasingly expensive technological support. However, accurately identifying different aspects of project costs, including start-up or set-up costs, ongoing or running costs and non-financial costs (including voluntary work), can be difficult, as demonstrated in the initial report on ISSP (Moore *et al.* 2004). Contracting out elements of supervision was a common feature of many ISSP schemes, and calculating the proportion of staff time spent on different parts of any programme was often complex. The other side of the economic analysis is the estimation of the financial benefits that can be reasonably attributed to the intervention. While there may well be benefits for the offenders, including increasing their chances of future and more lucrative employment, improving relationships with partners and family, and the health benefits of stopping the abuse of drugs or alcohol, these tend to be longer term and can only be properly calculated in longitudinal studies of offender cohorts. Emphasis has thus been placed upon estimating the shorter-term benefits of any reductions in the frequency and seriousness of re-offending.

Some of the smaller-scale studies of POPs have been able to use the Home Office estimates of the costs of crime in their evaluations of local projects. For example, the third evaluation of the Stoke-on-Trent project calculated that the project achieved a financial break-even point when it achieved 157 fewer offences (Worrall *et al.* 2003). Roberts (2006) has calculated that the Oxford Intensive Recidivist Intervention Scheme (IRIS), which was responsible for only 20 prolific offenders, achieved over a 12-month period a saving of almost £55,000 in police activity costs alone, as well as achieving an overall cost–benefit ratio of 1.35, offsetting the value of all benefits against the value of all economic costs, and 0.59 when only the benefits to direct victims and health services were included in the calculation.

A similar cost–benefit analysis was conducted as part of the ISSP evaluation. An average cost per start was calculated for each scheme by dividing the total scheme costs by the number of starts. Across all schemes this averaged just over £12,000 per start. Benefits were then calculated for each starter by considering the reduction in their offending during the following 12-month period. Standard costs of crime were used (Brand and Price 2000), and account was taken of reductions not just in offending frequency but also in seriousness. It was recognised that a combined reduction in offending frequency *and* offending seriousness would produce even greater cost savings than either on their own. An average saving of approximately £40,000 per start was calculated, equating to a benefit–cost ratio of 3.4, meaning that the benefits were over three times greater than the costs. This is encouraging if reliable, but it is by no means a final figure. For example, the calculation only relates to the reduction in offending over 12 months. In the 24-month follow-up, it appeared that the reduction in offending had continued, and the saving per starts rose to approximately £80,000. Second, the benefits measured were limited to reduced offending. Yet, as pointed out above, there are likely to have been other benefits, such as employment and health, which should ideally be costed. These would increase the return on investment.

Most notably, one needs to be aware of a major limitation of the studies so far described. The benefit–cost ratios are dependent on an assumption that the interventions have a *causal* connection with the reduction in offending. As McDougall *et al.* (2003) highlight, a similar analysis of costs and benefits should be conducted for the comparison group not receiving the intervention. In the ISSP study, the calculation could not be made due to difficulties in obtaining reliable cost data for the comparison groups. On the benefits side, as set out in the previous chapter, the comparison groups experienced a similar reduction in offending to the ISSP groups. When the benefits of reduced offending over 24 months were costed, the saving per start was approximately £82,000, almost exactly the same as for ISSP. Thus, while relatively expensive intensive programmes may be cost-effective if they target offenders with high-volume offending histories and are associated with significant reductions in the amount and seriousness of re-offending, it must be shown that there is a *causal link* with this reduced offending.

Summary

It was shown in the opening chapter that the political impetus behind the introduction of intensive community programmes has been strong with a desire to reduce levels of custodial sentencing and re-offending rates through tough and stringent community interventions that have credibility in the eyes of the public. A range of empirical studies, including the ISSP evaluation, have measured the extent to which these political demands are achievable. Crucially, while the evidence-base for intensive community programmes is continually developing, a number of key lessons have now emerged.

First, there is a need to set achievable and realistic aims and expectations. Given the prior behaviour of persistent and high-risk offenders, improvements in re-offending rates are likely to be gradual, while custody rates are likely to be affected by a range of other factors, with a degree of 'net-widening' likely to occur. Second, a clear theoretical model is required, ensuring that there is a strong rehabilitative component, adhering to a welfare-based model. Third, there is a need for precise targeting criteria. Notably, to have an impact upon re-offending rates, there are some research studies to support the 'What Works' principle of 'risk classification', but to have an impact upon custody rates and avoid extensive net-widening, the overriding criterion needs to be the likelihood of a custodial sentence. Fourth, difficulties can arise from the combination of supervision and surveillance, and from the complexities of multi-agency provision. Particular attention should thus be given to tackling any implementation or delivery difficulties, with careful thought being given to the managerial and more general staffing structures and the development of inter-agency relations. Fifth, to have a lasting impact upon custody rates and ensure programme completions, non-compliances should be dealt with through graduated responses, moving away from an authoritarian approach, with a range of incentives in place to try to prevent non-compliances from occurring in the first place. Sixth, to ensure the longevity of schemes, emphasis should be placed upon maintaining the confidence of the practitioners themselves, the local police, sentencers and the local communities.

Finally, collecting systematic evidence and information on individual cases should be viewed as crucial for practitioners, enabling them to tailor provision and monitor change. Aggregate data, at both individual programme and national levels, are also required to develop the evidence-base and the overriding 'What Works' agenda, which remains in need of further support and refinement. More specifically, there is a need to raise methodological standards and to employ integrated models of evaluation, combining quantitative and qualitative methods, and broader research designs, including economic analyses and longitudinal designs that follow offenders through the criminal justice system and also track changes in their personal and social characteristics.

Taken collectively, these emerging lessons should help to aid the design, implementation and delivery of intensive community programmes, hopefully raising effectiveness and satisfying the demands of politicians and key policy-makers. The challenge is considerable and unlikely to be ever fully achieved, but steps can be taken to ensure that the interventions avoid unintended consequences and are ultimately less wasteful of resources. Nevertheless, a number of important questions remain unanswered. It is to these outstanding critical concerns that the final chapter turns, re-engaging with the more theoretical considerations.

Chapter 8

Critical concerns

The first part of this book set out the various theoretical tensions and empirical uncertainties concerning intensive community programmes. While the ISSP case study and Chapter 7 have developed the empirical evidence and presented the emerging lessons, a number of wider, more theoretical concerns remain outstanding. These concerns encompass the difficulties of targeting, the dangers of labelling and net-widening, and the growing emphasis upon electronic forms of monitoring. There is also a lack of clarity as to how the effectiveness and value of intensive community programmes should be judged. While the theoretical foundations for intensive programmes are multi-faceted, further thought needs to be given to which of the rationales should be prioritised and whether the programmes should be promoted as welfare-based interventions, proportionate interventions, risk management interventions and/or authoritarian interventions.

The complications of targeting

Identifying persistent offenders

Intensive community programmes have varied greatly in the populations that they have targeted. Many have focused upon persistent offenders, indicative of the long-running interest in identifying and tackling such offenders. For instance, the Victorian criminal policy of England and Wales targeted 'habitual criminals', consisting of a 'small group of hard-core professional outlaws and a much larger group of inadequates, misshapen by both nature and nurture, who generally committed petty offences' (Wiener 1990: 300). Moving into the twenty-first century, the political interest in the persistent offender seems to have gathered further impetus. Notably, the *Home Office Strategic Plan* (2004d: 32–33) states that, 'A large proportion of crime is committed by a small number of people. In any one year, approximately 100,000 people commit half of all crimes and just 5,000 people commit about 9 per cent of all crimes – around one million crimes in total.' There have been particular concerns regarding Persistent Young Offenders (PYOs). For example, in 1975, the Magistrates' Association, giving evidence to the House of Commons Expenditure Committee, suggested that there was 'a minority of tough, sophisticated, young criminals [who] prey on the community at will, even after the courts have placed them in care. They deride the powerlessness of the courts to do anything effective' (quoted in Hagell and Newburn 1994: 51).

There have been a number of attempts at identifying persistent offenders and estimating the volume of crime for which they are responsible. Ann Hagell and Tim Newburn undertook one such attempt in the early 1990s. They studied a sample of 531 young people who had been arrested at least three times in the previous year. Within this group they tested several definitions of 'persistent offender', including the top 10 per cent in terms of offending frequency over a 12-month period, those committing ten or more offences in any three-month period, and those arrested eight or more times during the whole year. Their significant conclusions were as follows:

> First, and importantly, it appears that no two definitions of persistence will lead to the identification of the same individuals ... Secondly, the fact that it is extremely problematic to identify a discrete group of persistent offenders in this manner suggests that any definition of persistence will tend to be arbitrary ... Thirdly, the sentencing of juveniles on the basis of a definition of persistence will, therefore, potentially involve a degree of inequity ... Whilst the research results presented here once again confirm the existence of a fairly small group of juveniles who are responsible for a disproportionate amount of recorded crime, they underlie the difficulties which will need to be overcome in introducing any measures which impose definitions of persistence in the belief that this will identify a coherent group

of individuals that stand in need of special treatment. (Newburn and Hagell 1994: 335–6)

It is perhaps not surprising, therefore, that there is no commonly accepted definition of 'persistence', and that differing demarcations have been employed. For instance, the Government has defined a PYO as 'a young person aged 10–17 years who has been sentenced by any criminal court in the UK on three or more occasions for one or more recordable offences and within three years of the last sentencing occasion is subsequently arrested or has an information laid against him for a further recordable offence' (Home Office 1997a). More succinctly, the Youth Lifestyles Survey 1998/99 defined a PYO as 'someone who, in the last year, had committed three or more offences' (Home Office 2000). As was shown in Chapter 3, the YJB, in setting out the eligibility criteria for ISSP, eventually defined persistence in terms of 'offending episodes', requiring four or more such episodes in the prior 12 months. More recently, the national implementation guide for the Criminal Justice Act 2003 states very simply that persistent offenders are 'those who continue to offend over a period of time'. Interestingly, these offenders are distinguished from 'prolific' offenders, defined as 'those who offend with a high frequency, possibly committing a range of different offences, and rapidly building up a substantial history of convictions' (National Probation Service 2005b: 5). Within the Prolific and other Priority Offender (PPO) Strategy, no national eligibility criteria have been imposed, with these offenders having to be defined locally.

Further consideration was given to persistent offenders in the Carter Report (Carter 2003), using research conducted for the White Paper *Criminal Justice – The Way Ahead* (Home Office 2001). The research defined persistent offenders as those who had accumulated at least three convictions during their criminal careers. These offenders, it was calculated, formed about 10 per cent of the active offender population at any one time, and over their careers accumulated at least 50 per cent of all serious offences. However, it was again recognised that the persistent group was not stable, with 40 per cent of persistent offenders desisting from offending without official intervention and many being replaced each year by new persistent offenders. Michael Cavadino and James Dignan (2002: 341) reach the following conclusion: 'It should be borne in mind that out of this year's 100,000 most persistent offenders, as many as 20,000 will drop out of this Premier League of offending next year ... so our efforts on them may well be wasted. Again 50,000 of them are under 21, and even the most persistent young offenders usually grow out of offending, or at least persistent offending.'

Attempting to reduce offending levels by targeting persistent offenders is thus complicated by the transitory nature of this group. Even putting to one side this problem, Richard Garside (2004: 18) emphasises that the need for realism remains as strong as ever: 'in the context of crime rates that are measured in the tens of millions, it stretches credibility to breaking point to claim that it is possible to achieve meaningful reductions in crime by targeting a few thousand of the usual suspects'. He is also critical of (i) the way in which administrative data relating to criminal convictions are extrapolated to offending in general; and (ii) how persistent offenders are assumed to be committing the most serious offences.

Persistence vs. seriousness

The latter point made by Garside highlights the distinction between persistence and seriousness. The increasing emphasis that is placed upon the former at the expense of the latter can be seen as representing a 'shifting from acts to people' (Hudson 2001: 153). Notably, the assumption that persistent offenders are also those committing the most serious offences would appear to be often mistaken. Hagell and Newburn (1994: 131) have found, for example, that 'persistent offenders were not disproportionately engaged in serious offending'. As John Muncie (2004: 30) states, 'Most young offenders are not "hard core" in the sense of being continually engaged in serious crime, but are more likely to be repeat minor offenders.' Andrew Ashworth (2004: 525) is similarly critical of the promotion of persistence above seriousness as the dominant concern, concluding that, 'If the result is to visit unjustifiably heavy sentences on small-time offenders, this will violate the proportionality principle with insufficient justification.' It can thus be argued that notions of persistence and seriousness should be combined 'to ensure that participants have been convicted of sufficiently serious offences to warrant the level of intervention into their lives' (Bottoms, Rex and Robinson 2004: 413). Notably, such a recommendation was made in a recent process evaluation of Intensive Supervision and Monitoring (ISM) schemes in 15 probation areas (Homes, Walmsley and Debidin 2005). Returning to the theoretical framework for intensive programmes, under which the programmes can be classified as welfare-based, proportionate, risk management or authoritarian interventions (see Chapter 1), the arguments outlined here would clearly support proportionality as an important component.

To summarise, the focus of many intensive community programmes upon persistent offenders is questionable on a number of grounds: (i) the arbitrary definitions of persistence; (ii) the transitory nature of persistence; (iii) the reliance upon official statistics; and (iv) the disregarding of seriousness. With regard to the latter, it should not be assumed that defining 'seriousness' is without complication. In their analysis of the 2003 Crime and Justice Survey, Budd, Sharp and Mayhew (2005: 31) emphasise that, 'Identifying the relative seriousness of different offences is difficult. Some offence types seem more serious than others by virtue of their description (for example, assaults resulting in injury will be more serious than assaults with no injury, and actual thefts more serious than attempts). Nonetheless for many offences relative seriousness is likely to vary according to what actually took place.' Serious offenders in this particular survey were defined as those who had committed any of the following specified offences in the last 12 months: theft of a vehicle, burglary, robbery, theft from the person, assault resulting in injury, and selling class A drugs.

In the context of ISSP, in contrast, the YJB initially specified that serious offenders were those whose offence could attract a custodial sentence of 14 years or more in the adult courts. In 2005, the seriousness criterion was restricted to those offences that could attract a sentence of up to ten years for an adult. The impetus behind the introduction of this criterion, and its subsequent revision, was the desire to reduce custody rates, but the definitions employed encompassed some offences that, in reality, rarely led to a custodial sentence.

Identifying high-risk offenders

While many intensive programmes, such as ISSP, have targeted persistent and/or serious offenders, others have employed the terminology of risk, targeting the overlapping group of offenders who are at high risk of re-offending. The close relationship between identifying persistent offenders and high-risk offenders is emphasised by Barbara Hudson (2003: 52–3): 'The project of positivist criminology is centred on the search for reliable methods of sorting the hardened criminal from the one-time unfortunate, the corrigible from the incorrigible, and the contemporary terminology of high-risk/low-risk is a variation on an old theme, not a new motif.' There has, nevertheless, been a long-running interest in identifying high-risk offenders. Back in the late nineteenth century, for example, there were debates about special measures of confinement for 'those adjudicated to be a danger, or a menace, or some special risk over and above the ordinary' (Baker 2004: 29). It is true, however, that the interest in measuring risk has more recently gathered pace, particularly following the decline of the rehabilitative model in the late 1970s and the consequent emergence of an actuarial model of risk management that classifies groups according to levels of dangerousness (see pp. 26–27). Notably, this model promotes the three 'E's of economics, efficiency and effectiveness, dictating that resources should be concentrated upon high-risk offenders.

Those intensive community programmes that target offenders at high risk of re-offending can be seen, therefore, as adhering to a model of risk management. But this strategy is open to criticism, notably because of the difficulties in predicting further offending and identifying high-risk offenders. Such problems exist even with persistent offenders, Rod Broadhurst (2000: 121) noting that while their 'criminal careers ... often show offence patterns of preference (or specialisation), escalation (progression to more grave offences), as well as variation in the frequency of offending ... [these] offence patterns or transitions have proven complex and their predictive relevance from one event to the next limited'. Unfortunately, the difficulties become even more pronounced, 'the more specific the group and type of risk (offence) being assessed' (*ibid*.: 113). Whether those offenders who commit the more serious offences should necessarily be deemed high risk is particularly controversial: 'it is by no means clear that these serious type offenders represent a high risk for committing future crimes' (Altschuler 1998: 382). Notably, the ISSP evaluation found that offenders qualifying on grounds of seriousness but not persistence had fewer criminogenic needs and therefore a lower risk of re-offending, indicating that they may not have required the same intensity or range of supervision as persistent offenders. Support is again provided, therefore, to the view that the notions of persistence and seriousness should be combined when developing targeting criteria.

The difficulties of predicting an offender's risk of re-offending are further highlighted by Mark Brown (2000: 95): 'risk emerges as a label to denote the presence of particular circumstances of interest, circumstances that may differ considerably depending upon what view of the markers of threat and danger are being invoked by the risk assessor'. In other words, differing risk assessors can reach differing conclusions, and, more fundamentally, there will be variance according to which 'markers' or factors are taken into account. The introduction of standardised risk/needs assessment tools has clearly helped to ensure a more structured approach to measuring the risk of re-offending (see p. 197), but despite the claims of some proponents, they do not ensure complete objectivity, with the exercise of professional judgement remaining through 'the use of subjective rating scales (high/medium/low), interpretative categories and overrides' (Hannah-Moffat 2004: 36). Consequently, Robin Tuddenham (2000: 180) argues that there is a need for 'reflexive risk assessment', which is 'careful not to treat knowledge as immutable, and is realistic about its ability to minimize uncertainty, which increases as time passes. It acknowledges that our definitions and discussions about risk and dangerousness will determine how we respond to it. It recognizes that definitions can be contested, and are culturally relative.'

Perhaps we should not be taken aback by the difficulties encountered in identifying high-risk offenders: 'Given our tendency to miscalculate the risks faced in everyday life … it is perhaps unsurprising that assessment of more serious risks presents considerable challenges to both individual practitioners and organisations' (Baker 2004: 205). Nevertheless, the difficulties lend support to the argument that an emphasis upon risk management needs to be constrained to ensure that risk is seen alongside other social principles and priorities, such as justice and rehabilitation (O'Malley 1997; Robinson 1999). Ashworth (2004: 516–17), for example, states that 'the growing emphasis on risk assessment and risk-based penal policies not only tends to underplay the problems of effectively identifying and dealing with risk but has also led to a neglect of discussions of values and principles'. Hudson (2003: 49) further argues that the growing emphasis upon risk 'at the expense of due process and the principle of proportionality in punishment' signifies 'a shift from risk management to risk control'. While risk management 'recognises the uncertainty associated with risk situations' (Clear and Cadora 2001: 59), risk control seeks to ensure that offenders may not engage in any crimes through policies of containment. The arguments set out here suggest that neither a risk management nor a risk control model should be allowed to predominate.

The dangers of labelling

There are particular concerns that the attempted targeting of persistent and/or high-risk offenders is resulting in the detrimental labelling of a sub-group of offenders as 'innately criminal' (Downes and Morgan 2002: 90). Such concerns, while relevant to all those offenders who are referred on to intensive community programmes, are particularly strong in relation to those who consequently end up in custody. This latter group 'come to be viewed as having failed all attempts to reintegrate and are seen as constituting a new hardcore, intractable and dangerous element of the population' (Muncie 2004: 290–1). The promotion of intensive community programmes as 'last chance saloons' would thus appear especially unhelpful.

The most immediate danger of labelling is one of stigmatisation, encouraging offenders to develop 'a tough "macho" criminal self-image' (Cavadino and Dignan 2002: 35), consequently living up to the labels attached to them. Furthermore, in the youth justice field, Roger Smith (2003: 193) states that labelling will 'contribute to a growing obsession with the wrongdoings of the young – creating a further spiral of increased fear and renewed demands for "quick-fix" solutions'. More generally, Smith argues (2003: 192) that 'the preoccupation with risk is likely to generate a predisposition to seeing the worst in people and focusing unduly on the possibility of failure'. David Garland (2001: 135) uses particularly emotive language in considering the potential implications of crime-control policies: 'Individual offenders come to be seen as "career criminals", "drug addicts", "thugs" and "yobs" with few redeeming features and little social value ... offenders are treated as a different species of threatening, violent individuals for whom we can have no sympathy and for whom there is no effective help.'

These concerns have led to calls for the promotion of more inclusionary measures, through which labelling is avoided, rather than the more exclusionary populist punitive measures that often, as Smith notes above, only amount to 'quick-fix' solutions. A more inclusive approach would help to ensure that social inequalities are not simply 'framed as individual risks' (Kempshall 2002: 48), and that sufficient attention is given to the links between offending and socio-economic deprivation.

Even within the field of criminal justice, contrasts are evident, with youth crime-prevention measures such as Youth Inclusion Projects operating on (modified) inclusive principles, while at the same time, and possibly with the same young people, Intensive Supervision and Surveillance Programmes and 'tagging' are piloted and then 'rolled out'. In international terms, the 'inclusive' strategy borrowed from France can be contrasted with the 'exclusive' model operating in the United States (electronic monitoring and surveillance). Ultimately, these two positions are incompatible, and the policy conflicts they give rise to must be resolved in favour of a more comprehensively inclusive strategy. (Smith 2003: 200)

Intensification and net-widening

In 1979, Stanley Cohen published his highly insightful 'dispersal of discipline' thesis, employing the terminology of net-widening, mesh-thinning and penetration, in an attempt to explain the key features of the developing community corrections movement in England and Wales (see pp. 18–19). Similarly to various other recent developments, the proliferation of intensive community programmes, and many of the research findings, would appear to suggest 'that his predictions are now coming true' (Zedner 2004: 201). First, there are numerous examples of intensive programmes failing to target those offenders who would otherwise have received custodial sentences, and instead up-tariffing those who would have received a less intensive community intervention. Second, even when the programmes have been more successfully confined to those offenders at genuine risk of a custodial sentence, the evidence indicates that there is a consequent risk of 'catapulting the offender into custody when the enormous demands of the programme prove too much' (Cavadino and Dignan 2002: 304). Such an outcome is perhaps fairly predictable:

In order to comply fully with the 'piling up of sanctions', a level of competency and responsibility is required that may well be present in law-abiding citizens with higher education, stronger community ties, and greater financial resources but not in the typical offender participating in intermediate punishment. In essence, a 'middle class measuring rod' underlies what offenders are expected to accomplish as part of their punishment and rehabilitation. (Blomberg and Lucken 1994: 71)

More generally, the introduction of intensive programmes has clearly failed to halt the growing levels of custodial sentencing. The political desire to tackle prison overcrowding has, therefore, so far been thwarted. Some commentators believe that this is unlikely to change, with recent history consistently indicating that newly available prison beds do not remain 'available' for very long: Palumbo, Clifford and Snyder-Joy (1992: 240–1) conclude that, 'As long as the prison beds made available are not retired from service, intermediate punishments very likely add to the overall costs of corrections because they make it possible to increase the total number of people being put under correctional supervision.'

The evidence of net-widening, mesh-thinning and increased penetration have led a number of commentators to consider whether 'more' is necessarily 'better' or whether the general intensification of community penalties is in danger of causing more harm than good (Blomberg and Lucken 1994). For example, in relation to community interventions for young offenders, Cavadino and Dignan (2002: 304) state as follows: 'Even if some of this "tough early intervention" takes positive forms such as reparation or programmes to confront offending behaviour, the tougher you get and the earlier you get tough, the greater the likelihood that young offenders will suffer the adverse effects of stigmatizing "labeling" and accelerate "up the tariff" into overcrowded and damaging custodial institutions before they have a chance to grow out of crime.' Comparing community penalties with custodial sentences would appear to have been particularly unhelpful, as it has tended to divert attention away from the potential for the community options to be 'unwarrantedly punitive, intrusive, or degrading' (Zedner 2004: 203).

With regard to the sentencing of adult offenders in England and Wales, there are now further fears regarding 'sentence stacking' and 'condition creep' due to the introduction of the generic community sentence under the Criminal Justice Act 2003. Carol Hedderman (2005: 5), for example, states that the 'history of the Combination Order … shows that the temptation to overload is considerable and it is not obvious how it will be avoided as sentencers decide which of the many parts of a generic community sentence they should impose'. Seemingly recognising such concerns, the Sentencing Advisory Panel (2004), in its advice to the Sentencing Guidelines Council, has proposed 'three community sentencing ranges based on Low, Medium and High assessments of seriousness'. The Panel further emphasises that the resulting restriction on liberty should be a 'proportionate response to the offence that was committed'. There is close adherence to this advice in the National Implementation Guide for the 2003 Act, which states that the 'over-use of Requirements to address offenders' needs irrespective of the seriousness of the offending must be avoided' (National Probation Service 2005b: 7). Furthermore, the National Probation Service has sought to limit the use of intensive community orders under the 2003 Act: 'There may be occasions where an offender has a number of offending related needs but has not committed a serious offence, which would warrant an intensive community order. In these cases, staff should *not* propose an intensive order but ensure that the requirements proposed are proportionate to the seriousness of the offence and will meet the assessed offending related needs' (National Probation Service 2005a: 4). In other words, a welfare-based approach needs to be constrained by notions of proportionality.

Notably, a number of commentators would appear to favour a reversal of the trend towards intensification, in some instances placing greater significance upon the sentencing principle of parsimony, which requires the penalty imposed to be the least burdensome possible. For example, building upon Braithwaite's theory of 'reintegrative shaming', which favours less onerous levels of punishment, Cavadino and Dignan (2002: 304) advocate an approach that pursues more humanitarian goals with a minimum intervention bias. The principle of parsimony seems particularly relevant to young offenders, with Andrew von Hirsch recognising that young people have special 'developmental' interests. He concludes: 'A way of holding young persons accountable but seeking to reduce damage to their life prospects is to adopt less stringent punishment conventions for adolescents' (von Hirsch 2001: 230). More generally, and with a greater concern for resource limitations, Rod Morgan (2002) has argued that a shift in focus is required, with emphasis being placed upon developing *less* rather than *more* intensive supervision, possibly utilising agencies other than the Probation Service.

These arguments, whether related to the sentencing principle of parsimony or more practical issues such as resources, sit uneasily alongside the widespread adoption of intensive community programmes, particularly when their targeting is not confined to those offenders at genuine risk of a custodial sentence.

The emphasis upon surveillance

Another concept employed by Cohen (1979), in his 'dispersal of discipline' thesis, is that of 'blurring', referring to a breakdown of the traditional institutional/non-institutional divide. A clear example of such 'blurring', and also exemplifying a risk management approach, is the way in which politicians and policy-makers have promoted the surveillant aspects of intensive community programmes. This forms part of a more general promotion of community surveillance for offenders, especially through electronic monitoring (EM). In England and Wales, Jack Straw, the then Home Secretary, referred to tagging as 'the future of community punishment' (Home Office 1997c), while David Blunkett, during his time as Home Secretary, referred to satellite tracking as 'prison without bars' (Home Office 2004e). In assessing this promotion of EM, Mike Nellis (2004b: 15) concludes that it 'vividly symbolizes the way in which traditional humanistic elements in the community supervision field are now being displaced – not augmented – by surveillant elements'.

A number of commentators have raised concerns regarding the promotion of EM (Moore 2005). On the one hand, it has been argued that its benefits have been overstated. In particular, it has been noted that monitoring in the community, of whatever form, does not equate to custody in terms of control: 'The fact that communities are open systems where people have considerable freedom of movement, and not closed-system total institutions (as are prisons), is conveniently ignored by policymakers. Programs such as house arrest and electronic monitoring cannot offer the same level of temporary safety that a prison can offer' (Cochran 1992: 309–10).

More fundamentally, there are concerns that the use of EM can have detrimental effects. Zedner (2004: 221–2) puts forward the following forceful argument: 'the tag shames, but ... it has none of the qualities of "reintegrative shaming" promoted by Braithwaite and others. It labels the offender but provides no means for constructive dialogue with the offender's community, for the expression of remorse, or for eventual reintegration back into civil society ... it may be imagined that this form of observation is ultimately dehumanizing.' Within intensive community programmes, there are fears that EM will hinder the more promising rehabilitative components. Roger Smith (2003: 115), for example, concludes that 'Young people's noses are metaphorically held as the medicine (which is good for them) is forced down. The consequence, however, is that coercion and surveillance inevitably subvert the correctional and reformative aims of the specified intervention.' In support of his view, it was clear from the ISSP evaluation that from the young people's perspective the tag was a dominant feature of the programme, but in some cases it appeared to have only reinforced pro-criminal attitudes and anti-social behaviours.

Maintaining a balance between supervision and surveillance would thus appear crucial. Furthermore, attention needs to be paid to the forms of surveillance adopted. The electronic tag would not always appear appropriate, and there is evidence to support the use of human trackers. Notably, although not associated with reconviction, the ISSP evaluation found that the use of trackers aided completion of the programme, with the trackers providing the young people with valuable pro-social role models, closing the divide between the supervisory and surveillant aspects of the programme. This adheres to various other research findings: 'In work with young offenders, effect sizes have been shown to be larger when a "significant other" person in the young person's life works alongside him or her and also attends individual programmes ... This may be a close relative with whom they have a positive relationship or a mentor who is also familiar with the nature of the programme' (McGuire 2002: 26). A clear drawback of the tag and other forms of EM is that they cannot provide this humanistic element.

An alternative form of surveillance for the young people on ISSP was Intelligence-Led Policing (ILP). During the evaluation, a fully developed and integrated model of ILP had yet to be consistently delivered. Nevertheless, police officers were seen as able to bring to ISSP a number of benefits, including (i) a 'street-wise' knowledge of offenders and offending; (ii) access to police intelligence systems; (iii) a counter-balance to the 'softer' service-oriented values of other practitioners; and (iv) a measure of 'seriousness' and authority in the eyes of offenders. A danger, however, is that the greater involvement of police officers in intensive community programmes such as ISSP will affect the balance between control and care, disproportionately strengthening the first of these two dimensions.

In England and Wales the emergence of NOMS (Carter 2003; Home Office 2004f), with proposals for end-to-end management, the banding of offenders into risk categories, and the commissioning and contestability of probation services at a regional level, means that at present there is considerable uncertainty about how future forms of intensive supervision of both juveniles and adult offenders will be managed and delivered. One interesting question is about the level of joint work with the police that will be permitted or commissioned. At present the police involvement in Prolific Offender Projects (POPs) is considerable and, provided that the projects fit well with local police targets and priorities and the evidence indicates that they contribute to local crime reduction, the police will undoubtedly wish to remain prominent. If, however, police involvement in these schemes is lost, they will then revert to intensive probation schemes with 'policing at the margins' (Chenery and Pease 2000: 6).

Measuring effectiveness and value

While the previous chapter set out the emerging lessons for aiding the design, implementation and delivery of intensive community programmes, there are more fundamental questions as to how their effectiveness and value should be judged. The political interests have centred upon reductions in the levels of custodial sentencing and/or reconviction rates, but evidence of 'success' in relation to both remains limited. However, emphasis could instead be placed upon tackling underlying problems and the reintegration of offenders into the community. Antony Duff and David Garland (1994:24), for example, state: 'We need to ask not just "what works" to bring about for instance a reduction in the frequency of future offending, but also what we should count as "working". Should the penal system be concerned only with reducing future offending, or also with other kinds of improvement in offenders' conduct and circumstances?' In addition to asking whether intensive community programmes *work*, a further question is whether they are *justified*. It may be, for example, that the programmes can be justified solely on the grounds of managing risk or ensuring proportionality in sentencing, rather than other substantive outcomes.

The limitations of reconviction rates

In evaluating intensive community programmes, researchers have adopted differing measures of success and have interpreted their results in very differing ways (see Chapter 2). Attention has tended to focus upon reconviction rates, but on their own these rates cannot assess the processes underlying any change (Pawson and Tilley 1994). It is also important to recognise that reconviction rates have a number of well-known shortcomings, including 'being an undercount of actual offending; being affected by changes in police and prosecution practice; being an all or nothing measure; not accounting for severity or frequency of offence; and being a proxy for re-offending' (Harper and Chitty 2004: viii).

For intensive community programmes, it is important to bear in mind that the improved levels of surveillance may raise reconviction rates. Such improvements in the level and speed of detection can be viewed positively: 'As programs move away from rehabilitation and toward surveillance and control, some might argue that higher arrest rates should be seen as an indication of program success, not failure, especially when dealing with high-risk probationers' (Petersilia and Turner 1992: 656). In POP schemes, for example, high levels of arrests, convictions, breaches and prison recalls are identified as positive features of the schemes, helping to explain why they have received strong police endorsement. In many respects, this results in 'a "win/win" situation, complicating evaluation and raising clear questions about definitions of "success"' (Worrall and Walton 2000: 36). Lloyd, Mair and Hough (1994: 3) are thus surely right to conclude that 'it is all too easy to condemn one penal disposal for a reconviction rate of 70 per cent and praise another for a rate of 35 per cent without knowing anything about the disposals in question and what they aimed to do'.

Stephen Farrall (2003) notes that outcomes of probation have generally been conceptualised as dichotomous, rather than assessing any degree of achievement of a given programme. Unfortunately, such an approach significantly limits the interpretation of possible outcomes, both theoretically and in terms of substantive results. It is particularly inappropriate for those intensive community programmes that are targeting the most persistent offenders, for whom low reconviction and high completion rates are unlikely. It is more probable that, during the course of a programme, these offenders might reduce the frequency or gravity of their offending. When measuring such reductions, the complication of 'regression to the mean' needs to be recognised. Such regression is a common but not particularly well understood phenomenon, which is caused by the tendency for the offending frequency of persistent offenders to fluctuate from one time period to the next. Since the entry requirements for intensive programmes, such as ISSP, are often a period of frequent offending, it is not surprising that some reductions in offending should occur during the follow-up period (Loeber and Farrington 1998). Such fluctuations also help to explain those research findings that indicate that persistent offenders are a transitory group (see pp. 203–205).

Other outcome measures

It can be strongly argued that a limited impact upon reconviction should not necessarily be seen as indicative of programme failure, provided that progress can be shown to have been made in other ways. Such progress could, for example, take the form of improvements in the offender's behaviour, attitudes or social circumstances, all of which are potentially associated with offending (Underdown 1998). Promisingly, the ISSP study found quantitative evidence of inroads being made into tackling personal and social problems, while the qualitative evidence suggested that the young people and their families appreciated the support provided. A number of the ISSP schemes were found to employ much wider definitions of 'success'. In some of the 'more difficult' cases, any form of engagement with the young person was judged a success, as were any resulting changes in attitude or behaviour, criminal or otherwise.

> Success comes in many forms, it depends how you define it really. It's about support and awareness and being functional for some young people, it's about giving them a direction ... having one-to-one and building professional relationships with their workers and seriously attempting to change their behaviour. Success is sometimes the completion element. Success is seeing them turn around and changing from an obnoxious young person to enjoying doing sport, or music or whatever they're into ... Success is knowing that they're not in court every week for petty silly things. (ISSP manager)

In taking into account a wider range of factors, it is also worth considering the alternatives. Further research is needed to assess whether intermediate outcomes for intensive community programmes are better than those for the less intensive alternatives, although the qualitative evidence from ISSP would suggest much promise. As for the alternative of custody, the cost of incarcerating large numbers of high-risk offenders is politically prohibitive, and custodial sentencing is potentially damaging in other ways (see pp. 13–15). Notably, short-term custodial sentences are unable to provide any continuity in provision, frustrating rehabilitative aspirations.

Other reasons for adopting a range of outcome measures are provided by Michael Maltz (1984). Having listed a series of correctional goals which he groups into those relating to the offender, those relating to society and those relating to the correctional institution, he recognises that reconviction rates should not be used to measure the goals of the latter two categories, and cannot measure all the goals of the first category. On this basis, he concludes that further outcome measures are needed for a more in-depth analysis of effectiveness: 'With such diverse correctional goals one cannot expect a single measure of effectiveness to cover the waterfront; measures of similar diversity are required.' Adhering to this view, Joshua Meisel (2001: 242) states that, 'Even if the impact of relationships on recidivism cannot be established, there may still be value in improving the quality of relationship between case managers and youth', while Anne Worrall and Rob Mawby (2004: 285) argue that appropriate outcome measures should encompass 'on the one hand, health, educational and social benefits for participants and, on the other hand, improved multi-agency working and information exchange between project partners, and improved intelligence on prolific offenders'. In relation to youth justice, the value of examining a variety of outcomes has been highlighted by David Smith (2005) who recognises that 'effectiveness' could focus upon consequences such as behaviour change and crime reduction, or alternatively emphasise justice, symbolic values and victim satisfaction.

Taking into account wider institutional goals would appear to sit well with practitioners. For example, in the IMPACT probation experiment, the officers highlighted a wide range of outcome criteria, encompassing not only reconviction and personality changes in the offenders but also acceptance of new approaches by the probation service and increases in their own casework skills (Folkard *et al.* 1974: 45). In the US, meanwhile, a key factor for probation administrators has been the ability of intensive community programmes to present the function of probation 'in a new light', re-establishing the service and bringing it back to the policy table (Clear 1997: 131). It is perhaps questionable, however, whether such institutional factors should truly be seen as programme goals or appropriate outcome measures rather than useful by-products.

Ensuring proportionality

As for more general societal goals, it was shown in Chapter 1 that the theoretical foundations of intensive community programmes are multi-faceted and that programmes can be classified as welfare-based, proportionate, risk management or authoritarian interventions. Importantly, a number of the objectives of sentencing, including retribution, reparation, general deterrence and denunciation, cannot be measured by the use of reconviction rates (Lloyd, Mair and Hough 1994). This is particularly significant when one considers that some commentators have abandoned forward-looking considerations, arguing that intensive community penalties should be judged on more backward-looking retributivist grounds by considering the contribution to 'just deserts'. The emphasis here is upon delivering appropriate punishment rather than other substantive outcomes, and it can be argued that even if the research fails to demonstrate improvements in the offenders' underlying problems and/or offending behaviour, the programmes can still be seen as having value if they assist sentencers in tailoring sentences to differing types of offending. Notably, there is a perception among many sentencers, as confirmed by the ISSP evaluation, that the divide between standard probation and custody is too wide, and that the courts have lacked an appropriate middle option.

> Discussions about whether ISP is a promising direction for crime-control policy must therefore move from micro-level questions, such as whether programs benefit their subjects, to macro-level concerns about ISP programs' contributions to overall sentencing policy. The most compelling reason for continued development of ISP programs is the criminal justice system objective of just deserts, i.e., making the punishment fit the crime. (Petersilia and Turner 1992: 652)

The promotion of intensive community programmes as proportionate interventions would have the advantage of ensuring that sufficient attention was paid to the appropriate targeting criteria. Persistent petty offenders are very different from those who commit one-off serious offences, and it was argued above that to ensure a level of proportionality the concepts of persistence and seriousness should be combined. In promoting proportionality, an important debate is raised as to whether intensive community programmes should be viewed as having less punitive value than custody, potentially raising the spectre of Cohen's 'dispersal of discipline' thesis. As was set out in the CJA 1991, community penalties are traditionally seen as lying in a middle band of severity between fines and discharges at the low end and custody at the top end. However, practitioners and many of the offenders viewed ISSP as a very tough and punitive programme, and, in some cases, it was seen as the more difficult option for the offender when compared to custody, particularly when the intensive supervision was combined with an electronic tag. Sentencers, on the other hand, remained of the belief that a custodial sentence was the only option in certain instances, supporting the view of Hedderman (2005: 7) that 'it is time we recognised that there are no alternatives to custody as far as sentencers are concerned'.

While further debate is clearly required as to the punitive value of intensive community programmes, highlighting the issue of proportionality could, at the very least, help to draw attention to more general sentencing levels. Such a need has been increasingly expressed by a number of commentators in England and Wales, who have advocated the resurrection of the concept of proportionality:

> In our view it has become urgent to reintroduce the topic of proportionality into discussions on alternatives to prison. In relation to non-custodial sanctions, proportionality seems to have been overlooked lately, given the overwhelming late-modern emphasis on risk, and/or the eagerness to embrace new approaches to divert offenders from a custodial sentence ... Unless proportionality is accorded a significant role in sentencing, there is a real danger that non-custodial sentences will slip still further down tariff than they already have, and increasingly complex and intensive orders will be imposed on offenders who have been convicted of relatively minor offenders. (Bottoms, Rex and Robinson 2004: 419)

Summary

Despite the developing evidence-base for intensive community programmes, there are a number of outstanding critical concerns, reflecting inherent theoretical tensions. The targeting of such programmes remains problematic, with significant difficulties having been encountered in defining both persistence and seriousness and in identifying high-risk offenders. A degree of arbitrariness seems inevitable, and there are growing concerns that the targeting of particular groups is resulting in a labelling of a sub-group of offenders as 'innately criminal'. While risk management provides a theoretical basis for intensive community programmes, these difficulties and concerns suggest that any emphasis upon this model needs to be constrained to ensure that risk is seen alongside other social principles and priorities, such as justice and rehabilitation. More specifically, it can be argued that (i) notions of persistence and seriousness should be combined, helping to ensure that offenders are high risk while maintaining a level of proportionality in sentencing under the 'just deserts' model; and (ii) efforts should be focused upon developing more inclusionary measures.

There are accompanying fears that the expansion of intensive programmes is resulting in wider, denser and different nets of social control, with some offenders being up-tariffed into these programmes and other offenders being sent to custody for breaching their demanding requirements. It has become increasingly recognised that more is not necessarily better, and some critics have argued that the emphasis should shift to developing less rather than more intensive supervision. There are specific concerns regarding the role of electronic monitoring, with policy-makers tending to overstate its potential benefits under a risk management approach, set against growing evidence that it can have detrimental effects. The role of the police in intensive programmes also needs careful consideration, helping to ensure that a balance between control and care is maintained.

Doubts remain as to the optimum approach for measuring effectiveness. Notably, a focus upon reconviction rates can be criticised as not only too narrow but epistemologically flawed, with a number of commentators highlighting the need for a more integrated model of evaluation and the need to take into account further outcome measures. More fundamentally, general societal goals and a number of the objectives of sentencing cannot be measured by the use of reconviction rates. Some critics, for example, have argued that the contribution of intensive programmes to 'just deserts' should be viewed as a paramount concern. During the rapid proliferation of intensive community programmes, accompanied by uncertainties regarding the most appropriate targeting, the importance of maintaining a level of proportionality has arguably been forgotten. The value of intensive community programmes as proportionate interventions should, therefore, be more widely recognised, helping to refocus attention more generally upon sentencing levels.

Returning to the theoretical basis for intensive community programmes, it was shown in Chapter 1 that the programmes could be promoted as welfare-based interventions, proportionate interventions, risk management interventions and/or authoritarian interventions. Their theoretical foundations are thus multi-faceted, attempting to fuse consequentialist forward-looking rationales of deterrence, incapacitation and rehabilitation with backward-looking retribution and a promotion of 'just deserts'. The limitations of incapacitation and deterrence are clearly demonstrated by the empirical evidence, and the analysis set out in this chapter leads to the conclusion that less emphasis should be placed upon risk and greater emphasis upon proportionality. As Hedderman (2005: 6) states, 'Given that risk cannot be accurately assessed for individuals with much certainty, advice in court reports on suitable sentences should always be limited by a consideration of proportionality.'

Within the boundaries of 'just deserts', the intensity and flexibility of intensive community programmes also provide the basis for a strong rehabilitative dimension, adhering to a welfare-based model.

Efforts need to be made to ensure that programmes are tailored to the individual offender and his or her criminogenic needs. For young offenders, sufficient attention should be paid to their developmental needs, while for all offenders, emphasis should be placed upon their reintegration back into civil society, with all statutory services fulfilling their obligations. In this sense, it would appear that much could be gained from a careful balance of the traditional welfare and justice models of penology, ensuring that rehabilitative aspirations are not lost, while recognising the right of offenders not to be punished disproportionately.

References

Allen, R. (1991) 'Out of Jail: The Reduction in the Use of Penal Custody for Male Juveniles 1981–88', *Howard Journal*, 30: 30–52.

Altschuler, D. M. (1998) 'Intermediate sanctions and community treatment for Serious and Violent Juvenile Offenders', in R. Loeber and D. P. Farrington (eds), *Serious and Violent Juvenile Offenders: Risk Factors and Successful Interventions*. Thousand Oaks: Sage.

Armstrong, T. L. (ed.) (1991) *Intensive Interventions with High-Risk Youths: Promising Approaches in Juvenile Probation and Parole*. Monsey: Willow Tree Press.

Ashworth, A. (2002) 'Sentencing', in M. Maguire, R. Morgan and R. Reiner (eds), *The Oxford Handbook of Criminology*. Oxford: Oxford University Press.

Ashworth, A. (2004) 'Criminal Justice Reform: Principles, Human Rights and Public Protection', *Criminal Law Review*, 516–32.

Audit Commission (1996) *Misspent Youth: Young People and Crime*. London: Audit Commission.

Audit Commission (1999) *Children in Mind: Child and Adolescent Health Services*. London: Audit Commission.

Audit Commission (2004) *Youth Justice 2004: A Review of the Reformed Youth Justice System*. London: Audit Commission.

Baker, K. (2004) *Risk Assessment of Young Offenders*. Oxford: University of Oxford (unpublished D-Phil thesis).

Baker, K., Jones, S., Roberts, C. and Merrington, S. (2002) *Validity and Reliability of ASSET Findings from the First Two Years of the Use of ASSET*. Oxford: Probation Studies Unit, Centre for Criminological Research.

Bala, N. and Roberts, J. V. (2004) *Canada's Juvenile Justice System: Increasing Community-Based Responses to Youth Crime*. European Society of Criminology Meeting, August 2004.

Barnett, A., Blumstein, A. and Farrington, D. (1987) 'Probabilistic Models of Youthful Criminal Careers', *Criminology*, 25: 83–107.

Barnett, A., Blumstein, A. and Farrington, D. (1989) 'A Prospective Test of a Criminal Career Model', *Criminology*, 27: 373–88.

Barton, W. H. and Butts, J. A. (1990) 'Viable Options: Intensive Supervision Programs for Juvenile Delinquents', *Crime and Delinquency*, 36: 238–56.

Becker, H. S. (1963) *Outsiders: Studies in the Sociology of Deviance*. London: Macmillan.

Blomberg, T. and Lucken, K. (1994) 'Stacking the Deck by Piling Up Sanctions', *Howard Journal*, 33: 62–80.

Blumstein, A., Cohen, J., Roth, J. and Visher, C. (eds), (1986) *Criminal Careers and Career Criminals*, two volumes. Washington DC: National Academy Press.

Bonta, J. L. (1996) 'Risk-needs Assessment and Treatment', in A. T. Harland (ed.), *Choosing Correctional Options that Work*. Thousand Oaks: Sage.

Bonta, J., Rooney, J. and Wallace-Capretta, S. (1999) *Electronic Monitoring in Canada*. Canada: Public Works and Government Services.

Bonta, J., Wallace-Capretta, S. and Rooney, J. (2000) 'A Quasi-experimental Evaluation of an Intensive Rehabilitation Supervision Program', *Criminal Justice and Behavior*, 27: 312–29.

Boswell, G., Davies, M. and Wright, A. (1993) *Contemporary Probation Practice*. Aldershot: Avebury.

Bottoms, A. E. (1983) 'Neglected Features of Contemporary Penal Systems' in D. Garland and P. Young (eds), *The Power to Punish: Contemporary Penality and Social Analysis*. London: Heinemann Educational.

Bottoms, A. (1995) *Intensive Community Supervision for Young Offenders: Outcomes, Process and Cost*. Cambridge: Institute of Criminology Publications.

Bottoms, A., Brown, P., McWilliams, B., McWilliams, W. and Nellis, M. (1990) *Intermediate Treatment and Juvenile Justice*. London: HMSO.

Bottoms, A., Rex, S. and Robinson, G. (2004) *Alternatives to Prison: Options for an Insecure Society*. Cullompton: Willan Publishing.

Brand, S. and Price, R. (2000) *The Economic and Social Costs of Crime*, Home Office Research Study 217. London: Home Office.

Broadhurst, R. (2000) 'Criminal Careers, Sex Offending and Dangerousness', in M. Brown and J. Pratt (eds), *Dangerous Offenders: Punishment and Social Order*. London: Routledge.

Brody, S. R. (1976) *The Effectiveness of Sentencing*, Home Office Research Study 35. London: HMSO.

Bronfenbrenner, U. (1979) *The Ecology of Human Development: Experiments by Nature and Design*. Cambridge, MA: Harvard University Press.

Brown, M. (2000) 'Calculations of Risk in Contemporary Penal Practice', in M. Brown and J. Pratt (eds), *Dangerous Offenders: Punishment and Social Order*. London: Routledge.

Brownlee, I. (1995) 'Intensive Probation with Young Adult Offenders: A Short Reconviction Study', *British Journal of Criminology*, 35: 599–612.

Brownlee, I. D. and Joanes, D. (1993) 'Intensive Probation for Young Adult Offenders: Evaluating the Impact of a Non-Custodial Sentence', *British Journal of Criminology*, 33(2): 216–30.

Bryman, A. (1988) *Quantity and Quality in Social Research*. London: Unwin Hyman.

Budd, T., Sharp, C. and Mayhew, P. (2005) *Offending in England and Wales: First Results from the 2003 Crime and Justice Survey*, Home Office Research Study 275. London: Home Office.

Bureau of Justice (2004) *Prison and Jail Inmates at Midyear 2003*. Washington: Bureau of Justice.

Burnett, R. (2004) 'One-to-one Ways of Promoting Desistance: In Search of an Evidence Base', in R. Burnett and C. Roberts (eds), *What Works in Probation and Youth Justice: Developing Evidence-Based Practice*. Cullompton: Willan Publishing.

Burnett, R. and Appleton, C. (2004) 'Joined-Up Services to Tackle Youth Crime: A Case-Study in England', *British Journal of Criminology*, 44: 34–54.

Burnett, R. and Maruna, S. (2004) 'So "Prison Works", Does It? The Criminal Careers of 130 Men Released from Prison under Home Secretary, Michael Howard', *Howard Journal*, 43(4): 390–404.

Carter, H., Klein, R. and Day, P. (1992) *How Organisations Measure Success: The Use of Performance Indicators*. London: Routledge.

Carter, P. (2003) *Managing Offenders, Reducing Crime: A New Approach*. London: The Stationery Office.

Cavadino, M. and Dignan, J. (2002) *The Penal System: An Introduction*. London: Sage.

Chenery, S. and Deakin, E. (2003) *Evaluation of the Blackpool Tower Project: Final Report*. Blackpool Community Safety Partnership.

Chenery, S. and Pease, K. (2000) *The Burnley/Dordecht Initiative Final Report*. Burnley: University of Huddersfield /Safer Cities Partnership.

Children's Society (1989) *Penal Custody for Juveniles – The Line of Least Resistance*. London: Children's Society.

Clear, T. R. (1991) 'Juvenile Intensive Probation Supervision: Theory and Rationale', in T. L. Armstrong (ed.), *Intensive Interventions with High-Risk Youths: Promising Approaches in Juvenile Probation and Parole*. Monsey: Willow Tree Press.

Clear, T. R. (1997) 'Evaluating Intensive Probation: the American Experience', in G. Mair (ed.), *Evaluating the Effectiveness of Community Penalties*. Aldershot: Avebury.

Clear, T. and Cadora, E. (2001) 'Risk and Community Practice', in K. Stenson and R. R. Sullivan (eds), *Crime, Risk and Justice: The Politics of Crime Control in Liberal Democracies*. Cullompton: Willan Publishing.

Cochran, D. (1992) 'The Long Road from Policy Development to Real Change in Sanctioning Practice', in J. M. Byrne, A. J. Lurigio and J. Petersilia (eds), *Smart Sentencing: The Emergence of Intermediate Sanctions.* Newbury Park: Sage.

Cohen, M. A. (2001) 'To Treat or Not to Treat? A Financial Perspective', in C. R. Hollin (ed.), *Handbook of Offender Assessment and Treatment,* Chichester: John Wiley.

Cohen, S. (1979) 'The Punitive City: Notes on the Dispersal of Social Control', *Contemporary Crises,* 3: 339–63.

Cohen, S. (1985) *Visions of Social Control.* Cambridge: Polity Press.

Connell, J. and Kubisch, A. (2002) 'Applying a Theory of Change Approach to the Evaluation of Comprehensive Community Initiatives: Progress, Prospects and Problems', in J. Fullbright, K. Anderson, A. Kubisch and J. Connell (eds), *New Approaches to Evaluating Community Initiatives, Volume 2: Theory Measurement and Analysis.* Washington: Aspen Institute.

Cook, T. D. and Campbell, D. T. (1979) *Quasi-Experimentation: Design and Analysis Issues for Field Settings.* Chicago: Rand McNally.

Coulsfield Inquiry (2004) *Crime, Courts and Confidence: Report of an Independent Inquiry into Alternatives to Prison.* London: Esmée Fairbairn Foundation.

Councell, R. (2003) *The Prison Population in 2002: A Statistical Review,* Home Office Research Findings 228. London: Home Office.

Crawford, A. (1997) *The Local Governance of Crime: Appeals to Community and Partnerships.* Oxford: Clarendon Press.

Crawford, A. and Newburn, T. (2002) 'Recent Developments in Restorative Justice for Young People in England and Wales: Community Participation and Restoration', *British Journal of Criminology,* 42(3): 476–95.

Crawford, A. and Newburn, T. (2003) *Youth Offending and Restorative Justice: Implementing Reform in Youth Justice.* Cullompton: Willan Publishing.

Criminal Sanctions Agency (2003) *Annual Report of the Finnish Prison and Probation Services 2002.* Helsinki: Criminal Sanctions Agency.

Cullen, F. T. and Gendreau, P. (2000) 'Assessing Correctional Rehabilitation: Policy, Practice, and Prospects', in J. Horney (ed.), *Criminal Justice 2000.* Washington DC: Department of Justice, National Institute of Justice.

Dawson, P. (2005) *Early Findings from the Prolific and Other Priority Offenders Evaluation,* Home Office Development and Practice Report 46. London: Home Office.

Debidin, M. and Lovbakke, J. (2004) 'Offending Behaviour Programmes in Prison and Probation', in G. Harper and C. Chitty (eds), *The Impact of Corrections on Re-offending: A Review of 'What Works',* Home Office Research Study 291. London: Home Office.

Dhiri, S. and Brand, S. (1999) *Analysis of Costs and Benefits: Guidance for Evaluators,* Crime Reduction Programme – Guidance Note 1. London: Home Office.

Downes, D. (2001) 'The Macho Penal Economy', *Punishment and Society,* 3(1): 61–80.

Downes, D. and Morgan, R. (2002) 'The British General Election 2001: The Centre Right Consensus', *Punishment and Society*, 4(1): 81–96.

Drakeford, M. (1993) 'The Probation Service, Breach and the Criminal Justice Act 1991', *Howard Journal*, 32(4): 291–302.

Dubourg, R., Hamed, J. and Thorns, J. (2005) *The Economic and Social Costs of Crime against Individuals and Households*, Home Office Online Report 30/05. London: Home Office.

Duff, A. and Garland, D. (1994) *A Reader on Punishment*. Oxford: Oxford University Press.

Ely, P., Swift, A. and Sutherland, A. (1987) *Control Without Custody: Non-Custodial Control of Juvenile Offenders*. Edinburgh: Scottish Academic Press.

Errington, J. (1985) 'In Defence of Tracking', *Social Work Today*, 21 January: 3.

Fagan, J. A. and Reinarman, C. (1991) 'The Social Context of Intensive Supervision: Organisational and Ecological Influences on Community Treatment of Violent Adolescents', in T. L. Armstrong (ed.), *Intensive Interventions with High-Risk Youths: Promising Approaches in Juvenile Probation and Parole*. Monsey: Willow Tree Press.

Farrall, S. (2002) *Rethinking What Works with Offenders: Probation, Social Context and Desistance from Crime*. Cullompton: Willan Publishing.

Farrall, S. (2003) 'J'accuse: Probation Evaluation-Research Epistemologies (Part One: The Critique)', *Criminal Justice*, 3(2): 161–79.

Farrington, D. and West, D. (1993) 'Criminal, Penal and Life Histories of Chronic Offenders: Risk and Protective Factors and Early Identification', *Criminal Behaviour and Mental Health*: 3, 492–523.

Farrington, P., Ditchfield, J., Hancock, G., Howard, P., Jolliffe, D., Livingston, M. S. and Painter, K. A. (2002) *Evaluation of Two Intensive Regimes for Young Offenders*, Home Office Research Study 239. London: Home Office.

Feeley, M. and Simon, J. (1994) 'Actuarial Justice: The Emerging New Criminal Law', in D. Nelken (ed.), *The Futures of Criminology*. London: Sage.

Flood-Page, C. and Mackie, A. (1998) *Sentencing Practice: An Examination of Decisions in Magistrates' Courts and the Crown Court in the Mid-1990s*, Home Office Research Study 180. London: Home Office.

Folkard, M. S., Fowles, A. J., McWilliams, B. C., McWilliams, W., Smith, D. D., Smith, D. E. and Walmsley, G .R. (1974) *IMPACT Intensive Matched Probation and After-Care Treatment: Volume I. The Design of the Probation Experiment and an Interim Evaluation*, Home Office Research Study 24. London: HMSO.

Folkard, M. S., Smith, D. E. and Smith, D. D. (1976) *IMPACT Intensive Matched Probation and After-Care Treatment: Volume II. The Results of the Experiment*, Home Office Research Study 36. London: HMSO.

Friendship, C., Street, R., Cann, J. and Harper, G. (2004) 'Introduction: The Policy Context and Assessing the Evidence', in G. Harper and C. Chitty (eds), *The Impact of Corrections on Re-offending: A Review of 'What Works'*, Home Office Research Study 291. London: Home Office.

Garland, D. (2001) *The Culture of Control: Crime and Social Order in Contemporary Society*. Oxford: Oxford University Press.

Garside, R. (2004) *Crime, Persistent Offenders and the Justice Gap*. London: Crime and Society Foundation.

Gendreau, P., Cullen, F. T. and Bonta, J. (1994) 'Intensive Rehabilitation Supervision: The Next Generation in Community Corrections?', *Federal Probation*, 58: 72–8.

Gendreau, P., Goggin, C. and Fulton, B. (2000) 'Intensive Supervision in Probation and Parole Settings', in C. R. Hollin (ed.), *Handbook of Offender Assessment and Treatment*. Chichester: John Wiley.

Gibb, F. and Ford, R. (2005) 'Row Over Tagging After Fresh Youth Crime Spree', *The Times*, 28 October.

Gibbs, A. and King, D. (2003) 'The Electronic Ball and Chain? The Operation and Impact of Home Detention with Electronic Monitoring in New Zealand', *Australian and New Zealand Journal of Criminology*, 36(1): 1–17.

Glueck, S. and Glueck, E. (1950) *Unravelling Juvenile Delinquency*. New York: Commonwealth Fund.

Goodstein, L. and Sontheimer, H. (1997) 'The Implementation of an Intensive Aftercare Program for Serious Juvenile Offenders', *Criminal Justice and Behavior*, 24: 352–9.

Gottfredson, M. and Hirschi, T. (1986) *A General Theory of Crime*. Stanford, CA: Stanford University Press.

Graham, J. and Bowling, B. (1995) *Young People and Crime*, Home Office Research Study 145. London: Home Office.

Gray, E., Taylor, E., Roberts, C., Merrington, S., Moore, R. and Fernandez, R. (2005) *ISSP: The Final Report*. London: Youth Justice Board for England and Wales.

Hagell, A. and Newburn, T. (1994) *Persistent Young Offenders*. London: Policy Studies Institute.

Hancock, B. W. and Sharp, P. M. (2004) *Criminal Justice in America: Theory, Practice and Policy*. Upper Saddle River, NJ: Prentice Hall.

Hannah-Moffat, K. (2004) 'Criminogenic Needs and the Transformative Risk Subject: Hybridizations of Risk/need in Penality', *Punishment and Society*, 7(1): 29–51.

Harper, G. and Chitty, C. (2004) *The Impact of Corrections on Re-offending: A Review of 'What Works'*, Home Office Research Study 291. London: Home Office.

Heckman, J. (1979) 'Sample Selection Bias as a Specification Error', *Econometrica*, 47: 153–61.

Heckman, J., Ichimura, H. and Todd, P. (1997) 'Matching as an Econometric Evaluation Estimator: Evidence from Evaluating a Job Training Programme', *Review of Economic Studies*, 64: 605–54.

Hedderman, C. (2004) 'Testing Times: How the Policy and Practice Environment Shaped the Creation of the "what works" evidence-base', *Vista*, 8(3): 182–88.

Hedderman, C. (2005) 'NOMS and the Prison Population: Does NOMS Have the Courage to Keep the Prison Population Down?', *Prison Service Journal*, 162: 3–7.

Hedderman, C. and Hough, M. (2004) 'Getting Tough or Being Effective: What Matters?', in Mair, G. (ed.), *What Matters in Probation*. Cullompton: Willan Publishing.

Hill, D. (1992) *Intensive Probation Practice: An Option for the 1990s*. Norwich: Social Work Monographs.

von Hirsch, A. (2001) 'Proportionate Sentences for Juveniles: How Different Than for Adults?', *Punishment and Society*, 3(2): 221–36.

von Hirsch, A., Bottoms, A. E., Burney, E. and Wikström, P.-O. (1999) *Criminal Deterrence and Sentence Severity: An Analysis of Recent Research*. Oxford: Hart Publishing.

HM Chief Inspector of Constabulary *et al*. (2004) *Joint Inspection Report into Persistent and Prolific Offenders*. London: Home Office Communications Directorate.

HM Court Service (2005) *Effective Practice Guide – Breaches of Community Penalties*. London: HM Court Service.

HM Inspectorate of Probation (2005) *Inquiry into the Supervision of Peter Williams by Nottingham City Youth Offending Team*. London: HMIP.

Hollin, C. R. (1995) 'Reducing Re-offending and "programme integrity"', in J. McGuire (ed.), *What Works: Reducing Reoffending: Guidelines from Research and Practice*, Chichester: John Wiley.

Holt, P. (2001) 'Case Management: Context for Supervision', *Vista*, 6(2): 111–26.

Home Office (1990) *Crime, Justice and Protecting the Public: The Government's Proposals for Legislation*. London: HMSO.

Home Office (1997a) *No More Excuses: A New Approach to Tackling Youth Crime in England and Wales*. London: HMSO.

Home Office (1997b) *Tackling Delays in the Youth Justice System: A Consultation Paper*. London: The Stationery Office.

Home Office (1997c) *Electronic Monitoring – The Future of Community Punishment*, Home Office Press Release, 12 November 1997.

Home Office (1999) *Information on the Criminal Justice System in England and Wales: Digest 4*. London: Home Office.

Home Office (2000) *Crime Reduction Programme Guidance Note 3: Measuring Inputs: Guidance for Evaluator*. London: The Stationery Office.

Home Office (2001) *Criminal Justice – The Way Ahead*. London: The Stationery Office.

Home Office (2002) *Justice For All*. London: The Stationery Office.

Home Office (2003) *Prison Statistics England and Wales 2002*. London: The Stationery Office.

Home Office (2004a) *Probation Statistics England and Wales 2002*. London: The Stationery Office.

Home Office (2004b) *Offender Management Caseload Statistics 2003 England and Wales*. London: Home Office.

Home Office (2004c) *Managing Compliance and Enforcement of Community Sentences*, Probation Circular 43/2004. London: Home Office.

Home Office (2004d) *Confident Communities in a Secure Britain: The Home Office Strategic Plan 2004–08*. London: Home Office.

Home Office (2004e) *Eye in the Sky Launched to Monitor Offenders*, Home Office Press Release, 2 September 2004.

Home Office (2004f) *Reducing Crime, Changing Lives*. London: Home Office.

Home Office (2005) *Restructuring Probation to Reduce Re-offending*, NOMS consultation document. London: Home Office.

Homes, A., Walmsley, R. K. and Debidin, M. (2005) *Intensive Supervision and Monitoring Schemes for Persistent Offenders: Staff and Offender Perceptions*, Home Office Development and Practice Report 41. London: Home Office.

Hood, R. (2002). 'Criminology and Penal Policy: The Vital Role of Empirical Research', in A. Bottoms and M. Tonry (eds), *Ideology, Crime and Criminal Justice*. Cullompton: Willan Publishing.

Hough, M., Clancy, A., McSweeney, T. and Turnball, P. J. (2003) *The Impact of Drug Treatment and Testing Orders on Offending: Two-Year Reconviction Results*, Home Office Research Findings 184. London: Home Office.

Hudson, B. (2001) 'Punishment, Rights and Difference: Defending Justice in the Risk Society', in K. Stenson and R. R. Sullivan (eds), *Crime, Risk and Justice: The Politics of Crime Control in Liberal Democracies*. Cullompton: Willan Publishing.

Hudson, B. (2003) *Justice in the Risk Society: Challenging and Re-affirming Justice in Late Modernity*. London: Sage.

Joint Committee on Human Rights (2003) *The UN Convention on the Rights of the Child*, Tenth Report of Session 2002:03. London: The Stationery Office.

Jolin, A. and Stipak, B. (1992) 'Drug Treatment and Electronically Monitored Home Confinement: An Evaluation of a Community-Based Sentencing Option', *Crime & Delinquency*, 38(2): 158–70.

Kempf-Leonard, K. and Peterson, E. S. L. (2002) 'Expanding Realms of the New Penology: The Advent of Actuarial Justice for Juveniles', in J. Muncie, G. Hughes and E. McLaughlin (eds), *Youth Justice: Critical Readings*. London: Sage.

Kempshall, H. (2002) 'Effective Practice in Probation: An Example of "Advanced Liberal" Responsibilisation?', *Howard Journal*, 41: 41–58.

Key, J. (2001) 'The Rotherham Experience of Intensive Supervision: A Message from a Seasoned Practitioner', *Youth Justice Matters*, 10–12.

Knott, C. (2004) 'Evidence-based Practice in the National Probation Service', in R. Burnett and C. Roberts (eds), *What Works in Probation and Youth Justice: Developing Evidence-Based Practice*. Cullompton: Willan Publishing.

Laird, N. M. and Mosteller, F. (1990) 'Some Statistical Methods for Combining Experimental Results', *International Journal of Technology Assessment in Health Care*, 6(1): 5–30.

Latessa, E. J. and Vito, G. F. (1988) 'The Effects of Intensive Supervision on Shock Probationers', *Journal of Criminal Justice*, 16: 319–30.

Lee, C. and Wildgoose, K. (2005) *Prolific and Other Priority Offender Strategy Premium Service*. London: Office for Criminal Justice Reform.

Lewis, S., Vennard, J., Maguire, M., Raynor, P., Vanstone, M., Raybould, S. and Rix, A. (2003) *The Resettlement of Short-Term Prisoners: An Evaluation of Seven Pathfinders*, RDS Occasional Paper No. 83. London: The Stationery Office.

Lewis, S. (2005) 'Rehabilitation: Headline or Footnote in the New Penal Policy?', *Probation Journal*, 52(2): 119–35.

Lipton, D., Martinson, R. and Wilks, J. (1975) *Effectiveness of Treatment Evaluation Studies*. New York: Praeger.

Lipsey, M. W. (1992) 'Juvenile Delinquency Treatment: A Meta-Analytic Inquiry into the Variability of Effects', in T. Cook, D. Cooper, H. Corday, H. Hartman, L. Hedges, R. Light, T. Louis and F. Mosteller (eds), *Meta-analysis for Explanation: A Casebook*. New York: Russell Sage Foundation.

Lipsey, M. W. (1995) 'What Do We Learn from 400 Studies on the Effectiveness of Treatment with Juvenile Delinquents?', in J. McGuire (ed.), *What Works: Reducing Re-offending: Guidelines from Research and Practice*, Chichester: John Wiley.

Little, M., Kogan, J., Bullock, R. and Van der Lann, P. (2004) 'ISSP: An Experiment in Multi-Systemic Responses to Persistent Young Offenders Known to Children's Services', *British Journal of Criminology*, 44: 225–40.

Lloyd, C., Mair, G. and Hough, M. (1994) *Explaining Reconviction Rates: A Critical Analysis*, Home Office Research Study 136. London: HMSO.

Lobley, D., Smith, D., and Stern, C. (2001) *Freagarrach: An Evaluation of a Project for Persistent Juvenile Offenders*. Edinburgh: The Stationery Office.

Loeber, R. and Farrington, D. P. (eds), (1998) *Serious and Violent Juvenile Offenders: Risk Factors and Successful Interventions*. Newbury Park: Sage.

López-Viets, V., Walker, D. D. and Miller, W. R. (2002) 'What is Motivation to Change? A Scientific Aanalysis', in M. McMurran (ed.), *Motivating Offenders to Change: A Guide to Enhancing Engagement in Therapy*. Chichester: John Wiley.

Lurigio, A. J. and Petersilia, J. (1992) 'The Emergence of Intensive Probation Supervision Programs in the United States', in J. M. Byrne, A. J. Lurigio and J. Petersilia (eds), *Smart Sentencing: The Emergence of Intermediate Sanctions*. Newbury Park: Sage.

Mair, G. (2004) 'The Origins of What Works in England and Wales: A House Built on Sand?', in G. Mair (ed.), *What Matters in Probation*. Cullompton: Willan Publishing.

Mair, G., Lloyd, C., Nee, C. and Sibbit, R. (1994) *Intensive Probation in England and Wales: An Evaluation*, Home Office Research Study 133. London: HMSO.

Maltz, M. (1984) *Recidivism*. London: Academic Press.

Mannheim, H. and Wilkins, L. (1955) *Prediction Methods in Relation to Borstal Training*, Home Office Research Report. London: HMSO.

Marshall, T. F. (1996) 'The Evolution of Restorative Justice in Britain', *European Journal on Criminal Policy and Research*, 4(4): 21–43.

Martinson, R. (1974) 'What Works? – Questions and Answers about Prison Reform', *The Public Interest*, 35: 22–54.

Martinson, R. (1979) 'New Findings, New Views: A Note of Caution Regarding Sentencing Reform', *Hofstra Law Review*, 7: 243–58.

McCarthy, B. R. (ed.) (1987) *Intermediate Punishments: Intensive Supervision, Home Confinement and Electronic Surveillance*. Monsey: Willow Tree Press.

McDougall, C., Cohen, M. A., Swaray, R. and Perry, A. (2003) *Cost–benefit Analysis and Cost–Effectiveness of Sentencing: A Systematic Review of the Literature*. Available online at:
http://www.aic.gov.au/campbellcj/reviews/2003-12-sentencing.pdf

McDougall, C., Perry, A. E. and Farrington, D. P. (2006) 'Overview of Effectiveness of Criminal Justice Interventions in the UK', in A. E. Perry, C. McDougall and D. P. Farrington (eds), *Reducing Crime: The Effectiveness of Criminal Justice Interventions*. Chichester: John Wiley.

McGuire, J. (ed) (1995) *What Works: Reducing Re-offending: Guidelines from Research and Practice*. Chichester: John Wiley.

McGuire, J. (2002) 'Integrating Findings from Research Reviews', in J. McGuire (ed.), *Offender Rehabilitation and Treatment: Effective Programmes and Policies to Reduce Re-offending*. Chichester: John Wiley.

McMahon, M. (1990) '"Net-widening": Vagaries in the Use of a Concept', *British Journal of Criminology*, 30: 121–49.

McNeill, F. and Batchelor, S. (2004) *Persistent Offending by Young People: Developing Practice*, Issues in Community and Criminal Justice Monograph 3. London: National Association of Probation Officers.

Meisel, J. S. (2001) 'Relationships and Juvenile Offenders: The Effects of Intensive Aftercare Supervision', *The Prison Journal*, 81: 206–45.

Merrington, S. (2004) 'Assessment Tools in Probation: Their Development and Potential', in R. Burnett and C. Roberts (eds), *What Works in Probation and Youth Justice: Developing Evidence-Based Practice*. Cullompton: Willan Publishing.

Merrington, S. and Stanley, S. (2004) 'What Works? Revisiting the Evidence in England and Wales', *Probation Journal*, 51(1): 7–20.

Moffitt, T. E. (1993) 'Adolescence-Limited and Life-Course-Persistent Antisocial Behavior: A Developmental Taxonomy', *Psychological Review*, 100(4): 674–701.

Moore, R. (2005) 'The Use of Electronic and Human Surveillance in a Multi-Modal Programme', *Youth Justice*, 5(1): 17–32.

Moore, R., Gray, E., Roberts, C., Merrington, S., Waters, I., Fernandez, R., Hayward, G. and Rogers, R. D. (2004) *National Evaluation of the Intensive Supervision and Surveillance Programme: Interim Report to the Youth Justice Board*. London: Youth Justice Board for England and Wales.

Morgan, R. (2002) 'Do Not Go Straight to Jail, and We'll Collect £200', *The Times*, 19 November 2002.

MORI (2003) *Magistrates' Perceptions of the Probation Service*. London: National Probation Service.

Morris, A. and Gelsthorpe, L. (2000) 'Something Old, Something Borrowed, Something Blue, But Something New?: A Comment on the Prospects for Restorative Justice under the Crime and Disorder Act 1998', *Criminal Law Review*, 18–30.

Muncie, J. (1999) *Youth and Crime*. London: Sage.

Muncie, J. (2004) *Youth and Crime*, (2nd edn). London: Sage.

NACRO (2000) *Factors Associated with Differential Rates of Youth Custodial Sentencing*. London: Youth Justice Board.

Nagin, D. and Land, K. (1993) 'Age, Criminal Careers and Population Heterogeneity', *Criminology*, 31: 327–62.

National Audit Office (2004) *Youth Offending: The Delivery of Community and Custodial Sentences*. London: National Audit Office.

National Council for Crime Prevention (1999) *Intensive Supervision with Electronic Monitoring*. Stockholm: National Council for Crime Prevention (BRÅ).

National Probation Service (2005a) *Delivering Intensive Community Orders under the Criminal Justice Act 2003*, Probation Circular 56/2005. London: National Probation Service.

National Probation Service (2005b) *National Implementation Guide for the Criminal Justice Act 2003 Community Sentence Provisions*. London: National Probation Service.

Nellis, M. (2004a) 'The "Tracking" Controversy: The Roots of Mentoring and Electronic Monitoring', *Youth Justice*, 4(2): 77–99.

Nellis, M. (2004b) '"The Truly Remarkable Thing": Introducing Satellite Tracking of Offenders to England and Wales', *Vista*, 9(1): 9–16.

Nellis, M. and Lilly, R. J. (2001) 'Accepting the Tag: Probation Officers and Home Detention Curfew', *Vista*, 6(1): 68–80.

Newburn, T. (2002a) 'Atlantic Crossings: "Policy transfer" and Crime Control in the USA and Britain', *Punishment & Society*, 4(2): 165–93.

Newburn, T. (2002b) 'Young People, Crime, and Youth Justice', in M. Maguire, R. Morgan and R. Reiner (eds), *The Oxford Handbook of Criminology*. Oxford: Oxford University Press.

Newburn, T. (2002c) 'The contemporary politics of youth crime prevention', in J. Muncie, G. Hughes and E. McLaughlin (eds), *Youth Justice: Critical Readings*. London: Sage.

Newburn, T. and Hagell, A. (1994) 'Identifying Persistent Young Offenders', *Justice of the Peace & Local Government Law*, 334–36.

NOMS (2005) *The NOMS Offender Management Model*. London: NOMS.

Nutley, S. and Davies, H. (1999) 'The Fall and Rise of Evidence in Criminal Justice', *Public Money and Management*, 47–55.

O'Malley, P. (1997) 'Risk Societies and the Government of Crime', in M. Brown and J. Pratt (eds), *Dangerous Offenders: Punishment and Social Order*. London: Routledge.

Palmer, T. B. (1991) 'Intervention with Juvenile Offenders: Recent and Long-term Changes', in T. L. Armstrong (ed.), *Intensive Interventions with High-Risk Youths: Promising Approaches in Juvenile Probation and Parole*. Monsey: Willow Tree Press.

Palmer, T. (1992) *The Re-emergence of Correctional Intervention*. Newbury Park: Sage.

Palumbo, D. J., Clifford, M. and Snyder-Joy, Z. K. (1992) 'From Net Widening to Intermediate Sanctions: The Transformation of Alternatives to Incarceration from Benevolence to Malevolence', in J. M. Byrne, A. J. Lurigio and J. Petersilia (eds), *Smart Sentencing: The Emergence of Intermediate Sanctions*. Newbury Park: Sage.

Partridge, S. (2004) *Examining Case Management Models for Sentences*, Home Office Online Report 17/04. London: Home Office.

Partridge, S., Harris, J., Abram, M. and Scholes, A. (2005) *The Intensive Control and Change Programme Pilots: A Study of Implementation in the First Year*, Home Office Online Report 48/05. London: Home Office.

Pawson, R. and Tilley, N. (1994) 'What Works in Evaluation Research?', *British Journal of Criminology*, 34: 291–306.

Pearson, F. S. (1988) 'Evaluation of New Jersey's Intensive Supervision Program', *Crime & Delinquency*, 34(4): 437–48.

Pease, K., Billingham, S. and Earnshaw, J. (1977) *Community Service Assessed in 1976*, Home Office Research Study 39. London: HMSO.

Petersilia, J. and Turner, S. (1990) *Intensive Supervision for High-Risk Probationers: Findings from Three California Experiments*. Santa Monica: RAND.

Petersilia, J. and Turner, S. (1992) 'An Evaluation of Intensive Probation in California', *Journal of Criminal Law and Criminology*, 83: 610–58.

Petersilia, J., Turner, S. and Piper Deschenes, E. (1992) 'Intensive Supervision Programs for Drug Offenders', in J. M. Byrne, A. J. Lurigio and J. Petersilia (eds), *Smart Sentencing: The Emergence of Intermediate Sanctions*. Newbury Park: Sage.

Pitcher, J., Bateman, T., Johnston, V. and Cadman, S. (2004) *Health, Education and Substance Misuse Services: The Provision of Health, Education and*

Substance Misuse Workers in Youth Offending Teams and the Health/Education Needs of Young People Supervised by Youth Offending Teams. London: Youth Justice Board.

Pitts, J. (2002) 'The End of an Era', in J. Muncie, G. Hughes and E. McLaughlin (eds), *Youth Justice: Critical Readings*. London: Sage.

Pratt, J. (1989) 'Corporatism: The Third Model of Juvenile Justice', *British Journal of Criminology*, 29(3): 236–54.

Prison Reform Trust (2004) *Prison Reform Trust Factfile December 2004*. London: Prison Reform Trust.

Prison Reform Trust (2005) *Recycling Offenders Through Prison*. London: Prison Reform Trust.

Raynor, P. (1988) *Probation as an Alternative to Custody: A Case Study*. Aldershot: Avebury.

Raynor, P. (2001) 'Community Penalties and Social Integration: "Community" as Solution and as Problem', in A. Bottoms, L. Gelsthorpe and S. Rex (eds), *Community Penalties: Changes and Challenges*. Cullompton: Willan Publishing.

Raynor, P. (2004) 'Rehabilitative and Reintegrative Approaches', in A. Bottoms, S. Rex and G. Robinson (eds), *Alternatives to Prison: Options for an Insecure Society*. Cullompton: Willan Publishing.

Raynor, P., Lynch, J., Roberts, C., Merrington, S. (2000) *Risk and Need Assessment in Probation Services: An Evaluation*, Home Office Research Study 211. London: Home Office.

Raynor, P. and Vanstone, M. (1997) *Straight Thinking On Probation (STOP): The Mid Glamorgan Experiment, Probation Studies Unit Report 4*. Oxford: Centre for Criminological Research.

Rex, S. (1999) 'Desistance from Offending: Experiences of Probation', *Howard Journal of Criminal Justice*, 38(4): 366–83.

Rex, S., Gelsthorpe, L., Roberts, C. and Jordan, P. (2004) *An Evaluation of Community Service Pathfinder Projects: Final Report 2002*, RDS Occasional Paper No. 87. London: The Stationery Office.

Roberts, C. H. (1989) *Hereford and Worcester Probation Service Young Offender Project: First Evaluation Report*. Oxford: Department of Social and Administrative Studies, University of Oxford.

Roberts, C. H. (1995) 'Effective Practice and Service Delivery', in J. McGuire (ed.), *What Works: Reducing Reoffending: Guidelines from Research and Practice*. Chichester: John Wiley.

Roberts, C. H. (2004) 'Offending Behaviour Programmes: Emerging Evidence and Implications for Practice', in R. Burnett and C. Roberts (eds), *What Works in Probation and Youth Justice: Developing Evidence-based Practice*. Cullompton: Willan Publishing.

Roberts, C. H. (2006) *Displaying Effectiveness: Evaluation Report on the IRIS Project*. Oxford: Thames Valley Police and Probation Studies Unit/Centre for Criminology, University of Oxford.

235

Robinson, G. (1999) 'Risk Management and Rehabilitation in the Probation Service: Collision and Collusion', *Howard Journal*, 38(4): 421–33.

Robinson, G. (2002) 'Exploring Risk Management in Probation Practice: Contemporary Developments in England and Wales', *Punishment and Society*, 4(1): 5–25.

Robinson, G. (2003) 'Risk Assessment', in W.-H Chui and M. Nellis (eds), *Moving Probation Forward: Evidence, Arguments and Practice*. Harlow: Pearson Education.

Robinson, G. and Dignan, J. (2004) 'Sentence Management', in A. Bottoms, S. Rex and G. Robinson (eds), *Alternatives to Prison: Options for an Insecure Society*. Cullompton: Willan Publishing.

Rumgay, J. (2004) 'The Barking Dog? Partnership and Effective Practice', in G. Mair (ed.), *What Matters in Probation*. Cullompton: Willan Publishing.

Rutter, M., Giller, H. and Hagell, A. (1998) *Antisocial Behaviour by Young People*. Cambridge: Cambridge University Press.

Sampson, R. and Laub, J. (1993) *Crime in the Making: Pathways and Turning Points through Life*. Harvard, MA: Harvard University Press.

Sentencing Advisory Panel (2004) *New Sentences – Criminal Justice Act 2003: The Panel's Advice to the Sentencing Guidelines Council*. London: Sentencing Advisory Panel.

Sentencing Guidelines Council (2004) *Overarching Principles: Seriousness, and New Sentences: Criminal Justice Act 2003 (Draft Guideline 2)*. London: Sentencing Guidelines Council.

Sherman, L. W., Gottfredson, D., MacKenzie, D., Eck, J., Reuter, P. and Bushway, S. (1997) *Preventing Crime: What Works, What Doesn't, What's Promising: A Report to the United States Congress*. Washington, DC: National Institute of Justice.

Smith, D. J. (2005) 'The Effectiveness of the Juvenile Justice System', in *Criminal Justice*, 5(2): 181–95.

Smith, R. (2003) *Youth Justice: Ideas, Policy, Practice*. Cullompton: Willan Publishing.

Social Exclusion Unit (2005) *Transitions: Young Adults with Complex Needs: A Social Exclusion Unit Final Report*. London: Office of the Deputy Prime Minister.

Stouthamer-Loeber, M., Huizinga, D. and Porter, P. (1997) *The Early Onset of Persistent Serious Offending*. Washington DC: Office of Juvenile Justice and Delinquency Prevention.

Strauss, A. and Corbin, J. (1998) *Basics of Qualitative Research: Techniques and Procedures for Developing Grounded Theory*. California: Sage.

Swaray, R. (2006) 'Economic Methodology and Evaluations: The Costs and Benefits of Criminal Justice Interventions', in A. E. Perry, C. McDougall and D. P. Farrington (eds), *Reducing Crime: The Effectiveness of Criminal Justice Interventions*. Chichester: John Wiley.

Tarling, R. (1993) *Analysing Offending: Data, Models and Interpretations*. London: HMSO.

Tolan, P. and Guerra, N. (1994) 'Prevention of Delinquency: Current Status and Issues', *Applied and Preventative Psychology*, 3: 251–73.

Tonry, M. (1990) 'Overt and Latent Functions of Intensive Supervision Probation', *Crime and Delinquency*, 36: 174–91.

Tonry, M. (1998) 'Intermediate Sanctions', in M. Tonry (ed.), *The Handbook of Crime and Punishment*. Oxford: Oxford University Press.

Tonry, M. (2004) *Punishment and Politics: Evidence and Emulation in the Making of English Crime Control Policy*. Cullompton: Willan Publishing.

Torrance, D. A. (2000). 'Qualitative Studies into Bullying within Special Schools', *British Journal of Special Education*, 27(1): 16–21.

Travis, A. (2005) 'Nine out of 10 Teenage Criminals Reoffend', *Guardian*, 28 October.

Trotter, C. (1999) *Working with Involuntary Clients: A Guide to Practice*. London: Sage.

Tuddenham, R. (2000) 'Beyond Defensible Decision-Making: Towards Reflexive Assessment of Risk and Dangerousness', *Probation Journal*, 47(3): 173–83.

Turner, S. and Petersilia, J. (1992) 'Focusing on High-Risk Parolees: An Experiment to Reduce Commitments to the Texas Department of Corrections', *Journal of Research in Crime and Delinquency*, 29: 34–61.

Underdown, A. (1998) *Strategies for Effective Offender Supervision: Report of the HMIP What Works Project*. London: Home Office.

Utting, D. and Vennard, J. (2000) *What Works with Young Offenders in the Community?* Ilford: Barnado's.

Van Zon, J. (1994) *A Systematic Approach to Persistent Offenders that Works. Back to the Future: Annual Report of the Netherlands Public Prosecution Service*. Den Haag, Netherlands: Public Prosecution Service.

Vestergaard, J. (2004) 'A Special Youth Sanction', *Journal of Scandinavian Studies in Criminology and Crime Prevention*, 5: 62–84.

Walter, I., Sugg, D. and Moore, L. (2001) *A Year on the Tag: Interviews with Criminal Justice Practitioners and Electronic Monitoring Staff about Curfew Orders*, Home Office Research Findings 140. London: Home Office.

Walter, I. (2002) *Evaluation of the National Roll-Out of Curfew Orders*, Home Office Online Report 15/02.

Whyte, B. (2001) *Effective Intervention for Serious and Violent Young Offenders*, CJSW Briefing Paper 2: December 2001. Edinburgh: Criminal Justice Social Work Development Centre for Scotland.

Wiebush, R. G., Wagner, D., McNulty, B., Wang, Y. and Le, T. (2005) *Implementation and Outcome Evaluation of the Intensive Aftercare Program*. Washington: Office of Juvenile Justice and Delinquency Prevention.

Wiener, M. J. (1990) *Reconstructing the Criminal: Culture, Law, and Policy in England, 1830–1914*. Cambridge: Cambridge University Press.

Wikström, P.-O. (1990) 'Age and Crime in a Stockholm Cohort', *Journal of Quantitative Criminology*, 6: 61–83.

Wikström, P.-O. (2003) 'Individual Risk, Life-Style Risk, and Adolescent Offending: Findings from the Peterborough Youth Study', *Report of the Work of the Institute of Criminology, University of Cambridge*, 3–13. Cambridge: University of Cambridge.

Wilcox, A. and Hoyle, C. (2002) *Restorative Justice Projects: Summary*. London: Youth Justice Board.

Wilcox (2005) 'Are Randomised Controlled Trials really the "Gold Standard" in Restorative Justice Research?', *British Journal of Community Justice*, 3(2): 39–49.

Wolfgang, M., Figlio, R. and Stelim, T. (1972) *Delinquency in a Birth Cohort*. Chicago: University of Chicago Press.

Worrall, A. and Walton, D. (2000) 'Prolific Offender Projects, and the Reduction of Volume Property Crime: Targeted Policing and Case Management', *Vista*, 7: 34–7.

Worrall, A., Mawby, R. C., Heath, G. and Hope, T. (2003) *Intensive Supervision and Monitoring Projects*, Home Office Online Report 42/03.

Worrall, A. and Mawby, R. C. (2004) 'Intensive Projects for Prolific/Persistent Offenders', in A. Bottoms, S. Rex and G. Robinson (eds), *Alternatives to Prison: Options for an Insecure Society*. Cullompton: Willan Publishing.

Young, R. and Sanders, A. (2003) 'The Forester's Dilemma: The Influence of Police Research on Police Practice', in L. Zedner and A. Ashworth (eds), *The Criminological Foundations of Penal Policy: Essays in Honour of Roger Hood*. Oxford: Oxford University Press.

Youth Justice Board (2000) *Intensive Supervision and Surveillance Programmes*, unpublished.

Youth Justice Board (2001) *Risk and Protective Factors Associated with Youth Crime and Effective Interventions to Prevent it*. London: Youth Justice Board.

Youth Justice Board (2002a) *Corporate Plan for England and Wales 2002–03 to 2004–05 and Business Plan 2002–03*. London: Youth Justice Board.

Youth Justice Board (2002b) *Building on Success: Youth Justice Board Review 2001/2002*. London: Youth Justice Board.

Youth Justice Board (2002d) *Intensive Supervision and Surveillance Programme (ISSP): A New Option for Dealing with Prolific and Serious Young Offenders*. Youth Justice Board leaflet (updated June 2002).

Youth Justice Board (2002e) *Preparation for Initiatives on Street Robbery and Remands*, unpublished paper prepared for Youth Justice Board Meeting, 21 March 2002.

Youth Justice Board (2003a) *Corporate and Business Plan 2003/04 to 2005/06*. London: Youth Justice Board.

Youth Justice Board (2003b) *Education, Training and Employment: Key Elements of Effective Practice*. London: Youth Justice Board.

Youth Justice Board (2003c) *Mentoring: Key Elements of Effective Practice*. London: Youth Justice Board.

Youth Justice Board (2003d) *Intensive Supervision and Surveillance Programmes: Key Elements of Effective Practice*. London: Youth Justice Board.

Youth Justice Board (2004a) *New Scheme to Crack Crime and Support Families*, Youth Justice Board Press Release, 1 October 2004.

Youth Justice Board (2004b) *National Standards for Youth Justice Services*. London: Youth Justice Board.

Zedner, L. (2004) *Criminal Justice*. Oxford: Oxford University Press.

Index